COMFREY, WYOMING

BOOK TWO:
MARCELA'S ARMY

COMFREY, WYOMING

BOOK TWO:
MARCELA'S ARMY

DAPHNE BIRKMYER

atmosphere press

PART ONE:
SOLDIERS

CHAPTER ONE

HOUSE ON FIRE: COMFREY 1983

The crisp autumn air provided the oxygen, the old wooden house provided the fuel, and an extension cord, run over by a vacuum cleaner earlier in the day, provided the spark. It had been nine minutes since a neighbor made the call, four minutes since Armand Dubois gave up trying to start the ladder truck's engine. By the time the tanker trucks arrived and men leapt off to uncoil hoses and start the water pumps, tongues of flame licked the eaves and angry snaps and crackles peppered the sky with silver sparks and red embers. Larger, softer, black papery things swooped and fluttered in the thermals, catching in trees, dissolving into powder as they landed on the clothing of those who watched from across the street. Smoke roiled in waves up the pitched roof and spiraled in loose grey funnels into a cloudy leaden sky that withheld its rain.

Built almost a century ago, the houses on Franklin Street followed a similar plan. Between the sitting room on the right and the dining room on the left, a staircase led from a small square entranceway to three bedrooms on the second floor. As they watched in horror and fascination, neighbors envisioned the flames devouring their own homes, the fabric of their own lives. Those from a few blocks over gave thanks their houses were made of brick.

3

The fire arched and twirled with the passion of a flamenco dancer, its orange and red skirts consuming the furniture, catching the new curtains. It advanced to press against the glass, shattering the dining room windows, sucking in a great gulp of oxygen before belching a bolus of fire onto the narrow front porch, then retreating momentarily to tear upstairs and mock the crowd from the front bedroom window.

Wyatt Beauclaire, the only member of the Comfrey Volunteer Fire Brigade to draw a modest salary, and thus the de facto captain, had been taking a nap with his baby daughter when his pager went off. Her teething was wearing on the both of them.

He took the stairs three at a time, burst through the front door, and leapt over the boxwood hedge, yelling over his shoulder to his father, "Fire on Franklin. Half a can of formula in the fridge. No more Tylenol 'til six."

The elder Beauclaire stopped raking leaves and walked out into the street. As he watched his son disappear into the station house half a block down, he sniffed the air and scanned the sky. Smoke gathered seven blocks over, no fire hydrants in that old neighborhood. He had been a fire fighter; he knew two tanker trucks, a small water tender, and eight thousand gallons of water wouldn't be enough to put out a wooden house fire. Save people, protect neighboring homes—that would be the best they could do.

His granddaughter bellowed from inside the house and he allowed himself a proud grin since there was no one around to see it. Little one had a good set of lungs. He'd go inside, change her, fix her a bottle, and resist the temptation to take her over to watch the blaze. It wouldn't hurt her none, but his son wouldn't like it, so he'd just put her on his back in that baby carrier and she could grab at his hair with her chubby little fists as he finished his raking.

4

The Dubois brothers on hoses, four hundred gallons per minute, four men around the back holding a tarp as a net. Without the ladder truck, they hadn't a hope of reaching the man desperately trying to open the back bedroom window or the woman at his side with a baby in her arms.

"*Break it*," the firemen yelled up to the man. "*Break it*."

A shoe. Why didn't he use a shoe, an elbow, a fist? They looked at each other in confusion—he was taking too long. It was glass, just glass, didn't he know he was out of time?

The man held up a hand, as if asking them to wait, and disappeared. Presuming he'd turned away to grab something to break the window, they readied their net, but he must have opened the door to the hall for suddenly a brilliant flash of light filled the room and one of the firemen let out a long, anguished, "*Noooo...*"

The woman, a black silhouette against the flame, shouted something down to the men below and bowed her head, then for a moment, just a moment, she held her baby up high, before they both slid from view.

The men looked at each other, aghast. What had this woman been thinking? That if she raised her baby up high enough, she could save it?

The lashing and roaring of the fire drowned out the gentle hum of the water pumps and the shouts of the men behind the house. When the crowd saw the fire captain walk toward them, they paused from looking amongst themselves for members of the new family that had just moved in. They gathered close. Folk approved of Captain Wyatt Beauclaire, short, compact, tough like his father, calm, confident, an easy manner just like his dad. They'd share what they could; the family had been there less than a week. Related to Betty Ann Wolfe, they thought, the parents were called Rick and Jess, and true McNabbs, no doubt—the father and girl had the hair.

"A girl?" asked Wyatt. "A baby?" No, they assured him, a

girl of seven or eight, no one could recall her name.

"Ruth Creeley visited them yesterday, she'll know about the girl," they called as Wyatt tore back across the street to alert his men that they also needed to recover a young girl.

After the second floor collapsed onto the first and the roof gave way, part of the back wall fell out. Wyatt released a weary breath and removed a glove to draw a sweaty hand over his face. He'd call it, they'd give up on the McNabbs, pull the plug, cut their loses, accept the deaths. With an abrupt and violent shake of his head, he directed the Dubois brothers to use the rest of the water to hose down the roofs of the houses on either side.

The death of a *family*. Wyatt felt his stomach seize and clenched his jaws against the bile that rose in his throat. He shut his eyes and pressed his thumb and forefinger tight against his lids, trying to erase the image of Jess McNabb holding that baby up.

"Baptism by fire, Jesus Christ," he whispered under his breath. "Baptism by *fucking* fire," he repeated, knowing the idiom didn't really fit but unable to let it go.

When it was safe, the men in their vulcanized rubber-soled boots tromped through the blackened ruin, crunching over glass, avoiding galvanized pipes that connected to nothing. Their eyes watered from the acrid odor of wet ash as they skirted the contents of the upstairs bedroom, now lying on the kitchen tiles. Water, grey with soot, seeped from a ceiling fragment onto the charred bodies of two adults and a baby. Tyree and Armand Dubois used fire hooks to lift debris enough to shine their flashlights underneath, looking for the body of a seven- or eight-year-old girl.

When Tyree thought he heard crying from the basement, he and Armand walked around the foundation, calling "Honey?" and "Little girl?" They lay on their bellies, shone their flashlights into a black cavern, and hoped one of them wouldn't have to crawl inside if a child called back. Wyatt, dubious a living child could be found in the basement, held a slim hope she might have escaped, and she'd be hiding. If she were alive, she'd be hiding.

Leaving others to coil hoses and check for hotspots, Wyatt went to search the freestanding garage at the end of the driveway. He played his flashlight over the interior of a dusty old Buick that smelled of mildew and mice, and peered into a barrel that lay on its side. The floor at the back of the garage had been swept clean, and collapsed moving boxes, with 'kitchen' or 'upstairs' written on their sides, had been propped against a wall. He lifted a canvas sheet to find a potter's wheel, a kiln, and neatly stacked bags of clay. He climbed a narrow set of stairs to the loft. He called for her. Nothing.

Would the ladder truck have made a difference? When a cat needed rescuing the previous day, the ladder truck had started readily enough. They'd all known the battery didn't hold a charge as well as it should. He had asked the town council for funds for a new battery, a few hundred bucks, and they said to wait until next month. He should have demanded, refused to back down, but the truck had started yesterday, with the barest hesitation. Had it been the *barest* hesitation?

Wyatt emerged from the garage and stood a moment to watch the storm clouds, rimmed pink and gold by the setting sun, scud away, conserving their water for elsewhere in the Green River Basin. As he climbed the slope toward a decrepit shed that stood under a magnificent October Glory Maple near the property line, he staggered to the side to avoid stepping on a small creature. A pine squirrel lay on its side, panting, quivering. A hint of russet and grey remained in a solitary tuft of hair on its tail but a good portion of its skin had burned, exposing dark red muscle underneath. The squirrel fixed him with a round black eye, curled its tiny fists tight, and resumed its frantic gasps.

Wyatt unhooked a small, short-handled axe from his belt.

It was a multipurpose tool, designed for giving access through locked doors and hollow walls, equally handy for chopping the head off a small rodent. He dug a shallow grave near the base of the tree and carefully arranged the head back on the neck before covering the carcass with dirt and leaves.

He stood, re-hooked the axe to his belt, and instinctively ducked his head at the sound of an object dropping through the branches. It bounced off the shed's roof and, lying before him, was a child's canvas shoe. It had landed almost on top of the little grave. He shone his flashlight into the foliage above, and there she was, crouching on a branch a good forty feet up. He stepped back for a better view—she had one hand braced on the trunk, the other grasping a branch. A pale face peered down at him without expression. Wyatt looked from the face to the house and realized with a chill that the October Glory Maple would have offered an unobstructed view of the back bedroom window.

"So you think she's in that big old tree, the one that's leaves are turnin' red?" asked Tyree Dubois, craning his neck to look up at Wyatt. He'd thought he heard the whimpering again, but Armand, who couldn't hear worth a damn, said it was just the building shifting.

"I *know* she's there. I saw her and she doesn't want to come down," said Wyatt. "Fact is, when I called to her, she climbed higher."

"Well, what's the sense in that?" asked Tyree, stumbling awkwardly to his feet and reaching a hand down to his brother. "Why would she climb higher? She think we have a ladder that high? She think we're gonna be able to climb up and just carry her down?"

Wyatt struggled for patience. He had been in school with the Dubois brothers. He knew how Tyree got, innocent as a five-year-old, too eager to make friends, a brain that skipped from one topic to another so you pretty much had to shut him

8

out after a while. Armand was easier, quiet, courageous on and off the football field, even when rumors started to circulate that maybe he liked guys more than girls. But one thing about the Dubois brothers, they always showed up and didn't leave until it was over.

"Well now, Tyree, I reckon that little girl's scared shitless," said Wyatt. "And I don't know what she's thinking. She doesn't have to think right now."

Armand rolled his eyes at Wyatt and gave a nod, that's right.

"But you thinkin' she maybe watched the whole thing?" asked Tyree, his plump face wrinkling in concern. "Jesus, Mary, and Joseph, she'll be screwed up for life."

"The neighbors said Ruth Creeley visited the family yesterday," said Wyatt. "I just talked to her, she said the girl's name is Vera."

"Vera? You're kidding, I had a girlfriend named Vera. Remember her, Armand?" Tyree received a slight shoulder shrug from his brother. "Sure you do," Tyree insisted. "Big girl," he said, cupping his hands as if holding cantaloupes.

"Is Ruth Creeley coming?" Armand asked Wyatt, ignoring his brother.

"Yup. Betty Ann Wolfe's some kind of relative so Ruth's picking her up on the way. I'll go wait in the road. Can you guys ..."

Tyree interrupted, an edge of panic to his voice, "You're gonna tell me I'm the one gotta climb up there and get this little Vera girl down because I'm the youngest, but I'm too heavy, and Jesus, what if she gets dropped? We can't drop her, everybody'll go nuts."

"Tyree!" Tyree blinked as if he'd been slapped and his brother said, more gently, "Ruth will help us get her down."

"But what if ..." Tyree trailed off as his audience walked away, Armand toward the tree in case Vera opted to descend, Wyatt to the road to wait for Ruth and Betty Ann.

CHAPTER TWO

THE OCTOBER GLORY MAPLE

Wyatt had his ears tuned for the rattle of one of Ruth's old trucks, so the women snuck up on him when they arrived in a respectable-looking late model car, probably belonging to Betty Ann Wolfe. He was anxious to get Vera down from the tree before the coroner's van arrived, but he allowed the women a moment to absorb the destruction of the old wooden house before he approached.

Ruth emerged from behind the wheel, her face stricken. "My God, Wyatt," she said, her normally authoritative tone tempered with horror and disbelief. "Oh my dear, dear God, and I just saw them yesterday." She stared at the ruins a moment before leaning down to talk to her passenger through the open car door. "Betty Ann, better if you stay seated here while ..."

But the old woman interrupted with surprising firmness, "You go right ahead, Ruth. Go on and get little Vera down. All I need's a moment, then I'll be right on your heels."

Ruth straightened, closed the car door, and beckoned Wyatt to stand next to her. "More stubborn than a stone," she hissed. She closed her eyes and pinched the bridge of her nose. "This has been such an appalling shock but she insisted on coming. Had a stent put in her heart last week, apparently even pescatarians can block an artery. If you'd just give her a hand, Wyatt, but take a care. Let her set the pace, there's a good lad."

To be called 'good lad' by someone not ten years his senior would have made Wyatt release a chuckle if he'd had one in him. Wiry, tough little Ruth Creeley didn't look the mothering type, but she had that comfort about her.

Since the house no longer blocked the view of the October Glory Maple, Ruth pointed toward the tree and said in a much louder tone, "I'll go see what I can do to encourage the poor lamb to climb down."

Wyatt watched Ruth take off in short, determined strides before he walked around the car to open the passenger door. Robbed of its usual vitality, the old lady's face looked scary white and he hoped she wouldn't see the alarm in his eyes.

"Mrs. Wolfe," he said, offering his hand. Over twenty years ago, she had been his fifth-grade teacher—he'd never be able to address her as Betty Ann.

In a voice as thin as paper, she said, "You're sure that baby's gone too, Wyatt? You found his little body?"

"Yes, Mrs. Wolfe. We did find his body. I am so sorry."

She worked her mouth the way old people sometimes do, as if chewing on words before offering them up. Wyatt crouched down to hear her more clearly, feeling like he was back in elementary school as he looked up at her.

"We were planning a nice visit, they were coming over tomorrow, bringing a salmon salad and rolls, Ricky, Jess, the children." As if not wanting him to think less of her for not making the salmon salad herself, she added, "I'm not much up for cooking at the moment."

He remained crouched because she'd put her hand on his shoulder and was attempting to push herself into a standing position. He awkwardly put his hands around her middle and gave an assist. What was he doing? Stuck here with his old teacher, who looked like she'd expire any minute, leaving Ruth and the Dubois brothers to coax Vera down. He looked toward the tree and narrowed his eyes. He could just make out Ruth

11

being given a leg up by Armand.

"Mrs. Wolfe. I'm not so sure ..." Wyatt began as she swayed on her feet, but she righted herself and shot him her teacher look and said in her teacher voice, "Wyatt Beauclaire, all I ask is a minute or two to get my bearings. You're in such a blessed hurry? It seems to me this dreadful business is mostly over."

Wyatt could have easily carried her, but he shuddered to think how that suggestion would go over. They crossed the road haltingly; he tried to match her steps without appearing too obvious. By the time they started along the driveway, they had developed a rhythm of sorts, walking, pausing for breaths, walking.

As they skirted the house, she said she wanted to take a closer look but he said firmly, "No you do *not*, Mrs. Wolfe. Let's not make this any harder."

"Are their bodies still there, Wyatt? Isn't someone taking care of their poor bodies?"

"We're waiting on the coroner from Pinedale," he said, and for a moment her face crumpled. He didn't think he'd be able to bear it if she cried, but she surprised him when she tugged at his arm and demanded furiously, "What did the Lord need with that little baby? You ask Him that, Captain Wyatt Beauclaire. *You* ask him why he had to take that little baby too, because He sure as hell isn't talking to me."

Armand and Tyree Dubois watched in admiration as Ruth climbed. She stopped a few branches below the child and they could hear her beginning to talk in low, soothing tones, her words indistinguishable from the ground.

"Mom couldn't do that," observed Armand.

"You mean the climbing part? Because Mom could do the talking part," said Tyree loyally.

"Climbing part." Armand wasn't sure about the talking part. What could anyone say to a child who had probably seen her family burn?

"Yeah, well I remember Wyatt talking on how he helped Ruth re-roof her house a few months ago. Remember that? Said she climbed like a monkey, worked like a dog. Matched him tile for tile," said Tyree. "Ruth's a few years younger than Mom and she has superior upper body strength, Mom's just regular. Recommendable."

"Commendable, too," murmured Armand.

Ruth peered up at the weary little face looking down at her, pale and remote as the moon. "Hello, Vera," she called gently. "We met yesterday, remember? The chocolate chip cookies? That was me. I'm so very sorry, honey, I truly am. Life can be so cruel and there's nothing to explain it."

The child gave a slow blink and turned her face away. Ruth sighed and settled her back against the trunk. She watched Wyatt and Betty Ann make slow progress toward them. Smart young man, steering such a wide path around the ruins. From up here you could still make out the shapes lying on the kitchen floor, if you knew what they were.

"You see that lady down there, Vera?" Ruth called up. "The one walking with the fire captain? That's Betty Ann, my friend and some kind of auntie to you. She didn't come with me yesterday because she's recovering from surgery, but she'll be fine." Vera's attention shifted momentarily toward the small figures coming their way and Ruth continued, "When you decide you can come down, we'll go to Betty Ann's house. It's a nice house, comfy and safe."

Vera changed position, leaning back against the trunk like Ruth. It almost seemed as if the child were settling in, and Ruth felt a stab of alarm. Lightning flashed, thunder rumbled somewhere over the little town of Farson, to the south. The clouds continued their retreat so she and Vera were in no physical danger, but night approached. When the coroner arrived, he'd have to set up lights and the whole scene would be lit up like the final act of a macabre play.

Betty Ann gave Wyatt's arm a squeeze as they paused once again for her to catch her breath. "You're a sweet boy, Wyatt, always have been. And look at you now, giving up that big job as a fireman in Cheyenne, bringing your baby home to Comfrey when that silly girl up and left you both."

Wyatt nodded; silly girl just about summed Amy up. When she'd grown bored with motherhood after a few months and left, there had been no question he'd have to return to Comfrey to have his dad's help in raising little Sophie.

As the wind shifted and the odor of wet charcoal wafted over, Betty Ann looked back at the house.

"Do you remember how long that house stood empty?" she asked, her hand trembling on Wyatt's arm. "Ricky inherited it few years back from a cousin of my late husband. I'm not sure of the particulars, that side of my husband's family has always been a bit iffy. When the baby arrived, Ricky and Jess decided they needed a bigger house so they moved down from Montana, where she's from. Then as soon as they arrive in Comfrey, three of them are gone in a puff of smoke."

Wyatt grimaced. If only they had gone in a puff of smoke. Again he saw the blackened remains of the parents, indistinguishable from each other, the baby fallen away from his mother's arms, charred except for part of an arm and a tiny pale foot.

Betty Ann agreed not to attempt the sloping path to the maple and stood waiting as Wyatt went to see if there was anything to retrieve from the shed for her to sit on. Her voice reciting the 23rd Psalm followed him, "*He maketh me to lie down in green pastures: he leadeth me beside the still waters.*"

Wyatt shook his head ruefully—they couldn't be further from green pastures and still waters. She should have chosen the prayer of St. Francis, to sow hope where there is despair and light where there is darkness. He muttered under his breath his favorite part of the prayer, "*Grant that I may not so much seek to be consoled as to console; To be understood as to understand; To be loved as to love.*"

The shed door opened with a creak and Wyatt played his flashlight over a pillow, a crumpled blanket, and a book, *The Hidden Staircase*. He recognized the girl on the cover, in control, confident in her sweater and pleated skirt, her flashlight trained on something in the shadows. Wyatt's older sister had read him Nancy Drew books as bedtime stories. He would have had to leave town if his friends had found out he preferred Nancy to the Hardy Boys.

He heard something move, a restless sound. And there, under a shelf holding a box of graham crackers and a bag of dog food, cowered a familiar-looking dog, muscular, medium tall, medium brown, unexceptional except for the degree to which his lower jaw jutted out, hinting of a bulldog ancestry.

It was Porky's dog all right, but way skinnier than he'd remembered. The dog had disappeared from Comfrey's streets about the time Porky started spending time with a woman in Big Piney. People didn't like Porky much, but their dislike did not extend to his dog. Plenty of folks would have taken in the dog, but Porky was rumored to have dumped it somewhere in Wild Horse Valley. Porky was like that—he'd rather destroy something than give it away.

To Wyatt's, "Hey, there," the dog stood, stretched, lowered his head, and wagged his tail.

Wyatt looked around for something to use as a leash. Had Vera been holed up here reading Nancy Drew to the dog when the fire broke out? Had Nancy Drew saved them both?

The moment she spied the dog, Vera descended rapidly. Without saying a word, she sat on the ground, her arms wrapped around the dog's neck, her face buried in his fur. She still hadn't decided on a name for him but he was *her* dog, her very first dog. He had been waiting for her just outside the fence as she explored the backyard the day after they had moved in and he had been so shaky and so thin you could count each rib. Her father said the dog would have to sleep in the shed until they found out if he had house manners.

They fed him scraps the first day, but Vera knew a real dog needed real dog food, so her mother had let her do the vacuuming to earn money for a bag of Purina Dog Chow.

When the coroner's van arrived, Betty Ann saw the sense in letting Armand Dubois carry her to the car. He cradled her in his arms like a baby and Wyatt walked ahead, playing his flashlight over the ground so they wouldn't stumble. Ruth held Vera's hand in a vice-like grip as they marched rapidly past the burned house, Porky's dog following dutifully behind.

Wyatt bit back a grin when he heard Betty Ann saying to Armand, "The Lord has given me this task and He will walk this path with us."

Apparently, the Lord and Betty Ann were friends again.

CHAPTER THREE

PORKY'S DOG

The cat perched on the fence watching Vera, who sat in a garden chair placed within view of the kitchen window so Betty Ann could see her and not worry. The dog lay stretched out in a patch of sun near the linden tree and his feet twitched as he slept. He ran more in his sleep than when he was awake. Betty Ann called him a sedate dog and she said he suited their household perfectly, since the cat provided enough drama for all of them.

A gust of wind buffeted the leaves of the tree and shadows flickered on the ground. Another gust, more violent flickers, and Vera gasped as the shadows erupted into flames that danced around the dog's body. She couldn't move, she couldn't help ... her mother and brother at the window, the curtains on fire, the men shouting ... the sound of her screams as the second floor crashed down ...

Vera bent over and pressed her forehead to her knees. She opened her mouth and her throat ached as it managed to release a long, hollow, emptying moan. Behind the sooty black of her closed eyes, she thought of the pennies her father always had in his pocket, just for her. It was his joke, the joke that made her mother roll her eyes as he handed his pennies over, two by two, when he rendered his opinion.

"Which name do you like best?" she had asked him as they stacked clay in the garage that would become their pottery studio. She had chosen two names from the glazes they used that were closest in color to the new dog.

"Jasper or Phoenix. It's a big decision, Vera," her father had said, jingling the coins. "I'll render my two cents' worth after supper."

But the fire had stolen his opinion and now the dog would have to remain Porky's dog. People called him that anyway.

"Lucky for Porky's dog to have found a home," people said.

"Porky's dog has a little girl to take care of now."

Porky was a nothing, a nobody, so her dog could keep the two words that people called him, but now both would start with capitals: Porky's Dog. She would write it like that to show Betty Ann sometime. But not now. Now she could do nothing but eat, sit, or lie down. Had the coins in her penny jar melted as the fire flashed at the window and climbed up the curtains? Her mother and brother ... Vera pressed her fist to her mouth so hard she tasted blood ... the noise of the top floor crashing down ...

When Betty Ann called out the window lunch was ready, Vera stood and waited for Porky's Dog to get up. Soup was on the table, steam rising, rolls, two glasses of water. Vera took what had become her customary seat with its back to the woodstove. At night there would be a fire in the stove, but from her seat, she wouldn't have to see it.

Betty Ann paused on her way to the table and went back to the sink to dampen a cloth. "There, there," she murmured as she wiped tears from Vera's face. "There, there my love," she said in a voice that trembled like the leaves of the linden tree.

* * * * * *

When the social worker lady with all the papers and questions came over, Ruth came too. While the lady talked about school and all the reasons Vera should give it a try, Vera concentrated on removing the tiny bits of walnut from her piece of banana bread. She arranged them into a 'J' for Jada, the goldfish. She removed more until she had enough to turn the 'J' into a 'P' and make a 'D' for Porky's Dog.

"Often a child will talk to another child if they won't talk to an adult," the lady said to Betty Ann and Ruth when she had given up on including Vera in the conversation. Vera examined the walnuts. How could she talk to other children when she couldn't even talk to Betty Ann?

The following Monday, Vera accepted the brown bag lunch Betty Ann held out to her and attached the leash to Porky's Dog's collar. She found comfort in the leash tethering them together and she thought he found comfort in it too.

"School is just the thing," said Betty Ann, walking fast in her brown lace-up shoes. "Children in the classroom have fresh ideas, different ways of looking at things. You can't just have an old lady for company."

Vera cast a quick glance at Betty Ann. Fresh ideas? Those were words from the social worker's mouth. Ruth should have told the lady she came over a lot and she had fresh ideas. Betty Ann should have said there were Porky's Dog and the cat and Jada in his tank in the kitchen for company. Besides, Betty Ann was old and a lady, but she wasn't an *old lady*.

"No need to be nervous, Vera," Betty Ann continued, pausing to pick up a cigarette butt to put in the plastic bag she carried for litter. "I told you I've talked to the principal and your teacher. No one will press you."

Vera frowned. Betty Ann was talking a lot. Maybe *she* was nervous. Betty Ann said for the third time that she used to teach at Comfrey Elementary before teaching science at the high school. Again, she said the principal and her teacher were very nice and they understood about the not talking. She said over and over that the teacher would be waiting on the sidewalk to bring Vera inside.

There was the school, children were calling to each other, looking at her, the teacher was waving. Vera tugged at Porky's Dog's leash before handing him over to Betty Ann. He sat and looked up at her.

"I'll come home early," Vera said, watching her silent words drift down on his head like ashes.

After perusing her newspaper over a leisurely cup of coffee, Betty Ann went outside with the cat and dog at her heels. She needed to prioritize chores for Tyree Dubois. There was wood to split, the bookshelves she had bought for Vera's room to paint, and half a yard of topsoil to work into the beds along the driveway. The town tried to share the Dubois brothers equitably and Tyree was hers for half a day. In the winter, you'd be fortunate to get one of them for more than an hour.

The dog went to look for a sheltered patch of sun, but the cat followed Betty Ann to the log pile so he could climb to the top and look down on his domain. Betty Ann smiled at the cat. After a bit of a rough start, the cat and the dog had come to appreciate each other's warmth, and no doubt they'd be curled up together in a sunny spot soon.

"How do you think our girl's doing at school?" Betty Ann asked, writing 'a dozen big logs split smaller than last time will do for this week,' on Tyree's list. The cat had the grace to turn his attention from the tiny feathery puff chattering agitatedly from the Apache Plume bush to the one who fed him. "I'm a little worried, truth be told, but her teacher and the principal said they are prepared to deal with her silence. Did I tell you there's a goldfish in the classroom? It's not as magnificent as our Jada, but Vera should find some comfort in him."

The cat appeared to consider this; after all, he found the goldfish endlessly fascinating, which was the reason he was shut out of the kitchen at night. The wind picked up and the old lady's grey hair began to whip about until she pulled up her hood. The long pink seed heads of the Apache Plume parted, revealing the feathery puff, but the cat gave a languid stretch and leapt to the ground. Birds could wait and the dog should be warmed up nicely by now.

Betty Ann was trying to decide between the split pea soup Ruth had kindly supplied and a can of Campbell's tomato soup, which she honestly thought she'd prefer, when the school principal phoned. Vera had walked into the office during morning recess and taken a seat along the wall, where children waited if they were to be picked up early by their parents. It was now lunchtime, and she was refusing to join her classmates outside.

"We'll send work home for her," said the principal. "When you said she doesn't speak, we were perfectly willing to give her..." He paused, searching for words, "...time and space. We all appreciate what she has been through, but it's the fact that she looks right through us, as if we're not even here. It's somewhat unnerving. She's unsettling the other children."

Betty Ann very much doubted that final statement. Her experience as a classroom teacher for over forty years had taught her most children had more compassion and patience than adults gave them credit for. The principal had sounded as if his feelings were hurt.

"He'll have to be tougher than that if he wants to serve children," muttered Betty Ann to the dog as they walked back to the school to collect Vera.

Several more weeks passed, and, except her for murmurings to the goldfish, Vera had still not spoken a word. Comfrey's only doctor, a man who had said for years he was on the cusp of retirement, was unable to offer suggestions beyond "give her time, time and more time." But that was the problem with being old, Betty Ann pointed out—she simply didn't have time, time, time, and she needed to take a hand in Vera's recovery now.

"Well, if you truly feel time's winged chariot bearing down, I'd urge a visit to a specialist," the doctor said. "The closest pediatrician is in Pinedale. Have her give Vera another workup and see if she has some ideas about dealing with severe childhood trauma."

CHAPTER FOUR

SILENT SCREAM

Betty Ann needed two cushions to see over the steering wheel, and had just adjusted them to her liking when Vera let out an audible sigh from the back seat.

"All right, Vera? Something you needed to say?" asked Betty Ann, looking up at the rear view mirror and meeting Vera's eyes. "Are we forgetting something? Because if it's the dog's water, I've brought a bottle and a bowl."

Porky's Dog had collapsed with his head on Vera's lap and the girl tugged at his collar. "Oh, a leash," said Betty Ann. "Of course, clever girl. Hanging by the back door. Be a love and go and get it."

Vera returned to the car with the leash dangling loosely around her neck and climbed into the back seat. She buckled her seat belt and flicked a glance up to meet Betty Ann's eyes in the mirror.

"I thank the Lord every day, Vera, for the thoughtful and responsible child you are," said Betty Ann as she eased away from the curb.

Betty Ann had lived in parts of the Green River Basin for most of her life and she was looking forward to the hour-long drive to Pinedale. She never ceased to marvel at the bleak beauty of the high prairie scrubland. Sun sparkled off the hint of snow that remained along the edge of the road after last

23

night's dusting. With peaks shrouded in mist, only the rocky shoulders of the Wind River Range were visible a mile or so to the northeast. The steppes of the high prairie gently sloped south, red dirt, pockets of snow, dying grasses, gray bitter bush, and tough, broad-leafed forbs. In the spring, the stiff silver-white Sagewort would have yellow flowers and the Firecracker Penstemons would thrust narrow scarlet blossoms on two-foot stems into the sky.

They stopped along the way to admire a small herd of pronghorn antelope, one male, several females, a yearling.

"Shall we let the dog stretch his legs?" Betty Ann asked as they got out of the car.

Vera looked from the pronghorn to Betty Ann, put her finger to her lips, and slowly shook her head.

"Right you are," said Betty Ann. She peered through the window at the dog in the back seat. He had already given up and made himself comfortable on a plaid car blanket. The emergence of a good-sized dog from the car, even a dog as placid as this one, would test the patience of any prey animal.

As always, Betty Ann was struck by how handsome the pronghorns were, with their reddish-brown coloring and distinctive white markings, black cheeks for the male. The animals paused in their grazing, alert but not alarmed. No need to lift their tails to flash their white rump hairs and take off yet.

Vera closed her eyes and turned her face to the sun. She opened her arms and began to spin in slow circles, her umber brown curls blown into a froth. The male pronghorn chewed his cud and, Betty Ann fancied, tried to watch her eye, the two of them responsible elders watching a young creature glory in the high prairie wind.

They arrived in Pinedale earlier than expected, so they had time to walk to a nearby park. The dog and Vera ran ahead toward a magnificent oak in the process of dropping its leaves.

"I do believe this is a Bur Oak, Vera," said Betty Ann as the dog and child circled the tree's massive trunk. Betty Ann kicked some of the leaf litter out of the way and bent to pick up an acorn nearly two inches in length. The capsule covered most of the nut and had a wooly fringe like a knitted pixie cap.

"You can see why this tree is often called mossycup oak." Betty Ann handed Vera the acorn. "*Quercus macrocarpa.* Latin. Genus and species, only the Genus is capitalized. There are several of these magnificent trees in Comfrey. I used to collect the acorns for my students, even at the high school level, to make into Christmas tree ornaments. It's an almost perfect tree, drought-tolerant, fast-growing, an excellent hardwood, white oak they call it, and the largest acorn you could ever wish to see."

Betty Ann didn't add 'fire resistant' to the list of the tree's attributes. She prayed for the day where a mention of the word 'fire' wouldn't cause Vera to stiffen.

During Vera's physical examination, the doctor worked quietly and efficiently, her hands gentle, her comments encouraging. "Good girl ... that's right ... one more deep breath ... excellent, excellent ..." The doctor continued her mantra as she checked reflexes, listened, prodded, and probed. When done, she released Vera to rejoin the dog in the waiting room and she and Betty Ann moved into her office.

"The clinical term is 'Selective Mutism,'" said the pediatrician, rocking back in her chair and looking across the broad expanse of her desk to Betty Ann.

"Vera is not being very selective if she's not talking to *anyone*," said Betty Ann.

The doctor shrugged. "Nonetheless, that *is* the preferred term, somewhat broad. Or perhaps you're suggesting too specific?" The doctor raised an eyebrow at Betty Ann.

"It doesn't really ..." began Betty Ann, wishing this woman would get to the point.

"Whatever the case may be," said the doctor, cutting her off, "I assume sometime in the future Vera will speak. If you can separate the body from the mind—and that's impossible I might add—I'd say physically Vera's doing well. She's at an acceptable weight, she appears to hear well, heart and lungs are strong. Her throat's not inflamed but the musculature is tightly contracted."

Betty Ann tried to hide her irritation; she was a 'get to the gist' kind of person. She was grateful for the empathy the doctor had shown Vera during the exam but now the woman appeared to be lapsing into a meandering narrative.

The doctor steepled her fingers and looked over them. "I don't believe she's *choosing* not to speak, I believe she *cannot* speak until some relaxation of the larynx and vocal cords occurs," she said. "It's as if her throat is frozen in a silent scream. A frozen scream—it brings to mind that painting by Edvard Munch. I saw it in a museum in Oslo years ago. You surely know the painting I'm referring to, titled simply enough, *The Scream?*"

Betty Ann nodded; Art History 101, but her night vision wasn't as good as it used to be, and this digression into Edvard Munch raised the possibility that they wouldn't make it home before nightfall. Hoping to get back on track, she said, "But what can be done to help her?"

"I have the lithograph at my house," the doctor continued, undeterred. "Not really suitable for a pediatric office, I will agree with you. The colors in the original painting are stunning. In his diary, Munch wrote of an infinite scream passing through nature."

Ah, she's a lonely, disappointed woman, realized Betty Ann. She felt a stab of sympathy but she really did need to get home before dark. She opened her mouth to speak but once again the doctor got there before her.

"Really quite poetic, an infinite scream," the doctor mused. "Apparently Edvard was walking with friends when the sky

26

turned blood red—he describes it as tongues of fire above a blue-black fjord. A natural phenomenon on occasion in the far north I believe, but it gave Munch great anxiety. However, perhaps we are straying a bit far afield?"

"Yes, I ..." tried Betty Ann, only to be cut off again.

"Let's draw a more apt comparison then. Vera is rather like the person who refuses to eat. She too is trying to exert control over her environment. She's retreating into herself, insulating herself, *cushioning* herself with silence."

Determined to interject a few sentences, Betty Ann asked in a rush, "But how do we help her? It worries me no end that she can't share her suffering, and at some point I'll need to get her back in school."

The doctor shook her head. "In New York, my specialty was juvenile rheumatoid arthritis. In a town the size of Pinedale—not my choice of a place to live, but my husband's— I've had to become more of a general pediatric practitioner. But there you are, live in Pinedale and give up the luxury of specializing."

"So, do we ..."

The doctor held up a finger. "To be honest, I haven't a clue how to help Vera regain her voice, beyond letting time take its course. I've not had to ..."

"Then you'll excuse me, but we'll need to find someone who honestly *does* have a clue," Betty Ann interrupted. How could someone live with pain they couldn't share? How would Vera cope in school if she couldn't speak?

"I was going to say, if you'll allow me to continue ..." The doctor paused meaningfully, and Betty Ann offered an impatient, "Excuse me."

"I was *going* to say," the doctor repeated, peering at Betty Ann over her glasses, "I happen to have a young man living in my guesthouse at the moment. He has recently completed his doctorate in child psychology at NYU. I would imagine he's a top-notch trauma specialist."

"You have a trauma specialist living in your guest house?" asked Betty Ann, sitting to attention. She imagined Edvard Munch's man screaming, *'Why didn't you say so?'*

"Yes. His name is Bakari. Dr. Bakari Silberstein. He's my sister's adopted son. He's hiding out here from New York, writing. Before hanging out his shingle, he wants to finish his book about his experiences as a child soldier in Mozambique. He knows trauma, believe me." The doctor shook her head and added ruefully, "He has been quite fierce with me, as I expect most writers are at times. I am limited to a short conversation after supper, before he gets back to work. But he is my only nephew and we are really very fond of each other. I'm sure I can get him to meet with you."

Betty Ann and Vera walked slowly back to the car, stopping repeatedly for Porky's Dog to sample the odors and flavors of Pinedale and leave his mark. As they waited for him to complete his exploration of a particularly enticing gooseberry bush, Betty Ann rested her hand lightly on Vera's shoulder.

"I'm not sure how I feel about Doctor High and Mighty, but we must be charitable and she has given us a lead, Vera. We have an introduction to an African gentleman, a trauma specialist. What do you think of that?"

Betty Ann didn't expect an answer, she just wanted to sow a seed. A young man from across the sea, educated in New York and squirreled away in Pinedale, might lend a hand. The Lord had His ways.

CHAPTER FIVE

CHILD SOLDIER

Vera stood at the French doors of the very dark man's cottage. Porky's Dog sat outside, tied to a green wooden bench in front of a pond in which a large cement frog spouted water high into the air. The drops rained down onto real lily pads and made them bounce. Maybe there were fish in the pond too.

Vera was aware the man spoke to her but she couldn't speak and they *knew* she couldn't speak, so it would be better if she could just go outside and see if there were fish in the pond and sit on the bench with Porky's Dog. She liked water, she had a warm sweater, and it was sunny outside. She placed her hand on the ornate door handle and looked over her shoulder to Betty Ann.

"She'd prefer to be outside with Porky's Dog," Betty Ann said.

Vera heard the very dark man reply that he was just going to suggest that, so she opened the door and walked into the garden without a backward glance.

Betty Ann settled into a chair upholstered in a print featuring energetic brown rabbits jumping over roses, timid ones peering through bushes. The trauma specialist took the leather recliner. He sat with his legs crossed, an expensive tasseled loafer dangling from a raised foot, while she rested her highly polished, sensible shoes on a footstool. They smiled at each other, recognizing the need to take the other's measure before they got to work.

"Your aunt told me how busy you are and I'm grateful you found the time to meet with us, Dr. Silberstein," said Betty Ann, her voice strong, holding just a slight quaver of old age.

He smiled. "Bakari, please. No need for formality, we're not really meeting in an official capacity."

"Bakari, that's not a name you hear every day," Betty Ann remarked, leaning forward to adjust her footstool.

"It means 'promise' or 'he who will succeed.' I have a lot to live up to."

"It's a good name, very reassuring. I'm not sure what Betty Ann means, and I'm just plain Betty Ann, not *Elizabeth* Ann."

"Betty Ann," Bakari repeated solemnly. He liked old people, women in particular. His grandmother and her cronies had surrounded him with love, humor, and more treats than he deserved. "Your name reminds me of a nursery rhyme. I wouldn't be surprised if Miss Muffet's name wasn't Betty Ann."

The old lady appeared to consider this, looking at the ceiling and placing her thumb and forefinger on her chin, as if in thought. "Betty Ann Muffet. Hmm ... I agree the names go well together," she said slowly, then gave him a surprisingly youthful grin and added, "But upon further consideration, I'd prefer not to have my name associated with an arachnophobe. I am quite fond of spiders."

He laughed out loud. The old lady had an air of authority about her—he wouldn't be surprised if she had been a teacher.

"My uncle married a woman from Ghana," he said. "She told us tales of Anansi, who often took the form of a spider. Anansi gathered dew in her web and cast it into the heavens to create the stars. And she brought stories from the sky-god to earth. Can you imagine a world without stories?"

Betty Ann replied she could not and that when she had been teaching, she reserved the hour after lunch for storytelling. "Spider Grandmother is a powerful helper and teacher to Native people here, and of course, to other interested parties. I'm sorry now I didn't take the opportunity to share with my students her importance in African tales," she said.

Bakari promised he would send her a book when he got back to New York.

His voice was deep and soft, a blend of New York and an African tongue she supposed. Urdu? No, that was more likely for an Indian or Pakistani. Perhaps Swahili? Betty Ann felt a stab of shame. Africa, a continent of over fifty countries and the cradle of human evolution, offered a rich diversity of tongues, yet she could only name one. She had never met anyone from Africa before, let alone Mozambique. An exotic blossom in Pinedale, to be sure. A child soldier.

Bakari watched Betty Ann's eyes travel from the scar that ran from his mouth to his right ear, then to the scars on the backs of his hands. He was used to addressing 'the elephant in the room,' an English phrase he found particularly amusing, so he pulled up his sleeves to reveal more scars running the length of his forearms.

"You wonder about me, so I will tell you first, before we get down to the business of helping your Vera," he said.

He paused to take a sip of water, holding onto the glass, running his finger around its rim thoughtfully before returning it to a side table and clasping his hands loosely in his lap. With his face in shadow, Betty Ann could only distinguish his eyes, large and intelligent, the whites tinged with yellow.

"When I was a boy of ten, I walked to my Auntie's house in another village, half a day away, to bring her bread from my mother and to return the next morning with mango and avocado," he began.

Betty Ann settled back to listen; this was obviously a tale he'd told many times, his voice calm, almost flat, his eyes distant. He recounted how the walk back to his village had been cooler than the day before, the wind soft, the grass golden. He described scrub robins foraging for ants and termites in the dry yellow soil. Two cinnamon-colored hoopoe birds sang to advertise the territories they'd claimed, holes in the rocky shelves of a cliff. Near the path, another pair of handsome rivals faced off, long curved beaks stabbing at the air, their striped wings spread, their black-tipped crests opened into half-circles.

"I remember thinking, 'there is no place on earth more beautiful than this,'" he said.

He paused a long moment before telling of the complete and utter silence that greeted him as he descended the hill into his village. Betty Ann steeled herself for the horror she felt sure was to come. A child soldier.

Bakari described the sticky black sprays of blood along mud-stuccoed walls, the fly-covered pools of blood on the ground. All homes stood empty, all people vanished. He had fled into the bush, met up with another boy. For weeks, they circled homesteads, stealing food at night, sleeping in caves and trees during the day. Then just after dawn, on a day like so many others, their lives changed. The air had warmed and the boys had curled under a bush to sleep, trying to ignore the insects that landed on their faces to drink the moisture from their eyes, when Rebel soldiers found them, dragged them from their shelter and into the shadow of Commander Manjate.

He was a man to look up to, a strong man with drugs that took away the terror and made the boys feel powerful. Bakari had become a soldier for three years, killing people who would have killed him, some of them children like himself. Just before his fourteenth birthday, white men with food, cigarettes, and big smiles drove their UNICEF vans into camp.

Bakari shut his eyes to the sympathy he saw in the old lady's eyes. He didn't trust his voice to speak and he fell silent.

He hadn't wanted to leave. *He* had been a good soldier, stronger and braver than many of the other boys who'd been allowed to stay. He would never understand how Commander Manjate had chosen who would be given away.

He had been corralled for months in a UNICEF children's village, receiving treatment for malnutrition, parasites, and drug withdrawal as workers searched for an adult to claim him. He had watched American movies projected onto a sheet in the dining room before bedding down each night next to boys who would have killed him weeks before, unless he'd killed them first. Sometimes he felt afraid, sometimes angry, but usually he felt nothing at all.

One night, as the others watched the weekly showing of the camp favorite, *Butch Cassidy and the Sun Dance Kid,* he used the excuse he had to use the latrine to leave the dining room, and he had kept on walking. At some point he sensed someone following. The doctor, a volunteer from New York, who asked so many questions and took so many notes, followed twenty, thirty paces behind. They walked for over an hour down a dirt road to nowhere, the moon full enough to light the dusty track. Suddenly a hare startled him as it made a frantic dash out of the brush and across the road, and he collapsed to the ground, howling, pawing the dirt like a wild dog. Dr. Stephen Silberstein sat beside him as he'd wept like a child, until his eyes were parched and the skin on his face became hard and ached.

Bakari opened his eyes and looked at Betty Ann, grateful she had sat silently, allowing him time to gather himself.

"During the civil war that consumed my country, many of us did terrible things, fierce and dreadful things," he said, holding his hands in his lap, palms up as if in supplication.

Bakari got up and walked to the window. He watched the dog and child outside for a moment before turning to Betty Ann and saying formally, "God and the Silbersteins have helped me resurrect my humanity. Now I, who have participated in the most unspeakable acts, have the opportunity to make reparations for the evil I have done."

Betty Ann couldn't begin to imagine the unspeakable acts this calm, educated young man had committed to survive. The Silbersteins would have worked with him, given him techniques to block the sounds, the images that must come at night. He had probably heard a thousand times from well-meaning folk, "But you were just a child, you had to survive. Forgive yourself." She wouldn't say it too. She would read his book, she would make herself walk in his shoes. A burden shared.

"Thank you," she said.

He gave her a bleak smile. "Do they like lemonade?" he asked softly, gesturing to the window.

"*She* does, and so do I," answered Betty Ann.

"But not the dog?" asked Bakari with a smile.

He was teasing but he wasn't sure if she understood, for she laughed and said, "I assume the Silbersteins aren't dog people."

Bakari went into the kitchen to get the lemonade he'd made that morning.

In fact, the Silbersteins were very much dog people. When he had come to live with them, they already had a small dog with hair like a mop that covered its eyes. But when night after night his dreams threatened to consume him and he woke the household with his cries, they had taken him to an animal shelter so he could select his own dog, a companion to hold in his bed. He knew he had chosen a dog larger and younger than the Silbersteins had hoped, but the moment he'd seen her, a half-grown Irish wolfhound mixed with something else, he knew she would be big enough to fill that long, dark space between his bed and the wall.

His dog was the reason he had chosen NYU, close enough to home that he wouldn't have to stay in a dorm. She was now well past middle age and suffered from the arthritis one might expect in a very large dog. He missed her gentle warmth at night but he and the Silbersteins had agreed she wouldn't travel comfortably. He didn't expect to be in Wyoming more than a few months—he would be back with her soon.

Bakari opened the kitchen door and followed a flagstone path around the corner of the cottage and toward the pond. "Last soldiers standing," he murmured as he passed a berm of yellow daisies and purple Mexican sage. Most of the garden had already withdrawn to hunker down before the onslaught of the coming Wyoming winter.

The dog sat erect on the bench next to the girl. Long slender spikes of small white flowers clasped by furry purple calyces sprang from his collar and formed a graceful arc over his head. Vera had chosen the Mexican sage. She had left enough of the soft green leaves to form a doily that rested on the dog's muscular crown. The dog turned his head, flowers bobbing as he tracked the man's progress down the path. He greeted Bakari's arrival with a toothy, sheepish grin.

When Vera looked up, Bakari read the resignation in her eyes. She would be waiting for him to make an overly effusive, typically adult comment about the dog's headdress. Instead, he held out the glass and said, "Mostly lemonade."

Vera pressed her lips together, accepted the drink, and studied the bits floating across the top. She looked up quizzically.

"I didn't have quite enough lemons. I tried to borrow some from my aunt but she only had limes. Those are the green bits," he said.

Vera nodded. She took a sip, pursed her lips, and frowned.

Bakari laughed. "Is it the limes or not enough sugar? You Americans have such a sweet tooth. I can't do anything about the limes but I can bring you the sugar bowl."

Vera opened her mouth as if to speak and Bakari held his breath, but she merely let out a small puff of air, closed her eyes, and shook her head.

He returned to the kitchen encouraged by the flowers. It would have been easier to make a yellow daisy chain but Vera had fashioned a headdress out of sage. She still saw beauty, she adorned her dog, she played. This child would fight her way back, he was sure of it.

"My aunt tells me Vera hasn't spoken since the fire," he said, settling back into his chair after retrieving the sugar bowl from the kitchen at Betty Ann's request.

"Not quite true," said Betty Ann. She stirred several heaping teaspoons of sugar into her lemonade and tentatively took another sip. "She speaks to Jada, that's our goldfish."

"And to the dog also?"

"No, Porky's Dog is left out in the cold, like me and the rest of humanity," Betty Ann said, placing the spoon neatly on her napkin so it wouldn't leave a mark on the side table.

"And how did Jada get his or her name?" asked Bakari.

Betty Ann looked at him in surprise—again with the names. "I called him Jada because it's the Hebrew for 'he knows.' In the Old Testament, Jada is a son of Onam." She looked pointedly out the window—surely it was time to talk about Vera.

Following her gaze, Bakari explained, "I ask you about Jada, the fish that Vera can talk to, because when you tell me about the fish, I also learn about you. And then you and the fish and I hatch a plan."

Betty Ann picked up her spoon and gave her glass another vigorous stir. She had added so much sugar, much of it remained on the bottom.

"Right, I'll tell you how Jada earned his name," she said, taking a rapid sip of her drink before the sugar could settle again. "Jada *does* know. He is very interactive. You find yourself telling him all sorts of things. I keep him in the kitchen because he likes to be part of the action. They see well,

36

goldfish, they see colors, he watches us watching him."

"And you said you *won* him? What did you have to do?"

Betty Ann laughed. It had been a proud moment. She settled back in her chair and found herself telling Bakari how she hadn't wanted to go to the fair. Ralph, her husband, had died the month before and it was something they had always done together. But her neighbor had a grandson who was showing a heifer, and she needed a ride.

Not interested in watching the parade of calves and hogs that would be auctioned and eaten, Betty Ann had wandered, feeling each one of her seventy years. People glanced at her and looked away—they must have seen her lips moving as she asked God how long He was going to make her wait before allowing her to join her Ralph. But she hadn't alarmed the carny at the ring toss. She and her husband had never been sucked in that way, but this man had such a kind face. He called her over and told her she looked like she had a good arm. All she had to do was toss a ring over a milk bottle to win the goldfish inside; don't tell his boss but he'd give her five rings for the price of three.

"The carny was as surprised as I, when the fifth ring settled, easy as pie, around the neck of that bottle," said Betty Ann with satisfaction. "I didn't name Jada right away, I kept expecting him to die. So many of those tiny creatures die in the little plastic bags they give you before you even get them home."

"And how did you determine this little fish to be a boy?" Bakari asked.

"Little? Oh, he's not so little now." Betty Ann gave Bakari a rough approximation of Jada's six inches with her hands. "He's in a thirty-gallon tank that takes up half my kitchen counter. And how did I determine his sex? He has a slightly concave vent, the hint of a midline ridge running along his belly, and he's more slender than a typical female. The latter is only a clue, mind you, for the little feeder fish they give away at fairs. Male fancy goldfish can be grotesquely round and not nearly as healthy. That's what inbreeding does for you."

She paused to look at Bakari shrewdly. "I'm not one of those people who automatically apply the masculine pronoun when gender isn't apparent."

Bakari laughed, a deep, rich sound. "I wouldn't dream of thinking you were one of *those* people. And now to Vera, what is the family connection you share?"

"I simply call Vera my niece and that seems to satisfy people, but to be precise, her father was my late husband's second cousin's son."

Bakari took a moment to absorb this before asking, "And the dog? You call him Porky's Dog. Why is that?"

"Well, he's our dog now. Porky is a nasty piece of work, never gave that poor dog a name. Vera wrote Porky's Dog down for me, circled the capital letters, and went to sit with him. She does communicate when need be. I sense she's a child with plenty of imagination, so I assume she has her reasons for sticking with what people have called that poor animal for years."

Bakari nodded and murmured, "No doubt."

One more swallow and Betty Ann finished her lemonade. She gave a small cough, blinked hard, and managed to ask, "What language do you speak in Mozambique?"

"Portuguese, a gift from colonial times," said Bakari. "At least, that is the *official* language, but in my village in the North, we speak Makhuwa, a Bantu dialect. Some of us, myself included, learn rudimentary English in school. And of course many speak at least some Swahili, just to get along."

"Three languages and some Swahili and my poor girl speaks nothing right now," said Betty Ann. This was why they were here, after all.

"She's mute except to Jada and he will help her speak to us," said Bakari. "It will require your help and my tape recorder." He stood up. "More lemonade?"

When Betty Ann politely and firmly refused. Bakari picked up their glasses and disappeared into the kitchen, returning with the small black tape recorder he had used extensively in college.

"Vera needs to hear herself speaking to the fish," said Bakari.

"Are you suggesting I hide this tape recorder by the fish tank?" asked Betty Ann. "I don't like sneaky business."

Bakari said he didn't think it was necessary to hide the tape recorder. If left in the kitchen near the fish tank, the recorder would soon disappear into the background. Betty Ann could casually turn it on and off and, eventually, Vera's voice would be captured. If Betty Ann knew someone who was good with such things, she might consider minor edits to reduce extended pauses, or alleviate static if necessary.

"The diagnosis 'Selective Mutism' indicates exceptions and Jada is the exception. Is Vera's barrier anatomical, physiological, psychological?" Bakari asked with a shrug. "It doesn't really matter how we characterize it, this fish has broken through. Record her talking to him, then listen to her voice *with* her. Expand the circle, invite a friend, someone Vera knows, and the three of you listen together."

"We've been handed quite an honor, Vera," said Betty Ann as they walked to the car. "That nice young man has trusted us with the tape recorder he used in college. We'll leave it in the kitchen until we decide what we want to do with it."

Betty Ann adjusted her cushion and waited until she heard the click of Vera's seat belt before starting the car. She smiled as the engine purred to life. Her husband had always said a new car was a waste of money—it lost thousands to depreciation the moment it was driven off the lot. But last year, when she hit the three-quarter century mark, she *did* buy a new car and not an economy model. She had chosen a Caprice Classic, burgundy with a matching interior, power steering, power brakes, and heavy enough to mute the noise and bumps of the road. Even Ruth, who was happy to drive a truck with one wheel in the salvage yard, had licked her chops at the Caprice.

As they headed home, a low mist played along the side of the road and hinted of frost. The dog slept loudly with his head on Vera's lap. He woofed and snored, and at one point he retched.

"Do we need to pull over, Vera?" Betty Ann asked.

She caught the slight shake of Vera's head in the mirror. The retching proved minor. It became a short dry cough and the dog slept through it all, unperturbed.

Dusk tamped the countryside. "Eyes peeled for pronghorn," Betty Ann said as they passed the field where they'd seen the antelope the previous week, but a glance in the mirror showed Vera fast asleep. Only the seatbelt prevented the child from collapsing completely on top of the dog. She looked so peaceful, for a moment Betty Ann imagined her as any child, returning home after a tiring day afield, a visit to a relative, or perhaps a day of shopping and lunch in Rock Springs. But Vera wasn't any child—she had been dealt a savage blow, the lone survivor of a devastation that had stolen her voice.

Would Bakari's plan work? He seemed to think so. Betty Ann looked at the little black box on the seat beside her. Would she finally get to meet the little girl who, the day before the fire, had opened the door to Ruth's knock?

Betty Ann had been recovering from her surgery when Vera's family arrived in Comfrey, so Ruth had offered to go over and welcome them in her stead.

"Another wave of true McNabb hair has come to Comfrey," Ruth announced when she stopped by after her visit to the family. "Rick, his daughter, and the baby have masses of the stuff."

She relayed how the girl had opened the door and introduced herself as Vera. The child had politely said now wasn't a good time for a visit because a dog had found them. He was very dirty and thin, and she and her father were on their way to the feed store to buy dog food and worming pills.

"Tape worms?" Ruth had asked. "Long and flat?"

The girl nodded. She said when her mother had given the dog some beef stew, the food had given him diarrhea and he had pooped out lots of flat worms, so they had to get pills and real dog food right away.

Ruth had approved of the child immediately. She handed over the chocolate chip cookies she had baked and turned to go when the father appeared, car keys in hand. He said a brief hello, called "Jess" over his shoulder, and told his daughter to get in the car.

Jess arrived and insisted Ruth stay for coffee. In the kitchen, the baby slept in a bassinette, surrounded by boxes. Jess apologized for her husband and daughter's rapid departure, attributing it to shyness and Vera's obsession with the dog.

"I'd say Vera has shown excellent judgment in focusing on the needs of the dog," said Ruth.

"I guess you're right, a poor animal must be tended to even if it means not being sociable," said Jess, pouring coffee into chunky, slightly lopsided cups. "Anyway, me and the baby are the sociable ones. Vera and her father are in a different world than us. It's the artist in them. They don't mean to be rude or standoffish."

Her daughter hadn't gotten her interest in clay from her or the baby, Jess said—that was Rick all the way. As evidence of her daughter's talent, Jess removed a nativity scene from a box in the corner and arranged it on the table. The donkey, the oxen, and the camels were easily distinguishable as separate species, and although the human figures were somewhat crudely fashioned, the colors of their robes were stunning.

Vera had used brown clay, and the unglazed faces of the people contrasted with their clothing. Mary knelt in blue, Joseph stood at attention in orange. The Magi wore the most elaborate robes, striped red, yellow, and green. Before unwrapping the Baby Jesus, Jess warned Ruth not to be offended, but Jesus was brown too.

"I suggested a porcelain clay," Jess had said, frowning at brown Baby Jesus. "People expect a white Baby Jesus, but Vera said if I wanted a white Baby Jesus, I'd have to make Him myself. Stubborn, just like her dad."

Slowing for what might be a patch of black ice, Betty Ann remembered how much she and Ruth had chuckled at such clearly defined family alliances. Rick had Vera, and Jess had the baby. Betty Ann gave a shiver and turned up the car's heater.

A dog advocate, a child who insisted on a brown Baby Jesus—this was the Vera she waited to meet, Betty Ann thought as she pulled off the highway onto Comfrey Road. She looked forward to the warm house that would greet them. Rarely did she use the furnace after winter because the cat had his heating pad and Jada liked a cold tank, but with Vera and the dog to consider she was being indulgent with the heat these days.

"Not yet, Lord," she prayed under her breath. The good Lord would just have to wait a decade or so before taking her to join Ralph. Vera was on the scene now.

Betty Ann followed Vera and the dog as they stumbled sleepily up the path to the house. She almost dropped the tape recorder when her hip gave a twinge. The front door opened to the smell of chicken stew from the crockpot in the kitchen and Betty Ann thought she heard the child give a sigh of pleasure.

After supper, Vera retreated into the sitting room to listen to the soundtrack from *Doctor Doolittle*. Several weeks ago,

Wyatt Beauclaire, the fire captain, had dropped off the record, saying his ex-wife had sent it for their baby daughter, but at ten months, the child didn't seem interested. He'd get the record back from them in a couple of years. Although Betty Ann found Rex Harrison's dulcet tones more than compensated for the whiney parrot, listening to the record almost every night was becoming a bit much, so she elected to stay in the kitchen and become acquainted with the tape recorder.

She became so engrossed at testing the recorder at varying distances from Jada's tank, she didn't realize *Doctor Doolittle* had finished until she looked up to see Vera standing in the kitchen doorway.

"Nice little tape recorder, Vera. It must have been very useful to Dr. Silberstein in college," she said, smiling up at the girl. "We'll get you one when the time comes for you to go to college."

Vera walked over to give Jada a pinch of food and a murmur. She cast the tape recorder an implacable look before retiring to bed.

CHAPTER SIX

I WANT TO SWIM WITH YOU

Some days Betty Ann managed to capture just a few words, some days a sentence or two, several times a short monologue. It was three weeks before she had recorded enough of Vera's voice to hand the tape recorder over to Armand Dubois. When she told him many of the words were so soft they were almost impossible to distinguish, and increasing the volume only increased the static, his dark eyes smiled. He reminded her he was good with electronics and he would return with something worth listening to the following day.

"You're in for a treat," said Armand, standing at the door, tape recorder in hand.

He had managed to splice together over three minutes of Vera's voice. They listened together and the words, clear and sweet, full of earnest inflection, moved Betty Ann to tears. After he departed, she took some time in the kitchen to compose herself before she sought out the little girl.

Vera lay on her bed, flat on her back, eyes closed, arms outstretched, her mass of tawny hair aflame in the sunlight pouring through the curtainless window. Several weeks ago, Vera had taken down her bedroom curtains and stowed them neatly in her closet. When Betty Ann informed Ruth of the curtain removal, Ruth reminded her that from Vera's vantage point high in the October Glory Maple, the child would easily have seen the bedroom curtains burning during the house fire.

"This is a good sign," Ruth had said. "She's a proactive child and she's trying to protect herself. She's also protecting you, Porky's Dog. You're her only family now."

Betty Ann still shuddered to think of how the child had managed to reach the rods. She must have placed a stool on a chair and stretched herself to her very tippy toes. Porky's Dog lay on his side on the bed next to Vera and thumped his tail when Betty Ann knocked on the open door. A quick frown traced itself across the child's features, disappearing before she opened her eyes.

"I've made us hot chocolate Vera, waiting in the kitchen. Let's not let it get cold," said Betty Ann.

Vera obediently swung her legs over the side of the bed. She pulled her woolen socks up to her knees, smoothed the legs of her pants down, and with the dog padding behind, followed Betty Ann downstairs and into the kitchen.

Vera took a seat at the table and looked from the tape recorder to Betty Ann. One of those Dubois brothers, the quiet one, had come to get the tape recorder yesterday and now it was back. Vera knew Betty Ann had been recording what she said to Jada. People wanted her to talk, but she couldn't talk because her throat was too tight now. She'd used up all her people voice screaming in the tree. She was puzzled why anyone would be interested in what she said to Jada, but she didn't mind. Maybe the brothers had a goldfish and needed to know what to say to it.

Betty Ann played the tape and Vera sipped her hot chocolate, watching Jada cruise along the bottom of his tank, picking up pebbles in his mouth and dropping them, hunting for food. He would have to wait; it wasn't time for his snack.

"Hear your voice, Vera, just *listen* to how well you speak," Betty Ann urged as she played the tape again. Vera withdrew her gaze from the fish tank and looked at the tape recorder.

Betty Ann said, "Let's hear it one more time, then we'll phone Ruth and ask her over tomorrow. We'll share your beautiful voice with her and she can bring some of those muffins with the blueberries popping out the top."

Ruth arrived the next morning, half an hour later than anticipated. She held up a bag of muffins saying apologetically they were from her freezer. She hadn't managed to bake a fresh batch because her neighbor had gotten himself stuck in his bathtub this morning.

"Heard Frank's dog howling, bless her. I'd recommend anyone living alone get a dog," said Ruth cheerfully. "I had to phone the Dubois boys to come help me get him out, very embarrassing for all involved. Of course Frank would be better off if he lost fifty, sixty pounds, especially with that dicky knee of his. Otherwise, stick to showers I say, although there's nothing like a bath on a cold November morning."

Jada, excited by the number of people in his kitchen, swam rapid circuits in his tank, sunlight glinting off his scales. After the muffins had been warmed in the oven, Porky's Dog circumnavigated the table, eyeing them hopefully. Vera got him a biscuit from a canister on the counter and he took it delicately and carried it over to his cushion in the corner, already partially occupied by the sleeping cat who wasn't the least bit interested in dog biscuits.

"I always find it remarkable how a piece of magnetic tape can record the human voice," said Ruth as she liberally applied butter to her muffin.

She asked to hear the recording again, this time with more volume. Partway through, she held up a finger and Betty Ann paused the tape.

"Did you say, 'I went to Timbuktu?'" Ruth asked Vera. The girl bit her lower lip and shook her head.

"Hmmm, no, I believe it was 'I want to swim with Sue,'" said Betty Ann.

Vera stared at the old lady. *Traitor!* They'd heard the tape together yesterday, *three* times.

"Sue is the fish? I thought its name was something more gender-neutral," said Ruth.

Vera looked incredulously back and forth between the two women. Jada swam to the top of his tank and smacked at the surface of the water with his gaping mouth. She got up to put a little pinch of food in the tank, then walked back to the table and examined the buttons on the tape recorder. She rewound the tape and pressed PLAY and there was her voice, clearly saying, "I want to swim with you."

Betty Ann and Ruth looked at each other. "Timbuktu," said Ruth.

Betty Ann shook her head. "Swim with Sue," she said.

Vera dragged a kitchen chair over to the fish tank and stationed herself in front of it. The women ignored her and played the tape again. The little girl's voice filled the kitchen as they sipped their tea.

As Ruth prepared to leave, she walked over to the fish tank and said to the lovely orange creature, "You're really very lucky to have someone like Vera conversing with you every day. She's a strong girl with a long, safe life ahead. You and Vera will be great friends."

Jada nibbled on an aquarium plant and gazed at Ruth. He had a surprisingly cognizant eye, with a large, perfectly round black pupil surrounded by a golden, almost metallic iris that reflected light as the eye shifted to track Ruth's movements.

"You know, I've seen this fish for years, but I'm not sure I've ever really appreciated the depth of his personality before," said Ruth, looking down at Vera.

The girl pulled at Ruth's sleeve so she would lean over. "I told him...I said, I want to swim with you," she whispered in Ruth's ear.

"Of course you did, Vera. Betty Ann and I were just playing. You speak very clearly." Ruth looked at the earnest little face and smiled. "You told him not to eat too much, because his tummy is no bigger than his eye. Something I didn't remember, although Betty Ann must have told me that at some point. And you reassured him he wasn't *trapped* in a tank, he has his own special world."

Vera nodded and opened her mouth as if to speak again. When no words were forthcoming, Ruth said to the fish, "Listen very carefully, Jada, because we are about to hear something important."

The fish made a rapid circuit and Vera took a deep breath.

"And he doesn't have to be scared," she said.

"And why is that?" asked Ruth.

"Because he can't burn in water." Vera placed her hand protectively on the tank and Jada hovered behind it, pectoral fins fluttering, tail fin beating a languid tattoo.

CHAPTER SEVEN

THE JOURNEY HOME: 1995

Porky's Dog managed to get Vera through elementary school and high school, but when Vera left for college, the old dog felt his duty was done. Severely arthritic, deaf, almost blind, and recently he had become incontinent. He slept in a sheltered spot outside in the sun with the elderly cat when the weather permitted; otherwise, Betty Ann managed to keep him comfortable on towels next to the woodstove in the kitchen. But this morning he had refused to eat his breakfast.

When Ruth arrived to see how the dog was faring, Betty Ann explained why she was considering not keeping her promise to phone Vera if he took a turn for the worse. "She has midterms in two days. She's the best player on the women's softball team and they have a pivotal game this evening. If she leaves after her game, she'll be driving for over four hours in the dark. That strip of highway just outside Laramie can get icy, even this time of year."

"Then I imagine she'll consider skipping the game and come immediately," said Ruth crisply. "The coach will understand if she says a loved one is about to pass." Squatting down, she placed a hand on the dog's grizzled head. "This old boy deserves a chance to say goodbye. They both do."

There was nothing wrong with his nose, and Porky's Dog

raised his head and tested the air when Vera opened the kitchen's backdoor. Then he gave the grin that always made him sneeze. Vera shed her coat and sat down next to him. With her back against the wall and her legs extended, there was plenty of room for the old dog to lay his head in her lap.

Before she went to bed, Betty Ann stoked the woodstove. It was April but temperatures promised to drop into the low thirties tonight. Vera nestled down under the quilt that Betty Ann tucked around them and lost herself to sleep.

Betty Ann woke up early and got out of bed slowly, carefully. Oh, how she ached. She gave herself a rueful smile in the mirror. Eighty-nine years—her old bones could give her a few more. She needed to see Vera graduate college, establish herself as a potter. The girl had a good head for business, she would do well. And if it wasn't too much to ask the Lord, she prayed Vera would find a special someone, man or woman, it didn't matter, but someone kind. Someone hardworking and loving who wouldn't mind Vera's silences.

Wrapping her robe around her, Betty Ann tied the sash securely and placed her feet in the slippers Vera had bought her, the ones with the non-skid soles. She reached for her aluminum cane, another recent gift from Vera. It had a four-pronged foot, comfort grip handle, and was touted as being the most stable cane on the market.

Betty Ann had chuckled when she read the pamphlet out loud to Ruth, who had come by to adjust the cane's height. "A lifetime unconditional guarantee is a safe bet to take on those of us with one foot in the grave."

"And a very stable foot it will be," Ruth had said, testing the cane in an attempt to make it waggle.

Still, Betty Ann preferred her wooden stick, an old friend and less unwieldy in narrow passageways, but with Vera home, there was no question she would use the new one.

The moment she entered the kitchen, Betty Ann realized

only one living soul slept by the wood stove. She stooped to put a hand on the dog's nose. Not a quiver, but he was still warm, so it hadn't been long since he had departed.

The Dubois brothers said they'd be over within the hour to dig the grave. Ruth promised to bring some of the fragrant pink, white, and red dianthus from the tub outside her back door. Betty Ann looked out her kitchen window. The salvia by Vera's ceramics studio would lend some lovely shades of blue to the burial.

Leaning heavily on her cane, she managed to wipe up a puddle Porky's Dog had left behind, then shook Vera gently on the shoulder.

"Wake up my love," she said. "Our old boy has passed."

Ruth entered the kitchen with a basket full of flowers to find Vera sitting motionless on the floor. The young woman's mass of hair hid her face and her hand rested on the bundle beside her.

"How long has she been like this?" Ruth whispered to Betty Ann.

"Since I woke her." Betty Ann smiled at the flowers. "You must have picked all your dianthus."

"He's a good-sized dog, and he always liked flowers," said Ruth. "Imagine him covered."

At that, Vera turned an expressionless face toward the women and slowly nodded her agreement. Porky's Dog had *loved* flowers.

"If they had another good pitcher, I wouldn't go back," said Vera the next day as she accepted the brown bag lunch Betty Ann held out to her.

"A degree gives you options, Vera," said Betty Ann, because it was the right thing to say. "And it gives you the opportunity to meet…"

Vera cut her off. "Next time I come back he won't be here

51

to greet me."

A gust of wind parted the canopy of the linden tree and sunlight dappled the ground. The cat sat on the fence by the woodpile, the tip of his tail showing a hint of agitation. Loss was in the air.

After Vera settled behind the wheel, Betty Ann patted the roof of the truck and said, "Eventually Ruth will find us not a...not a replacement of course, but someone who needs a home."

Vera shook her head.

"I know, too soon, too soon," said Betty Ann, closing her eyes briefly and taking a step to the side, not a stagger precisely, but there had been a sudden wave of exhaustion. For not the first time, she was grateful for the cane with the four-pronged foot. She squared her shoulders and gave Vera a determined smile, ignoring the alarm she saw in the young woman's eyes.

"I'm not leaving," said Vera, making to get out of the truck.

"I made you a lunch. You'll be home in a month and we will discuss the future *in* the future." Betty Ann stepped away from the truck and looked pointedly to the east, where Laramie lay.

"I will finish the semester, but that's it." Vera rested her hand on the gear shift and cast Betty Ann a long look.

"As you wish," said Betty Ann, when they both knew what she meant was, "We'll see."

Vera gripped the steering wheel and said to the windshield, "Don't let anything happen to you ... or to Ruth, but mostly to you. Promise."

Betty Ann raised her hand in a salute and held it as Vera backed down the driveway, then she turned to the gently mounded oblong of dirt edged with tulip bulbs that Vera had planted before supper last night. The Dubois brothers had moved the heavy metal garden bench next to Porky's Dog's grave and Vera must have placed the cushion on it this morning.

Betty Ann smiled at the cat curled up on the cushion with his paw over his nose. She picked him up and settled him on her lap. She knew her duty. She'd sit here awhile, pay homage, and let the sun warm her shoulders.

CHAPTER EIGHT

DEARLY DEPARTED

On a cool day in mid-April, Comfrey's citizenry gathered to honor a good woman who had been a school teacher to so many of them and their children, and even their grandchildren. Pneumonia had taken Betty Ann Wolfe less than a year after Porky's Dog had passed.

The funeral guestbook lay open on a table just inside the church's front door and Heidi signed her name. Crow, her new last name, no longer looked foreign to her eye and it had been a relief to discard Vogel. She handed the pen to the children at her side and smiled at an elderly couple patiently waiting their turn. Six-year-old twins, Amadeus and Marcela, laboriously printed their names next to hers.

A young man in a dark suit stood at the head of the main aisle leading to the altar. He blushed furiously when Heidi looked over and flashed him a smile. When she approached, he handed her a memorial booklet with Betty Ann's face looking solemnly from the cover. Heidi asked if she could have two more for the children, if he had enough.

"S-Sure," he stammered, handing them over.

"May we sit near the front, or is that only for the family?" Heidi asked, putting a restraining hand on Marcela's shoulder as the little girl started to march forward.

"The front's fine, I mean Mrs. Wolfe only has Vera for family, so I guess you can sit anywhere, and um, welcome to

Comfrey." He looked at his friends, who'd craned their necks to see the blonde. They waggled their eyebrows at him and he waggled his back.

People in the pews tracked the woman with the two little Native kids as they walked down the aisle toward Betty Ann's coffin lying before the altar. Heads came together to murmur comments—this must be the German woman moving to Comfrey next month—the kids are her niece and nephew—they don't look like they have much white in them. Is the school going to make her cut the boy's hair? It's as long as his sister's.

Heidi ushered Amadeus and Marcela into a partially filled pew, the second from the front. A garland of flowers ran the length of the coffin. Sunflowers, blue hydrangeas, red roses, and...Heidi narrowed her eyes and leaned forward...were those sprays of huckleberries? She heard the twins whispering to each other. They would be well behaved—they saved their rebelliousness for her—but perhaps she shouldn't have brought them. Why had she? To let the townspeople get a glimpse of them and ask their questions to Ruth Creeley before she and the children moved into their apartment above the restaurant next month? To show the congregants of the Comfrey Free Church that the Crow family understood the importance of showing respect to a beloved member of their community?

There hadn't been a funeral for Nara, the twins' mother. She and Richard, Nara's nurse, had gone alone to say goodbye at the crematorium. There had been no memorial, no people gathered in song and prayer. Women hadn't dabbed their eyes, men hadn't shifted in their seats, pulling their collars away from their necks, scratching and adjusting their ties. She watched the children look around curiously. She had already explained to them what she knew from Ruth. Betty Ann had lived a good, long life—no, she hadn't been in a car accident like their mother; no, she hadn't been in a coma in the hospital; she had died peacefully in her sleep at home. Yes, their mother had been peaceful in her coma, too. No, Heidi promised the twins, she wasn't going to die in her sleep. She was going be alive to take care of them for a very long time.

"The lady's dead body is in there," Marcela whispered to her brother, pointing to the coffin.

"I know," said Amadeus. He looked at the lady's face on the memorial booklet. She didn't look special, she just looked old. They didn't have a booklet for Mama, he'd tell Aunt Heidi to make one. They had pictures of Mama and he and Marcela and Aunt Heidi would write their names in Mama's booklet. So could all the kitchen crew at Saint Gemma's in Riverton, and also this new lady Ruth—she could write her name too. There would be lots of names in Mama's book.

An old man at the end of the row dropped his hymnal and let out a loud, "*God dammit* to hell and back." The twins grinned at each other in delight.

At Heidi's nod, Amadeus wormed his way through the narrow gap left between the pew in front and the knees of the fat lady who sat next to him and disappeared from view. He emerged victorious with a shabby red hymnal in his hand. He shook his long black hair out of his face and offered the book back to its owner, who said, "Thank you, young lady."

Amadeus sidled his way back, eyes downcast. Marcela giggled and mouthed, "Thank you, young lady," to her brother, and received a scowl in return.

Heidi leaned over and whispered, "Did you see how thick that old man's glasses are?"

Amadeus bit the inside of his cheek, looked at his hands, and gave a nod.

"Look over there in front," Marcela hissed to Heidi. "There's Ruth, between a lady and another lady and a little kid. He keeps staring at us."

Heidi looked where Marcela pointed across the aisle and smiled at a sharp-featured little boy with shaggy, very pale blond air, who was indeed staring boldly at them. The child responded with an impish grin and slid from view.

"Who are those people? How come they get to sit with Ruth?" demanded Marcela in a harsh whisper. "What color is that lady's big hair? It's not red, it's not brown."

Heidi looked at the back of the woman sitting so very still next to Ruth and felt a stab of sympathy. Ruth had told her Vera McNabb's tragic story.

"The color is called auburn," Heidi said. "I think it is very lovely. The lady's name is Vera and she is Betty Ann Wolfe's niece."

"Auburn isn't a color," said Amadeus. "Just say red-brown."

"No, it's auburn," retorted his sister. "Who's the other lady?"

"I think she must be Ruth's niece, Elizabeth," said Heidi, "and I believe Ruth said the little boy is called Lucas."

The twins watched in fascination as the little head began to reemerge, but froze when a loud crash of chords announced the beginning of the first hymn. The congregants rose to attention, big people blocked little people, and Marcela and Amadeus quickly forgot the little blond boy and his bold stare.

After the service, Heidi ushered the children out a side door and into a narrow alley that led to the street.

"How come we didn't have to go out the big door?" asked Marcela, dancing sideways with the relief of being outside in the fresh air. She had a new blue dress and the skirt floated around her legs.

"I think if we go out the front door, we will be here a very long time. We need to get back to Riverton before it is too dark and I must also check on the apartment to make a list of jobs for the Dubois brothers for next week. Then we change our clothes and take Gering to the lake and eat our picnic."

The children yelped with delight and hooted to Heidi to

hurry up as they chased each other to the large black Mercedes parked in the deep shade of a linden tree. They circled the car, sticking their fingers through the gaps at the top of the windows, calling to Gering, the little dog inside. The miniature dachshund peered up, mouth open, tail wagging madly.

Heidi released a long sigh of hope and trepidation. If they could keep Marcela's secret safe in this little town, this would be a new start for them. The congregation would become her customers, and she and the children might eventually move to a house similar to one of these. She looked approvingly at the houses lining the block. Even the shabby ones had well-tended front lawns, except for one that had allowed an abundance of thistles to spring up along its fence. Were the thistles worth fighting? Once she had tried.

She smiled at the memory of Nara watching from a chair on the patio as she had struggled to remove the native thistles that had invaded a corner of the backyard. After a tremendous tug at a particularly large plant, she had fallen backward, letting out a loud German expletive as she hit the ground hard.

"You okay?" Nara called with barely controlled laughter. "From the size of those leaves, you're looking at a primary root going down ten to fifteen feet, not to mention the laterals. Take a break, the babies are sleeping on their blanket next to me and I've made lemonade."

Heidi had stamped up the slope, muttering how no thistle would have dared to invade her father's well-tended garden in Germany. She accepted a glass of lemonade and collapsed next to the twins. She had known she was in for a lecture. Largely self-taught, Nara had an astounding breadth of scientific knowledge.

"Think of a tap root as an anchor," Nara began, after settling back in her chair. "Unless you're committed to using herbicides, which I commend you for refusing to do, I'd say those thistles are there to stay. Many a Wyoming backyard has given up the fight. Besides, the bees love their thistles, bless their adorable little dorsal hearts. Anyway, this yard's much bigger than you need for a tiny dog."

Heidi refrained from saying she knew Gering did not need such a large backyard, but she had been thinking of the twins, when they were no longer babies and beginning to explore. She had bowed her head and allowed Nara's dissertation on the coevolution of plants and their pollinators to drift over her. There had never been an assurance Nara and the babies wouldn't leave. And always at the back of Heidi's mind had been the option of returning to teach at her cousin's culinary academy in Munich. But when Nara and the babies did disappear, the thought of abandoning Wyoming had become unthinkable, not if there was a chance of Nara and the twins returning.

Her baby son, born so sick and now the twins, full of life ... children had been controlling her life for years. Heidi looked over at the Mercedes where Marcela conversed with Gering through the car window. Amadeus sat on the hood of the car, which he was not supposed to do. She leaned over the low fence to admire these Comfrey thistles, not quite as spikey and daunting as those in her Riverton backyard. She placed a fingertip on a rambunctious purple tuft that sprang from a bulbous, clasping base atop a spiny stem. The thistles were abuzz with bees—perhaps the homeowner had left them with purpose in mind. When Amadeus slid off the car hood and sprinted toward her with an impatient holler, Heidi withdrew from the fence. She held the car keys high and the boy jumped to grab them. Marcela howled at the injustice of her brother always being the one who unlocked the car.

People filtering out of the church onto the sidewalk watched them as they drove by. No doubt they thought the Mercedes a fitting car for the German woman who was about to reopen Comfrey's only restaurant. Standing apart was Vera McNabb, her lovely cloud of auburn hair lifting in the breeze. Ruth Creeley's niece, Elizabeth, was saying something to her little boy, who was yelling and enthusiastically waving a sunflower their way.

CHAPTER NINE

LUCAS IS BEWITCHED

The day before Betty Ann Wolfe's memorial service, Lucas Darcy fell out of a pear tree during his attempt to look into a robin's nest. He lay on the ground, the wind knocked out of him and rather liking the stars that swirled.

His mother phoned her Aunt Ruth and reported no bleeding, no broken bones, Lucas hadn't appeared to lose consciousness, but both women agreed, perhaps Doctor Tom should check him out.

Tom Magroot had recently returned to Comfrey for good to take over his father's practice and this would be his first look at Lucas. The little boy lay peacefully on the examination table, eyes closed. The doctor ran his hands over the child's limbs, then gently cradled his head and moved it side to side. Elizabeth and Ruth stood nearby, Elizabeth smiling bravely and Ruth watching Doctor Tom, waiting for his reaction when he examined Lucas's eyes.

"Good God," said the doctor, looking up in wonderment.

"Good God, indeed," said Ruth with a grin.

"Aunt Ruth says Greta's diaries mention amber-colored eyes in the next generation or two," said Elizabeth.

"But these irises aren't amber, they're more a golden yellow. Yellow irises weren't even mentioned in medical school, amber is rare enough. He is so very pale, but not albino, so he expresses some melanin, but perhaps not in the eyes."

"Aunt Ruth and I have an albino mouse called Snowball," said Lucas.

He told Doctor Tom they had found Snowball in Aunt Ruth's garden shed. Aunt Ruth said an albino mouse didn't have a chance in the wild so they had connected three cages with tubes so she had lots of room to play.

"His language is extraordinarily advanced," said Doctor Tom to the women. "He's not yet five?"

"A little over four," said Ruth.

"He's a leapling," said Lucas. "His birthday is on February twenty-ninth."

The doctor had the good grace to look embarrassed. "I apologize, Lucas. By rights I should be addressing the patient."

"That's okay," said Lucas. "Snowball has pink eyes 'cause she's albino, but I'm not."

"Extraordinary," the doctor muttered under his breath. To Lucas, he said, "Tell me about your friends and what you like to do."

"I play the piano, I draw, and I grow sunflowers," said Lucas. "I have five friends. Aunt Ruth and her cat and Bef and my dad and Snowball."

"He calls me Bef," Elizabeth interjected. "It's just his endearment, I suppose, and I like it, actually. I don't drive and since Toots is a little out of town, there aren't really many friends his own age close by, but he plays with his cousins when my husband takes him to Gillette."

The doctor looked over his glasses at the young woman. "Have you thought about learning to drive, Elizabeth? It'd be a chance to open your horizons and Lucas's a bit."

"Lessons are starting next week, Tom," Ruth broke in. "We thank you for giving us the nudge we needed. We're hoping to convince Heidi Crow to hire Elizabeth for a few waitressing shifts or whatnot when her restaurant opens sometime this summer. I can take care of Lucas if Fred's away when Elizabeth's working, but I'm not carting her hither and yon."

Elizabeth frowned at Ruth. She didn't want to learn to drive. Fred or Ruth picked up the groceries, took them to the library, and this was the first she'd heard about trying to convince Heidi Crow to allow her to waitress at her restaurant. With Lucas, she had all she needed.

"I want to be more with Aunt Ruth and Snowball," Lucas chimed in. "You learn to drive and work for the lady, Bef. And I have a question." Lucas looked at the doctor, and his mom and his great aunt. "Are there just two big families? Everybody old is Magroot or McNabb, except for my Dad, so are there just two big families unless you marry someone?"

"I've explained about Comfrey's founders, Lucas," said Ruth.

"I know, but if my dad was Magroot or McNabb, would he like it more here?"

"Your father likes Comfrey fine," said his mother, flushing. "In fact, he loves it here."

Ruth held back as Elizabeth and Lucas walked to the truck.

"Sorry about the dirty laundry, Tom," she said, looking up at her old friend.

"Being a newcomer in a town as insular as Comfrey ain't for sissies," he said mildly.

Ruth pushed her glasses in place and said Comfrey might not be for everyone, but Fred Darcy was a good father and he'd stick around. She chose to interpret Tom Magroot's noncommittal shrug as agreement and went on to ask what he thought of Lucas.

"I'd say a savant, but he's so exceedingly verbal and, I'd venture, loving and empathetic," said Tom slowly. "He should be getting some experience with children of his own age, not only for his own sake, but so the kids can get used to him before he starts school."

"I'm working on it," said Ruth. "Most families live the other side of town, nearer the school. Heidi Crow, the woman opening the restaurant, has two kids. They'll be living in the apartment above the restaurant for the time being, so they won't exactly be in the thick of things either. They may be the youngest people in proximity to Toots. They're six but it wouldn't be unheard of for kids of that age to take on a younger fellow."

"You cooking anything good for dinner tonight, Ruth?" he asked as he walked her to the door. "Because I'm free as a jaybird."

"I think the expression is more commonly 'naked as a jaybird.'" She grinned up at him. "I'll cook if you keep your clothes on."

She chuckled as Tom Magroot gave another one of his noncommittal shrugs.

* * * * * *

On the morning of Betty Ann's memorial, Ruth went by Toot's Lucky Thirteen to collect the sunflowers and roses Lucas and Elizabeth had picked. She would add them to the blue hydrangeas and huckleberry branchlets she had picked from her own garden. There would be a lovely array of flora on her dear friend's coffin.

When she returned to pick up Lucas and Elizabeth for the service, Elizabeth looked dubiously at the green truck. She said she thought they would be driving in the car Betty Ann had kept in immaculate condition and bequeathed Ruth. It was surely more respectable. Ruth laughed, reminded Elizabeth green was Betty Ann's favorite color, the truck was vacuumed and cleaned, and color trumped respectability every time.

Lucas sat between the two women, squinching his skinny little legs to the side whenever Ruth had to shift gears, and listened to the talk above his head.

64

"Are we sitting in front with Vera?" Elizabeth asked. "Because if we are, you sit next to her and Lucas and I will sit on your other side. If Vera starts to cry, I'll cry and that'll upset Lucas."

"I'll be okay," said Lucas.

"Heidi Crow will be there with her two kids," Ruth said, to change the subject. She herself would struggle not to cry. "The church will be pretty packed, but if we get a chance, I'll introduce her to you. Then Lucas can say hello to the children. They're older, but full of beans. The boy, Amadeus, shinnied up my pear tree last fall, and got me several Anjou from the very top."

"Our tree makes Bosc pears," said Lucas, who was very fond of pears. They smelled so good and they were gritty, not crisp like an apple or smooth like a peach.

"So Heidi Crow is German and the kids are Indian?" asked Elizabeth.

"Arapaho," said Ruth.

"What's Arapaho?" asked Lucas.

Ruth snorted her frustration. "Elizabeth, don't tell me you haven't introduced Lucas to the Indigenous people of the area. The Reservation is just over the mountains."

"Well," said Elizabeth slowly, "I think he knows about the Shoshone, because some of our guests last year were Shoshone, and they were very nice. The man and his little girl made s'mores at the fire pit down by the dock and invited Lucas and Fred to join them. I forgot about the Arapaho."

"Arapaho," Lucas whispered, exhaling on the 'o' so it sounded like the wind.

They sat in the front pew with Vera. Betty Ann's body lay in the coffin in front of them. Lucas concentrated on how the sunflowers and roses were arranged among the blue flowers and huckleberries. He would draw a picture of them when he got home and give it to Vera.

Once the flowers were committed to memory, he became conscious of the organ playing softly. He let out a long sigh. He didn't like organ music. Aunt Ruth had taken him to the church to see the organ once and she said air filled up the big pipes to make sound. All that air trapped in pipes took away the music's edges.

He liked the upright piano he and his father had found under a blanket in the shed much better. Bef had come out to look when they found it and said her father had put it away because her mother used to play it and the sight of it made them sad. Lucas had said he wanted to play it and it wouldn't make him sad.

A man had come to tune it and Lucas had watched, fascinated. "You need a strong ear and lots of patience to tune two-hundred-plus strings," the man said as he removed the front panel and exposed many, many dusty strings. The man used a feather duster and they both laughed as dust motes danced in the air. Then the man ran his fingers up and down the keyboard and Lucas watched the hammers strike the strings. With his head tipped to the side, the man began to make tiny adjustments to the pins.

"Don't wiggle or twist 'em," the man said. "Turn to the right, raise the pitch, to the left, lower it, check the tone, check the tone, steady hands, steady hands."

Lucas nodded. He could hear every tiny change in pitch.

"That's quite a little boy you have," the man said to Bef before he left. "I'd venture to say, perfect pitch. Very unusual, but with eyes that color, you'd expect something special."

Not only didn't Lucas like the sound of the organ, he didn't like the music being played. It all blended together and made it hard to breathe. The people behind him began to whisper. When the whispering got louder, he turned around and there, walking down the aisle, was a most beautiful girl. Next to her was a boy with the same long black hair. The girl had a dress that was blue on top, and the lower part was lighter blue. The dress had a red stripe at the bottom. The stripe was the same color as the red ribbon in her hair.

"Heidi and the children," he heard Aunt Ruth whisper to Bef.

Lucas focused on the woman for a moment. So that was what German looked like—her skin was a little bit darker than his but her hair was as light. The woman and the girl and boy went into a pew across the aisle and one row back. Lucas turned around, got on his knees, and clamped his hands on the back of the pew. He stared, his body filling with happiness at the sight of Heidi Crow and the Arapaho twins. The girl saw him first. She said something to her brother and Lucas smiled and lifted his fingers in a wave. They didn't smile or wave back. Lucas slunk down so they would probably look away and then he'd sneak his head up again to look some more.

But just he raised his head, the organ started and Bef told him to turn around and stand up. After everyone sang, they sat again and people walked up to the front to say nice things about Betty Ann. Lucas concentrated on the sunflowers. When it was time to go, he was going to run up and grab a flower to give to the girl—a sunflower to go with her beautiful brown skin and her long black hair.

The service ended and people began to leave, but Ruth said they should sit a few minutes with Vera and wait for the aisles to clear. Lucas could see the girl and her brother and the German lady going toward a side door, but by the time he got away from Bef and grabbed a sunflower, they were nowhere to be seen. He refused to put the sunflower back on the coffin. It belonged to the Arapaho girl now.

He saw them drive by in a big black car and he yelled, but the car didn't stop. On the way home, Aunt Ruth said the girl's name was Marcela Crow and the boy was called Amadeus. They were going to live in the apartment above the restaurant, and would enter first grade in the fall.

Lucas relaxed and looked at the sunflower on his lap; the girl was not going to go away.

"How old is first grade?" he asked.

"Usually sixish," said Aunt Ruth. "The Crow twins may have been able to get into second grade because they turn seven in October but they didn't go to kindergarten, so their aunt thought first grade was best."

Lucas thought first grade was best, too. He wasn't going to be in Kindergarten until next year and he didn't want to have to catch up too much. He nodded with satisfaction. When he grew up and reached high school, Marcela Crow would still be there.

CHAPTER TEN

LEGACY: TOOT'S LUCKY THIRTEEN 1992

Before her father's death, and before she had become a wife and a mother, Elizabeth Magroot had found her solace in walking. With a sandwich, a Jane Austen novel, and Chip and Dale, her two black Labrador Retrievers, she dreamed of life away from the confines of Toot's Lucky Thirteen, the cabins her father offered to the small number of visitors who preferred unassuming little Comfrey, with its modest airstrip and seldom-used hiking trails, to the bigger towns that backed into the Bridger-Teton National Forest. A tapestry of lichens, their colors rivaling the gold and red of the finest brocade, grew on the granite boulders that dogged her favorite path as it climbed into the Wind River Range.

Although Fitzwilliam Darcy was her true love, her most cherished quote came not from *Pride and Prejudice,* but from *Emma,* her second favorite of Jane Austen's books. *"If I loved you less, I might be able to talk about it more,"* avowed the valiant George Knightley to Emma, such an achingly perfect thing to say. Elizabeth used Knightley's words to excuse the tongue-tied young men she dated. "If they loved me less ..." she repeated to herself as they fumbled with her clothing, unable to express their love in words.

She hiked until she found a suitable spot to lie down; the dogs were content to rest nearby. With her head on her knapsack, she closed her eyes, her arms flung wide to embrace Jane Austen's world. She wiped her senses of the resinous herbaceous smell of sage, the raspy cry of a red-tailed hawk, the images of the tough bunch grasses that sucked the rocky soil dry, and gave way to what she imagined to be the scent and sounds of an English countryside, roses and lavender, soft grasses bejeweled by dew, English robins chirping from a hedgerow. She could hear the creak of her carriage; smell the leather of its seats. Wrapped in a heavy velvet cloak, she saw herself leaning forward as the carriage rounded a bend and through the window, a manor house standing on a rise coming into view. Inside, in a room lined floor to high ceiling with leather-bound books, a tall, elegant, dark-haired man anxiously awaited her, ready to declare his anguished love. He had come to terms with her humble breeding and modest circumstances. Now bewitched by Elizabeth's beauty, her intelligence, and essential goodness, he found the vapid snobbery of the women thrust at him by his family repellant. Brooding and powerful, haughty yet capable of great tenderness, he paced and yearned for her.

But somewhere on Elizabeth's rambles, Fitzwilliam Darcy and George Knightley became one heroic figure that she held in her heart a little too long. The tolerable boys from high school married or moved away. After her father died, she was left to maintain Toot's Lucky Thirteen on her own and she had to be content with just an evening with Jane Austen, George Elliot, or Charlotte Bronte to fortify her for each day that followed. She swept cabins, cleaned bathrooms, and changed bedding with only a transistor radio for company. When minor repairs in the cabins were required, Elizabeth phoned her Aunt Ruth.

Ruth watched with alarm as Elizabeth's world contracted after her father's death. Having helped her older brother raise his only child, Ruth took her role of mentor seriously and continued to dispense advice liberally whenever asked to lend a hand.

"Consider reading something more contemporary, Elizabeth, you seem to be wedded to the nineteen century," Ruth said as she added another *Welcome* mat to the stack in the wheelbarrow. "There's plenty of fine cowboy romance available at the library. You're more likely to find yourself a hardworking cowboy than a Lord of the Manor."

"I know that, Aunt Ruth, I just ... it's just that it feels so real to me, like I lived that life, reincarnation, something like that," Elizabeth answered, a dose of woebegone entering her voice.

"If you already lived it, no need to live it again," Ruth stated flatly. "And how's this dreamy stuff working out for you, you being alone, running this place. Are you happy with all this?"

"Toot's has been in our family for generations, it's my legacy. Toot and Greta Magroot had their homestead here, way back when."

Ruth stopped the wheelbarrow in front of the first cabin in the row of thirteen that stretched down the gentle slope to the pond.

"Don't sound so gloomy, Elizabeth," she chided. "Vera will be heading to college next year, I think you need to at least consider giving it a try."

"Next you'll say Vera and I should be roommates."

"Wouldn't dream of it," said Ruth. She lifted a *Welcome* mat off the pile in the wheelbarrow and handed it to her niece, who stood on the cabin's small porch.

"Why wouldn't you dream of it?" asked Elizabeth. "Except you know I'm not going to go. Anyway, Vera's story's so tragic, if we shared a room, I'd be sad all the time." Elizabeth placed the mat in front of a newly painted red door. "Although now Daddy's dead, I'm an orphan too, unless I'm too old to be an orphan. But I feel like an orphan and ..."

Ignoring her niece's morose tone, Ruth wrinkled her nose and cut in, "See anything wrong with the placement of that mat, my love?"

"Oh." Elizabeth turned the mat so the word WELCOME faced toward the porch steps. She removed the comb that held her soft strawberry blond curls at bay and allowed the wind to tousle her hair. "Do you think she's pretty?"

"Who? Vera?" Ruth picked up the handles of the wheelbarrow and prepared to trundle down to the next cabin. "If you can get her to smile, she's as pretty as a picture. Nothing prettier than a smiling face on a man or a woman."

Elizabeth sighed. That was just the sort of thing her aunt would say. "I mean, would other people think she ... oh, never mind, there are no other people."

"What on earth are you talking about, girl? Comfrey's full of other people. My concern is that you're tying yourself to running Toot's when you should be off at college, or exploring the country on a Greyhound Bus. We can hire someone to run the place while you're gone."

"I don't want to be a freshman in my twenties when everybody is younger. Anyway, I told you, this is my legacy." Elizabeth trailed behind the wheelbarrow. "I don't want to get swallowed up by some big city. I want to live in a village."

Ruth chuckled at Comfrey being called a village—so very Jane Austen. Why not a hamlet? She handed her niece another mat, which Elizabeth dutifully placed in front of the bright blue door to Cabin 2.

Red doors for odd-numbered cabins, blue doors for the evens—Elizabeth had insisted on the colors and Ruth had to admit the change from brown was pleasing.

"A legacy can be a burden, Elizabeth," Ruth continued. "When your father was alive, you had time to take your walks, read your romances, dream your dreamy dreams. Now you're a proprietress at only twenty-one."

Elizabeth considered the word 'proprietress,' and found

COMFREY, WYOMING: MARCELA'S ARMY

she rather liked it.

"Jane Austen didn't write just about romance," Elizabeth protested, always feeling obliged to defend Jane to whomever listened. "She wrote about real feelings and how unfair life can be. She would have understood about a young woman, left alone."

To put an end to Elizabeth's wallowing, Ruth said briskly, "Let's get this mat business done, I still need to help Betty Ann prune an aggressive blackberry that's threatening to overtake Vera's pottery studio."

The mat replacements took only a little longer than if Ruth had worked alone.

"What next?" she asked when the mat replacements were done.

At Elizabeth's silence, Ruth whipped around quickly and caught her niece with her tongue out. "*Aha*, got you, my girl! Why do I bother coming by?"

"'Cause we're family and you love me. The toilet keeps running in Cabin 2 but you said you had to help Betty Ann."

"I fibbed. I just needed to move us along. Let's get to that toilet, the chain may have slipped, or maybe the float's stuck. We'll take a look and you'll push the wheelbarrow back to the shed, it's empty and won't tip this time."

They walked back up the drive, the wheelbarrow only tipping over once. Ruth grabbed her toolbox from her truck and decided to try another tactic with her niece as they walked back to Cabin 2.

"If you don't meet a man, you're not going to have an heir to pass this magnificent family estate down to. I'll bet in your books they're always going on about producing an heir, male preferred no doubt, but you'll produce no one at all unless you loosen up, my love."

She opened the door to Cabin 2 and frowned at its squeak. She ferreted in her toolbox for a can of WD40 and handed it to Elizabeth.

73

"Give the hinges a spray," Ruth said. "Screen door too."

"Do I have to?"

"Yes, and I'll sit right here on the edge of this nice comfy bed to watch," said Ruth, wondering how a Magroot could be so helpless.

Elizabeth looked quite pleased with herself when she'd completed her task and the doors opened and closed soundlessly. At her aunt's instance, she followed Ruth into the bathroom. They peered inside the toilet's tank.

"*Ha*, look at that, chain slipped off," said Ruth. "We'll bend the hook a little more and re-hook it, shouldn't happen again. Hand me my needle-nosed pliers, no, those are channel locks, Elizabeth, how's that going to do the job? Blue handles, pointy, that's right."

Ruth fiddled with the hook, flushed the toilet twice, and gave a sigh of satisfaction. As they left the cabin, Ruth looked around for something to compliment her niece on. "Well look at that, what a lovely detail you painted along the doorway here."

Elizabeth flushed with pleasure. "English primroses and ivy," she said. "I'm working my way through the cabins, four more to go. I've started a Cavalier King Charles Spaniel over the bed in Cabin 8."

"There's no denying your talent, Elizabeth," said Ruth. "I'll look forward to seeing that when you're done." She regarded her niece solemnly a moment before continuing, "Elizabeth, let's give a young man from this century a chance, or not so young, how about taking a look at Booker McNabb? From Pennsylvania, sure, but he claims an uncle who was brother to our Faolin McNabb in the mid-1800s. That path you used to walk runs right along his property in Wild Horse Valley. When he bought that twenty acres right out from under that Chinese gentleman, that was an unpleasant business, I can tell you." Ruth shook her head. "Well, let's not get into that now."

"Booker McNabb is not very friendly," Elizabeth said as

74

she trailed Ruth to the truck.

Ruth stowed her toolbox behind the seat and turned to regard her niece. "He's a nice-looking man and pleasant enough," she said. "He's a private sort of fella, think of him as brooding. I suppose I can see how some would view him as standoffish." She took a look at her watch. "Oh Lord, look at the time. Now I've really got to get a move on, got a date tonight." Ruth tried unsuccessfully to sound nonchalant.

"Doctor Tom?" asked Elizabeth.

"That's right, back in town to cover for his dad so the old man can go fishing for a week. Probably should have married Tom, being only a fourth cousin. I could have remained a Magroot, but Creeley got in there first. And look at me giving you advice, if I loved you less, I'd shut up."

CHAPTER ELEVEN

MR. DARCY COMES TO TOWN

Several months later, a flesh-and-blood Mr. Darcy rode into town, a taciturn Fred in a white pickup, not a brooding Fitzwilliam on a steed. He arrived as part of a maintenance crew, hired to grade and re-pave Wild Horse Valley Road, up to and including the Lake Cheynook parking lot. When he signed into her registration book, Elizabeth had to re-read his name twice—F. Darcy he had written, using an economy of letters.

"The 'F' stands for ...?" she asked, holding her breath.

"Fred," he said, blushing to the roots of his very fair hair and giving her a shy smile.

Elizabeth exhaled; of course, *of course* no one was called Fitzwilliam these days, certainly not in Wyoming. He was of medium height and far from elegant in his baseball cap, khaki shirt, and jeans. She found it difficult to imagine the man standing awkwardly before her engaged in an anguished tumult as he tried to reconcile his noble lineage with her reduced circumstances. But Fred Darcy was here, and as her Aunt Ruth never hesitated to point out, Elizabeth was alone, and unless Fred was one of those men who eschewed a wedding ring, so was he.

From behind the office curtains, Elizabeth watched the men park next to their cabins. They unloaded their belongings and stood in their doorways smoking a cigarette, drinking a beer, waiting for someone to suggest it was time to eat. The sound of the pond, a synchronized rhythmic pulsing that had started a few days ago when the male frogs deemed it finally warm enough to emerge from their burrows, drew several of the men onto the dock to throw stones. The frogs swallowed their song and dove deep among the reeds; calling for a mate was second to survival. The pond fell silent. Elizabeth shivered as the men's unaccompanied voices wafted up the hill, raw and too loud.

After the crew left to hunt dinner in town, Elizabeth paced around the office, stopping each time she passed the tall antique mirror, which hung as it always had on the wall behind the front desk.

"I believe my countenance favorable enough, to please the likes of he," she said to the mirror, in what she thought to be a passable English accent. "Be brave Elizabeth, be not a timid lass, and ... Oh, for God's Sake, stop being so ridiculous."

She glared at herself. "So *bloody* ridiculous," she amended.

She made a circle around the front desk and stopped in front of the mirror again. When Darcy first set eyes on Elizabeth Bennett, he had said to his cousin, "She is tolerable; but not handsome enough to tempt me," but oh, how fiercely his love had come to flame. She moved close to stare into her eyes, almost as blue as the English delphiniums she'd planted from seed by the garden gate. Miss Elizabeth Magroot of Comfrey, Wyoming had no one to introduce her to gentry at a ball in an English manor, she wouldn't be offered a chance at Pemberley, she would have to take matters into her own hands.

"I am *more* than tolerable, I *will* be handsome enough to tempt you, Mr. Fred Darcy," she said to her reflection, her voice caught between a giggle and a sob. A shiver ran through her.

"Just you wait 'enri 'iggins, just you wait," she said, dusting off her best cockney accent. She grinned at herself sheepishly—Eliza Doolittle had a habit of cropping up whenever Elizabeth was in need of a dose of gumption.

The men returned after dark, trucks edging cautiously down the gravel drive. They brought a male energy with them, raucous laughter, the slamming of truck doors, cabin doors. Bereft of warmth, the sounds of a Comfrey night crept in, bringing the dry rasp of leaves buffeted by wind, the mournful hoot of an owl.

Elizabeth watched her pupils grow large with daring as she applied mascara to her lashes. She exchanged her t-shirt for a blouse and debated how many buttons to leave undone, settling for three, a spritz of rose water behind her ears, too little? She applied more. The temperature outside hovered in the mid-thirties and she reached for her jacket, hesitated, then decided against it.

"Make haste, oh make haste," she whispered as she scurried down the gravel drive to knock on Fred Darcy's cabin door.

Elizabeth gave a little laugh as Fred stood before her, pink from his shower. "Do you mind if I check to see if the fridge is still working?" she said through chattering teeth. "It's late, I know, but we've had problems with it, and I've been so busy."

To Fred, it all happened so quickly, like in the porno flick he had rented with two of his buddies at the hotel in Casper. Perfect title, *I Want To Be Your Handyman,* in which a heavily muscled man, shirtless, with low-slung jeans and a tool belt, knocks on an apartment door. As a woman opens the door, her robe parts, and she stands there more naked than any woman Fred had ever seen. She's embarrassed and tries to close her robe, but the handyman reaches for her hand, soothes her, tells her it's alright, nothing to be ashamed of. And then the camera pans to his jeans, and an enormous erection straining to be freed fills the screen.

The movie just kept getting better, people actually doing

all the things Fred had dreamed of, and you could tell the actors were really feeling it, you couldn't pretend all that heat, engorgement, and fluid. It was his first porno movie, shocking and thrilling—he had to go to the bathroom to jerk off halfway through, he couldn't help it. It had been torture waiting for his friends to go back to their rooms so he could watch the movie again in private.

The next day at Walmart, he bought a tape of the James Taylor song, "Handyman." "*Hey girls gather round ... Come-a come-a come-a come-a come come.*" He felt free to play it anytime; no one would know what he was thinking.

And now, here was this woman, Elizabeth something, knocking on his door, talking about his refrigerator, shivering so much he could hardly understand her. Pretty little blond thing, she had forgotten to button her blouse all the way and a pink-laced bra peeked out at him. He offered her a beer, she spilled a little down her front, he mopped it off with the red-striped towel from the kitchenette, and she caught his hand, held it to her breast. She turned her head to the side, exposing a delicate white neck. He moved closer—she smelled of roses—and he trembled as she pressed her hips into him. He brought his lips to her neck, hesitated, and took a lick. She tasted of salt and beer. He heard himself groan as she pulled at the cord on his sweatpants.

They did everything, everything he'd seen in the movie and, toward the end, when she knelt before him and took him in her mouth, he realized he had found a reason to get married. To have this, every day, forever.

* * * * * *

By the time Elizabeth realized Fred had little to say about his love for her, because he simply had little to say about *anything*, she was pregnant. The distraction of her baby's fluttering kicks, his twists and turns, the miracle of seeing his

79

tiny hand waving to her from his sonogram, filled her days and she couldn't wait to meet the tiny being growing inside her, stretching her skin, pressing on her bladder.

When she told Fred she wanted to name their son Beau, he surprised her by shaking his head.

"Don't think so," he said.

"The baby feels like a Beau," she insisted, putting her hands on her belly as a little limb pushed against the inside of her uterus. "It means 'handsome' or 'sweetheart.' The long form is Beauregard, but I'm just thinking Beau, or that could be his nickname."

It was rare for Fred to push back, but he shook his head again, this time saying, "No way, Elizabeth."

Since her body was doing all the work, Elizabeth felt she had the right to name the baby. Each time, or at least more than half the time, when she said "Beau," the baby moved. Perhaps if she gave the semblance of considering a suggestion or two from Fred, she might be able to wear him down.

She asked him for possible names and he shrugged. "I'll think on it. But not Beau and not Fred."

When he had nothing for her the following day, she went to the library and got a book of baby names and their meanings, and spent a happy few hours reading.

She handed Fred the book when he got home, saying, "We'll each pick out ten, then compare lists." She felt a burst of affection when he nodded and took the book.

Elizabeth came up with a list of names that she was sure Fred would dismiss out of hand. She couldn't see him agreeing with the book's assurance that Addison, Brook, Carol, Frances, Hillary, and Leslie were gender-neutral names. With the addition of Wilbur, Krishna, and Mordecai to the list, Beau stood a good chance.

At breakfast, she put her list on the table and asked Fred for his, but he handed her paper back without looking at it.

"I'm not ready," he said. "Still on the 'K's. It takes time,

Elizabeth."

Two days later, Fred handed her his list. "Choose one of these," he said.

He had printed three names and their meanings in block letters:

ELWOOD = MAN OF THE FOREST

HUNTER = A HUNTER

LUCAS = LIGHT GIVING

"I said *ten* names, and you haven't even looked at mine," Elizabeth said.

"I know that, but this is my list, and you get final say on my list." Fred poured coffee into his thermos and turned to look at her. "Elizabeth, you get to choose from my list," he repeated. "Whichever one you want."

"Elwood, they'll call him 'Woody,' like an old man or some penis joke," Elizabeth said. He wasn't taking the naming of their child seriously.

"So don't choose it. Man of the Forest sounds English, so I thought you'd like it." Fred looked at his wife, at his thermos, out the window to his truck and freedom. "Gotta go," he said, trying for a smile. "Meeting the crew in Farson. Maybe overnight in Rock Springs, I'll let you know."

CHAPTER TWELVE

LEAPLING

Fred said 'No thanks' to cutting the cord when the delivery room nurse poked her head into the waiting room, announcing his son had arrived. The nurse disappeared, presumably to get someone else to do the deed, and returned a few minutes later.

"He's just getting a wash, they're cleaning up your wife. You're welcome to go in or you can meet your little family in Room 14 in half an hour or so," she said.

"Think I'll get some coffee and let things, you know, get taken care of. Maybe track down some flowers or a balloon," said Fred.

"Flowers," said the nurse.

"Okay. Room 14?"

"That's it. The lactation nurse will be dropping by around two-thirty."

"I think I may be gone, a meeting," said Fred, sitting down abruptly.

"Do try to stay, Mr. Darcy, breastfeeding really is a family affair," the nurse said with an encouraging smile.

Fred's hands shook visibly as he stopped to fill a flimsy paper cone with water from the cooler, before setting off to hunt for flowers.

Elizabeth lay on her side and reached her hand toward him

as Fred entered the room. Her bangs were damp against her forehead and she looked very young, like a teenager, not the mother of a little boy. Fred fervently hoped she knew what to do. She didn't really have any girlfriends; Ruth would help and his mother had offered to come, but Elizabeth turned her down.

Fred grasped her outstretched hand, surprising both of them by raising it to his lips and kissing it.

"Oh," said Elizabeth, giving his hand a squeeze, rewarding him with a pleased smile. She rolled on her back with a grunt and looked at the five pink carnations springing from the slim white plastic vase Fred held in his other hand.

"Pretty—do they smell nice?" Elizabeth murmured and Fred held the vase to her face. "They smell just like they're supposed to, like soap," she said around a yawn. "The soap in the bathroom at home? If you move the water, you can put them next to the bed. Thank you, Fred."

Fred was relieved he'd chosen the pink carnations and not the blue-dyed daisies, which hadn't smelled good at all. He kissed Elizabeth awkwardly on the forehead and placed the flowers close enough so she could smell them. He looked around for the baby.

"They took Lucas to weigh him again, the scale in the delivery room was on the fritz," said Elizabeth. "They'll be back soon, the lactation nurse is coming early because the labor nurse said you might have to leave."

"Ah ... I thought I'd better get back, in case people ..." Fred avoided looking at his wife.

"Aunt Ruth told you, we're not to worry. She'll stay at Toots until we're back," Elizabeth reminded him, raising herself partway up on her elbows, pushing her heels on the bed before collapsing.

"What are you trying to do, Elizabeth?" Fred asked, sure she should just lie there for now.

"Sit up. I want to sit up, and you're not helping, Fred. Be

83

happy you didn't just give birth, my bottom's sore, but if you bring that donut thing over and put it under me, it's supposed to help."

Fred picked up the foam rubber donut she pointed at, and winced at every groan she made as he rolled, lifted, and hoisted.

"Okay?" he asked when he was done.

"Hmm, better. Could you pull the curtain a little? The sun's in my eyes."

Fred returned from the window and looked critically at Elizabeth's thin blanket. "Warm enough?"

"Yes, thanks. Come sit, Fred, you'll love our baby, he's perfect," Elizabeth said, closing her eyes.

"Picked up our little leapling from the nursery on my way over," said a large, grey-haired woman as she pushed a glass-sided cart into the room. Through the glass, a baby, wrapped tightly in a blue blanket, peered blearily out from under a knit cap, his tiny pink tongue probing the air.

"We're hungry, we'll have to wake Mommy," the woman said, extending her hand. "Patty Sweet, lactation specialist."

"Did you say 'leapling'?" asked Fred, shaking her hand and looking at the baby, not expecting him to be quite so small and red-faced.

"February twenty-ninth, he's born on Leap Day, a leapling. I always feel they're special, these little leaplings, no science behind it of course, but my niece is one and I've tracked several others, my own personal little study. They're gifted, very stubborn and independent. You'll see," she said, lifting Lucas out of the cart and handing his tightly swaddled body to Fred.

"Support the head," she said as Fred took the bundle gingerly. She watched in amusement as Fred held the baby in front of him as if holding a log he was about to put on a fire. Fred hefted the bundle with both hands, assessing its weight.

"And how much would you say he weighs?" Patty asked.

"Ummm, 'bout six pounds, twelve ounces?"

"That's almost it on the nose, six pounds, four ounces, add for blanket and diaper, and you've got it. You'll make a very good father, not all men can come that close to figuring their baby's weight," said lactation specialist and daddy-reassurer Patty Sweet. "Just you wait, you'll see this is the best thing you've ever done."

Lucas proved to be a good-natured baby. He smiled at his parents in the morning when they looked in his crib, he laughed uproariously at peek-a-boo. He searched Elizabeth's face as he nursed, as if trying to read her thoughts, which were usually focused on him and his remarkable beauty.

Elizabeth basked in her baby's total dependence. She slept when he slept, ate when he ate; she sang to him and he rolled his head and made sounds. In the late afternoon after Fred returned from work, they sat on the sofa, Fred with his bottle of beer, Elizabeth with her peppermint tea, staring at their son on his blanket on the floor, waiting for him to do something. Elizabeth would list the events of the day; Lucas holding his head up, almost rolling over, waving his hands to music. They were both there when Lucas crawled to the coffee table and pulled himself upright. They clapped, he wavered and collapsed on his rump, and the three of them laughed.

When he was old enough to ride in a backpack, Lucas would reach his hand over Elizabeth's shoulder to stroke her cheek or gently tug at her hair, pushing his little feet against her back to get a better vantage point. She was alone when Lucas took his first toddling steps unaided, and was unprepared for the alarm she felt at his budding autonomy. He could walk. He could walk *away* from her.

Shortly thereafter, Lucas refused to eat the pancakes she'd dyed pink and green with food coloring, as her father had done for her. He would wriggle out of her lap when he heard his father's truck in the driveway. He called Fred 'Daddy,' but insisted on calling her 'Bef' instead of Mommy.

"I think he's saying Beth, he hears Elizabeth and knows it's you," said Fred.

"How would you like him to call you Fred?"

Fred shrugged. "Fred rhymes with dead, it's not that good sounding."

"Dead? *That's* the reason you like Daddy more than Fred?"

Fred looked at the clock again—time to go, but he felt he had to stay and say a few words in Lucas's defense. "Elizabeth, Beth, that's nice-sounding, and Bef is cute."

"Cute, you said *cute*, you never say cute."

"I know, sorry, I'm just trying to...you know, he's just a little kid. He knows you're his mom, his mommy."

"I'd say you should call me Mommy, exclusively, until he gets the idea. Except he *has* the idea because he calls you Daddy."

Fred carefully poured coffee in his thermos and turned to her. "Okay. *Mommy,* then. I won't call you Elizabeth."

Elizabeth watched him hold his stupid old battered thermos and look at the clock.

"This so isn't fair," she muttered to the table as she put her head down, immediately ashamed of herself, a woman, a *mother* in her twenties. She heard Fred quietly close the door behind him.

Fred walked to his truck, refusing to examine the frustration he so often felt with his wife these days, and thought about Lucas instead. He wasn't sure what was fair, but he didn't think Lucas was trying to be *unfair*—the boy just probably liked the sound of Bef. Fred didn't know anything much about kids. His sister's boys were more...not normal, exactly, but more what you'd expect with the mommy-daddy business. He'd never loved anything or anyone as much as he loved his son. Fred got in the truck and let out a long sigh. Without Elizabeth, he wouldn't have Lucas. They were a package deal and he'd make the best of it.

CHAPTER THIRTEEN

AUTONOMOUS LUCAS

Several months later, Fred and Lucas drove to Gillette for the weekend to visit Fred's sister, Sandy, and her family. Elizabeth rarely accompanied them because she said the sprawling city, which claimed to be "The Energy Capital of the Nation," was too depressing.

Sandy regarded her nephew, who sat at her kitchen table with his sketchpad as she and Fred waited for the coffee to brew. Lucas had taken her fruit out of their bowl and arranged them in a precarious stack. He was sketching them as fast as he could as the banana perched on top threatened to topple them all.

"Do you think he's getting even more different?" asked Sandy. "My boys ..." She paused, not wanting to alarm her brother.

"Your boys what?" Fred got two mugs out of the dish drain.

"Well, you know when they were his age, they did all the regular things, coloring books, practicing staying in the lines ... unless they got frustrated, then it was scribble, scribble, scribble."

"I don't think we have coloring books at home. He likes fruit and his fruit looks like fruit," said Fred, looking over at his son, who was now using one hand now to hold the banana in place and still managing to draw. "I told you that nurse at

87

the hospital said he'd be artistic because he's a leapling."

"Mom and I were talking about that," said Sandy, pouring their coffee. "We think it's just an excuse you guys are using to let him be different. When he gets to kindergarten, they'll have coloring sheets and he'll be expected to color with the other children. Does Elizabeth believe all this leapling business?"

"We don't really talk about it. She doesn't have friends with kids so she doesn't compare him to anybody. It's pretty much her and Lucas most of the time, until I get home from work. Her aunt looks in a lot."

"Lucas should be with kids, Fred. Elizabeth should make more of an effort. Does he get to be outside?" Sandy stirred a teaspoon of sugar into both their mugs, licked the spoon, and put it in the sink.

"Of course." Fred sounded somewhat defensive. "He's got his own section of the garden. He just planted sunflowers."

"He's so pale, I wondered. Anyway, Mom's dropping off some age-appropriate coloring books in the morning before you leave." Sandy turned her back to the kitchen table and leaned close to whisper to Fred, "Try to get him interested so he won't be a little weirdo in kindergarten."

Lucas, whose hearing was very acute, looked up and asked, "Wassa weirdo?"

Elizabeth examined the coloring books that Fred handed her upon their return.

"Age-appropriate? Do your sister and mom think I can't be trusted to pick out age-appropriate coloring books for our son if I wanted to?"

"They were just trying to be helpful, Elizabeth," said Fred. "My sister says in kindergarten the kids sit and color, learn to stay within the lines, that sort of thing."

Elizabeth opened her eyes wide and blinked. "Oh, I hadn't thought about school," she said.

They watched their son, who had lined up his blueberries in a row and was in the process of sticking his tongue on them and managing to flick them into his mouth, one by one. After a moment Elizabeth took *Farmer Frank and Moo* off the little stack of coloring books and opened its cover.

"Do you want to color with me?" she asked Lucas.

Lucas looked over and shook his head.

"Your aunt sent new crayons too." Elizabeth took a red one out of the box and held it out to Lucas. "This one is called *Fire Engine Red,* but I expect we can use it to color Farmer Frank's tractor." She glanced at Fred and they smiled at each other.

Lucas took the crayon and sniffed it. "It smells bad. You color, Bef," he said, handing the crayon back. "First I eat blueberries and then I get paper and I draw Farmer Frank's trakker."

Eventually, Elizabeth managed to convince Lucas to use the crayons to color his own drawings—at least he wouldn't wrinkle up his nose at the smell of crayons in kindergarten. She made a determined effort not to worry too much about her son fitting in with the other children in school, which was, after all, more than a year away.

At Lucas's insistence, they began taking the transistor radio out to the garden. They only received three stations—a talk show, pop music, and classical. Lucas showed a marketed preference for classical and often stopped in his digging or weeding to conduct. His sunflowers flourished, her roses bloomed as never before, even Fred seemed more interesting, and Elizabeth kept away the gloom that had hovered after losing her mother so young. The gloom had reappeared after her father's death but dissipated once and for all with Lucas's arrival.

After lunch one day, Lucas spied "book-inna-bag" on top of the bookshelf, and asked Elizabeth to get it down.

"The book's broken," Elizabeth said, puzzling at how her son had determined the bag held a book.

"I want to see the broken-book-inna-bag," he insisted.

"No, it would break even more. Let's read about Mowgli and Baloo," she said, holding up *The Jungle Book*.

The following day, Lucas pointed to the bag again, promising to be careful, and once more, Elizabeth refused.

"It's not really a children's book," she said. "It's not a happy book."

"It's a bad book?" he asked.

"No, I wouldn't say *bad*, it's just a broken, boring book. Let's read more about Mowgli and the wolves."

After they finished *The Jungle Book*, Lucas dug himself in. He wouldn't help Elizabeth select any more books from the children's section at the library and he refused to listen to those she insisted on bringing home.

"I want to read book-inna-bag first," he told her.

Since Elizabeth couldn't dispose of the book in the bag—it was far too old—part of the Magroot Legacy—she moved it to the garage for storage. She was unprepared for Lucas's look of horror when he noticed the bag had disappeared.

He flew at her, crying, "I hate you, I hate you. I want book-inna-bag. You're *bad* Bef, *bad*," punctuating his misery with his little fists.

"What's going on?" asked Fred, appearing at the backdoor to find his son under the kitchen table and his wife in tears.

"He wants that old book, the one in the canvas bag. It's too scary for a small child. The horrible drawings, all those characters that don't make sense," Elizabeth wailed. She hiccupped and blotted her face with the dishtowel crumpled in her hand.

She took a deep breath, trying to ignore the little presence skulking under the table, and said, "My father found it after my mother died—he said my mother told him she loved it when she was a little girl, but she must of had a good copy, an

English one, I'm sure she did. It wasn't like this one, old and moldy, she wouldn't have liked this one."

The week after her mother had died, her father found the book in one of their old trunks as he was storing her mother's clothes away. He brought it in the house, carrying it as if it were a wounded animal.

"Your mother had a book like this when she was a little girl in England," he had said. "She would have wanted me to read it to you."

Night after night after night, they sat on the sofa and her father read the book aloud, his voice tight and sounding strange. When he looked away to wipe his eyes, they would pretend he wasn't crying. She had been afraid if she didn't sit quietly and listen, her father would disappear, like the county nurse who stayed and played awhile after taking care of Mother, or the other one, the pretty lady who cleaned and made food, she had gone away too, leaving only Aunt Ruth to come by and check on them.

"I *hated* it, Daddy's copy. I *wanted* to like it, I wanted ... oh, I don't know. And Lucas says he hates me," Elizabeth finished miserably. She looked at the dishtowel, blew her nose on it, and threw it in the corner.

"He doesn't hate you, he ..."

But Elizabeth shook her head and plowed on. "It's not really a kid's book, it's just one of those books that adults think is clever, imaginative, but it doesn't make sense. Like a bad dream, an acid trip."

"Like LSD?" Fred sighed. "Really Elizabeth?"

"Those trips are supposed to be scary, plus I've had plenty of bad dreams, *especially* after that book," said Elizabeth. Becoming Lucas's mother had shut the door to her own childhood and she didn't want it opened, not even a crack.

From the corner of his eye, Fred saw his son peek out from

under the table. "Just let Lucas look at the book, Elizabeth, you don't have to read it to him."

"The pictures are creepy," Elizabeth said half-heartedly, aware she was losing ground.

"Maybe not so bad, now you're all grown. Get the bag, Elizabeth."

"You never read, you don't know."

"Get the bag. I'll show the book to Lucas. If he's okay, I'll read it to him."

"No, you won't. If he still wants it after he's seen the wretched thing, *I'll* read it to him," said Elizabeth, struggling for some kind of traction. "You can get the measly old book if you want, it's in the cabinet over the sink in the garage."

Fred retrieved the bag and placed it before his wife. Lucas crawled out from under the table and climbed onto a chair, eyeing the bag and his mother expectantly.

"Say sorry to your mom," Fred said.

Lucas whispered under his breath.

"Louder, Lucas," his father said. Lucas whispered his apology a little louder.

"Okay," said Fred. "We okay, Elizabeth?"

The book was an original American printing, dated 1866. One evening, while her father attempted to read, the book's innards fell from their binding and page 188 lay exposed on the floor. As her father went to get something to put the book in, Elizabeth leaned over the edge of the sofa to stare at the page—another drawing of a frightened little girl. Elizabeth could count to ten; she focused on the digits, 1 and 8 and 8, 1 and 8 and 8. Her father returned with a canvas bag, looking almost cheerful.

"Just the thing for your mama's book," he said, waving the bag at Elizabeth. "Held my wedding shoes, but who, except your mother, puts shoes in a bag?"

They placed the book inside the canvas sack and Elizabeth

pulled the drawstring tight.

"Tie a knot, Daddy, so it can't get out," she said and her father did.

Effectively silenced in its dark cocoon, the book had gotten what it deserved, remaining for years crouched on the top of the bookshelves, the mockery of a Cheshire cat, until it had piqued the curiosity of a sharp-eyed little boy.

Elizabeth removed the bag's contents carefully. An abbreviated title, *Alice Wonderland,* had been written in ink on the coarse muslin cover someone had sewn for the book long ago. The writing had bled into the cloth and looked fuzzy, not like a proper book title at all.

Once, when her father left the room to deal with someone who'd rung the bell on the desk in the office, Elizabeth had peeked under the muslin in an effort to see the book's original red cover. In the center, stamped in gilt, stood a small Alice, holding a struggling animal. Some of the gold had flaked away but the animal might have been a pig, legs in the air, and Alice, only one eye and a corner of her mouth remaining, looked horrified. The muslin tore as Elizabeth tried to investigate the book's back cover. She hadn't really thought her father would be angry but she'd shoved the book away hastily, disliking Alice even more.

"Open book, Bef," said Lucas impatiently, kneeling on his chair, elbows on the table.

"What do we say?" asked Elizabeth absently; the book was smaller than she remembered.

"Please."

"That's right, please," said Elizabeth, touching the muslin cover, yellowed, stained, almost powdery in places.

She opened to the title page and showed Lucas the inscription, written in a precise hand:

"To our darling Cora on her 8th birthday,
How you have lit Our Lives!
Your loving Grandparents, 17 July, 1867"

"This was written by Greta," Elizabeth said softly. "You've heard of her, a great, great, oh sooo many times great, grandmother of yours. Do you want me to tell you about her? Her husband, Toot ..."

"Not now," interrupted Lucas. "Read, Bef."

She didn't remind him to say please. He had climbed onto her lap and was pulling at her cardigan so it would partially cover him too.

Tentatively, Elizabeth peeked at page 188. There was Alice, her arms up to ward off an attack by a deck of playing cards, a wide-eyed hare fleeing in one direction, a rat and a duck escaping in the other. Was the lizard about to bite her foot? As a child, Elizabeth had thought so, but now she wasn't so sure.

Lucas put an impatient hand on his mother's arm.

"No, start at front," he said.

Elizabeth turned to Chapter 1: *Down The Rabbit-Hole.*

The print was still small and mean upon the page. She started to read of Alice's boredom, sitting on the riverbank as she watched her sister read a book, but Lucas spied the first illustration and wanted to turn to it right away. Drawn in pen and ink, the White Rabbit looked at his pocket watch. The rabbit's eye had appeared so angry all those years ago, but now it merely seemed to be scrutinizing the watch's face.

The next illustration was of Alice pulling a curtain back to discover a little door.

"Her head's too big," said Lucas critically. "Silly Alice."

Alice's head *was* too big, and her feet were too small, realized Elizabeth.

She turned to the next picture; Alice holding a bottle in her hand.

"Read that, Bef," instructed Lucas, pointing to the label

around the bottle's neck.

"It says 'DRINK ME.'"

"Oh no, that's bad. Bad for Alice," said Lucas with the authority of a young child who had recently been chastised for almost drinking a similarly sized bottle of cherry cough mixture.

Elizabeth realized that in many of the illustrations, Alice—with her high, straight forehead, huge, deep-set eyes, and sullen mouth—looked ill. As ill as her own mother had, as she wasted away, confused and frightened, like Alice.

And here were the animals, although most a little less frightened or frightening, the mouse, the lizard, the frog-footman, the fish-footman.

Lucas pointed to the hands on the Dodo and laughed, "Dodo has hands *and* wings. You can't have hands *and* wings," and Elizabeth laughed too.

"Which should he have?" she asked.

Lucas shrugged. "Can't have both. Silly book."

"Silly book," agreed his mother.

For a time, *Alice's Adventures in Wonderland* became Lucas's favorite book. He examined the illustrations over and over, using parts of the text to point out details Elizabeth hadn't seen before.

"Rabbit gloves and fan," he said, pointing to the illustration of the rabbit dropping his belongings as he fled from Alice's gallons of tears.

"Red King sleeping, Man with the eel," he would say, and wait for his mother to find the king, curled up at the base of a tree with his mouth open, or the portly Father William balancing an eel on his nose.

"Poppies," Lucas exclaimed when he first saw the flowers on Father William's waistcoat. "Bef likes poppies," he said, snuggling next to his mother.

"Cat piller smoking on mushroom, cat in tree, Alice scary

hand over rabbit, long neck Alice." He asked for these ones so often that Elizabeth placed the caterpillar smoking its hookah and the Cheshire cat grinning from its branch together with his other favorites, not bothering to keep them with their original chapters.

CHAPTER FOURTEEN

SUBSTITUTE TEACHER

Ruth crouched down to check the lug nuts on her snow tires. Snow was forecasted for tomorrow's drive to Rock Springs Community College. She shook her head at the hubris of thinking a week of unseasonably warm days meant western Wyoming was done with winter in late April.

The four baby opossums, which had been delivered to her yesterday by Sublette County Wildlife Rescue, had come at an inopportune time. Each weighed less than thirty grams, so they required tube feeding every two hours. It was a routine she was familiar with, but one she could do without since she had already agreed to substitute once more for the Mandarin teacher at the college.

Because the babies were so very young, Ruth had briefly considered taking them in their incubator with her to the college—the contraption was light enough— but what if she got stuck somewhere along the way? The tiny animals would cool down rapidly and they were clinging to life as it was, so Vera would have to help out again.

"What do you think, Betty Ann?" Ruth whispered as she placed the lug wrench back in its spot behind the front seat of the truck. "Do I put too much on our girl?"

"She is yours now, she needs to help so she knows she belongs," she heard her old friend saying.

Ruth washed, dialed Vera's number, and left her request on the answering machine. No doubt the girl was busy in her studio, but she'd be in the house soon for lunch.

"I'd be grateful for your help with baby opossum feeding again, same routine as last semester," said Ruth when Vera called her back. "I'll be gone three times a week, but this time only for a month. Mrs. Ling is taking the baby back to Taiwan to visit her sick father, who may not last much longer."

"Okay," said Vera.

"Initially the babies will need tube feeding three to four times each day I'm gone, and perhaps a fifth time if I get delayed. We can probably start regular bottles in a couple of weeks and that will be easier."

"Not a problem," replied Vera.

"Would you be able to drop by later today for a refresher on the tube feeding?"

"Yes," said Vera.

Ruth hung up, smiled at Betty Ann's picture, and remarked, "Still a girl of few words, but once more our Vera's stepping up."

After Betty Ann's death, Ruth had made a habit of bringing Vera meals several times a week. Usually she found the young woman in her pottery studio behind the house she had inherited from Betty Ann. Often they shared the meal, Ruth shouldering much of the conversation. In turn, Vera helped Ruth with her animals and shared the largess from Betty Ann's garden. For her birthday, Vera had surprised Ruth with a grey ceramic mug she had made. The handle had the grace and texture of an opossum's tail.

"Darjeeling or Assam?" asked Ruth when Vera came through the kitchen door.

"Assam," said Vera, putting a bag of triple ginger snaps on the counter, courtesy of one of her customers.

Ruth's eyes brightened in anticipation. "From Mrs.

Ichikawa?"

Vera nodded.

Several cups of tea and all the cookies later, they put their cups in the sink and went into Ruth's bedroom, where the incubator sat on a card table near the bed.

"Tiny," Vera said, looking at the sparsely-haired infants nestled in a towel in their incubator.

"Tiny, with a will to live and assume their role in the ecosystem," said Ruth, taking one of the four small bottles of milk out of a pan of warm water and screwing on a nipple with a short length of spaghetti tubing attached. "Would you get me one of the babies, please?"

Vera reached into the incubator, picked up one of the little creatures, and handed it to Ruth.

"Take care to miss the trachea, can't have milk getting into their lungs. Remember to tilt the head like this." Ruth demonstrated, holding the tiny creature in one hand. "Ease the tube in."

The little animal's eyes opened in alarm as Ruth slid the tube behind its trachea into its esophagus.

"Like last time," said Vera.

"Last time the babies weren't quite so young."

"I know." Vera attached a tube to another bottle and picked up a second baby. Ruth watched with pleasure; here was another example of the competence and confidence Betty Ann had so often praised Vera for.

"You're a natural, my girl," Ruth said when Vera was done, giving the young woman a pat on the back.

"Thank you," said Vera, with the hint of a smile.

After they finished with the feedings, Vera asked, "Have you put your snow tires on?"

"I have indeed. You'll be stuck with my pestering for many years to come."

Looking away, Vera nodded.

On her way out of town early the next afternoon, Ruth

stopped at Raul Diaz's law office on Main Street. The lawyer had just returned to Comfrey after three months visiting his son in Hawaii and he might not have heard the news that Heidi Crow was finally moving to town.

"The good-looking blonde with the little Indian kids?" Raul asked, raising his eyebrows. "She was in here last October asking to use the phone. I don't remember her using the last name Crow."

"The children are Arapaho, and yes, she is a lovely young woman, so I assume we are talking about the same person. She recently changed her last name to Crow from Vogel. Shedding the vestiges of an unhappy marriage, I imagine. She and the children came to Betty Ann's memorial two weeks ago." She looked at her watch. "Anyway, I haven't much time before I'm off to subbing a Mandarin class in Rock Springs again. I stopped by as a courtesy since you'll more or less be neighbors."

Raul rocked back in his chair with a grin. "I know you subbed a group of oddballs last year, but seriously, that class at the community college is still going on?"

"When opportunity knocks, some people will answer," replied Ruth.

"How many students?"

"Thirty started the class last fall, twelve remained at the end. Nine of the twelve have signed up again."

Raul snorted. "How is that cost-effective, running a class with nine students?"

Ruth sighed. It was *Mandarin*, for heaven's sake—every American who learned it was taking a step onto the world stage. "Nine people in Sweetwater County have re-committed to taking another semester of the most widely spoken language in the world," she said, "so I imagine the forward thinkers in administration at the college think it well worth the money."

Raul chuckled and gestured to a chair. "Never mind, take

a seat, you have some time, let's talk about something more interesting. What's taking our Miss Crow so long to reopen Taylor's Refresher?"

Ruth looked at her watch again—she could give Raul ten minutes or so. He had been a few years behind her in school, but age eclipses time, and now they were contemporaries and friends. She said the name of the restaurant would now be The Crow's Nest, not a unique name on the coasts where restaurant names often had a nautical reference, but in this case Heidi was referring to her family name.

"Okay, I get that. It has a nice little ring. Cozy. But why in hell is the restaurant not open by now? I come back from living the life in Hawaii, and I'm still forced to open a can of beans." Raul placed his hand on his belly as it gave a loud rumble.

"She took the kids to Munich for her cousin's birthday and they decided to stay a month. Then she had to move a small side business she had in Riverton into the little building behind Wilson's Feed Store. It's been vacant for years, so there was work to be done."

"Jesus, Ruth, my head's spinning." Raul raked a hand through his unruly bounty of greying auburn hair. "What's the side business? What's a woman with two kids need with both a restaurant *and* a side business? How does she have time for any fun?"

"She exports a lingonberry shortbread to the coasts. You'll soon see a white van with Hebeka on the side trundling down Main Street on its way to Denver airport a couple of times a week." Ruth narrowed her eyes. "As to when and if Heidi has time for fun, you're not a kid person, Raul, so I'd say she hasn't time for fun with you. Your boy turned out as well as he did because your ex-wife got custody."

"That's true," agreed Raul, his Hawaiian tan giving him the look of a man of leisure. "But my boy and I are best buds now, plus you should see his house in Hawaii, he has his own private beach, it's amazing. I might move out there in a few years. And you can't blame a man for fantasizing about a woman that looks like her."

"Nobody's blaming you, Raul, just keep your fantasies to yourself," said Ruth, who was considering Booker McNabb for Heidi Crow. "I'm hoping she'll hire Elizabeth for a few waitressing shifts a week. Fred and I can take care of Lucas, and I've promised Heidi I'd find her some kitchen talent. I need someone who can do more than wash dishes and serve—someone with a real interest in food. Heidi was an executive chef in New York before she came out here."

"An executive chef in Comfrey?" Raul's face split into a broad grin. "Who woulda thunk it? Did you try Armand Dubois? Didn't he have a boyfriend or something who was a hoity-toity chef in Jackson?"

"I agree Armand has the work ethic required and he's eager to learn new things, but he's helping a friend open an aquarium in Pinedale. I've managed to get several people for Heidi's shortbread bakery. I'm thinking of approaching someone from last semester's Mandarin class as co-chef, or whatever that position would be called. I haven't yet seen the roster, but I'll bet he's on it this year. He was my most talented student. He has a natural linguistic ability and he has a bold and experimental way with food."

"Food?"

"Food and culture are inextricably intertwined, so last semester, I had some feast days with my class. This semester I'm only covering a month, so we'll have a single feast at the end. If this man is back in class and up for grabs, I intend to get him for Comfrey."

Raul chuckled. "Poor guy won't have a chance. Is he Chinese? Is he going to be interested in cooking regular food?"

"Have you always lacked this much flexibility in your thinking, Raul, or are you attempting a joke?"

"I don't know, a joke maybe?" said Raul good-naturedly.

"I like Chinese food, just not all the time."

Ruth checked her watch again and rose to go. "He is Shoshone, actually, and although he did pull together exceptional Chinese dishes for class, my sense is that he has a broad appreciation for fine food from many ethnicities."

Raul walked Ruth onto the sidewalk and they shuddered as wind gusts blew up the road. Ruth turned her face to the sky and stuck out her tongue to capture some of the snowflakes that had begun to fall. She wrinkled her nose and grinned when she saw Raul doing the same thing.

They both knew if he moved to Hawaii he wouldn't have this.

The copse of dormant bog willows in the swale half a mile out of town looked the better for their silvery-white dusting. Before Ruth reached the highway, the snow began falling in earnest. The wind caused flurries to skitter across the road and she slowed, grateful she had given herself an hour longer than she had thought she could possibly need. She ducked her head and peered up at the sky. The drive back to Comfrey that night might not be too challenging if the clouds kept moving.

She collected her roster from the office and examined it as she walked down the hall. She felt a rush of warmth when she saw her plans coming together. She wouldn't approach Esau Aoah until the last day of class, then *whoosh* ... she'd lay out an unassailable offer he wouldn't refuse.

She arrived early enough to arrange the desks in a circle and down her cheese sandwich before the students entered the room. She welcomed the familiar faces, three men and six women, ranging in age from early twenties to mid-seventies, two Natives, seven whites, no blacks—not surprising, this was Wyoming. They grinned at her—a warmer welcome than she had received in the fall.

* * * * * *

Last fall, when she'd met these people for the first time, she knew she hadn't inspired confidence. She had stood before them, a scrawny little white woman, wearing khakis and a neatly tucked-in white cotton shirt, subbing for a woman who looked much more like a Mandarin teacher, the elegant Mrs. Ling from Taiwan.

Ruth had introduced herself in Mandarin and said her stepfather, Jerome Lee, had been Chinese and taught her to speak both Mandarin and Cantonese. She was no longer married and her grown daughter had moved away. She was a realtor, the town of Comfrey's historian, and she rescued abandoned animals. In fact, she currently had a little black and white terrier mix, who had been picked up wandering along Highway 191. He was as friendly as could be and he was looking for his forever home. She repeated herself in English, then once again in Mandarin.

She felt the students relax during her second repetition in Mandarin. From their faces, she could see she had used many words new to them, but she had sounded as authentic as their 'real' teacher. She had smiled encouragingly at an older man in a blue bow tie. She would start with him—a blue bow tie said, 'look at me.'

"Using as much Mandarin as you can," she had said, "tell me why you are taking the class and something about your family and the animals you share your life with. Then tell me a hobby or a particular interest of yours."

In halting Mandarin, most students said they had a cat or dog, half were married or had been married, several had children, they gardened, hiked, watched sports, some liked to travel. The last student to talk gave the most fulsome answer.

"My name is Esau Aoah, father of none," he had said, shaking his long black hair back to reveal a startling array of scars. They covered much of his face and disappeared down the right side of his neck into his collar. "I am Shoshone. My family crossed the Bering Land Bridge 10,000 plus years ago.

I have a corn snake named Bill, three feet long, one inch high. If I had my own place, I would consider a black and white terrier mix. I speak English, two native tongues, and I am taking this class to challenge my brain. I like to ride my bike and I really like to cook."

Ruth listened with appreciation. The man spoke almost entirely in Chinese and he had a good ear. Despite the remarkable scars that limited his facial mobility, he had mastered the distinctive pitch contours of the four major tones of Mandarin. Say a syllable using the wrong tone and a word's meaning could change dramatically. *Ma* said in a high flat tone meant 'mother,' *ma* in a falling, then rising tone meant 'horse.' Use one of the other tones and it could mean 'hemp' or 'scold.'

Before class ended, Ruth had handed out a selection of recipes. She explained they would have four Chinese potlucks, each highlighting a different region of China. These recipes were for the first one. They could trade their recipe with another student if they liked and she herself would participate. She would also take care of napkins, paper plates, bowls, and chopsticks.

"This is Rock Springs. What if we can't find the right ingredients?" a woman had asked nervously.

"Learning a language means appreciating a culture, and much of culture is embedded in food," Ruth said patiently. "I am sure you will be able to improvise with ingredients."

"Most of us work during the day, that's why we're taking a night class," another student pointed out. "There's a couple of Chinese restaurants in town, can I just buy something to bring in? Mrs. Ling didn't make us cook."

"I have a job *and* kids at home," a woman joined in. "My husband doesn't mind babysitting so I can take this class but if it looks like I'm cooking for us and not for him, he's going to have a true hissy fit."

The Shoshone caught Ruth's eye and she nodded at him.

"Tell you what," he said. "I have extra time on my hands

and I really like to cook. If it's okay with you," he had looked at Ruth and then to his fellow students, "anybody who wants can give me their recipe. If they chip in for the cost of ingredients, I'll prepare their dish."

Ruth had realized she'd have to reassess her expectations as she examined the faces of those who had chosen to take a night class rather than putting their feet up and giving themselves over to a television set. Childcare, employment—many had already faced a full day. The students looked at her hopefully and after a moment she had acquiesced.

She said she had no issue with handing over the food preparation to someone who sounded as if he'd enjoy the challenge. Even if they hadn't prepared the food themselves, they would all still gain a true appreciation for the diversity and complexity of Chinese regional cooking if Mr. Aoah could handle the intense spicy, garlicky flavors of Sichuan cooking, or the salty, vinegary dishes of Shandong, modified for what is available from fish markets in Rock Springs.

"How about shark fin soup?" a young man asked. "My uncle is going fishing in the Gulf, maybe I can get him to bring back a fin or two. Last time they were there they saw Hammerheads swimming along the side of the boat. The captain shot one."

"How perfectly imbecilic of him." Ruth suddenly felt each and every hour of her very long day. "What a terrible waste of a life. An absolute no to shark fin soup. After its dorsal fin is sliced off, the shark is released to the ocean bleeding and unable to swim properly and it dies in agony. The fin has no flavor and little nutritional value. Many shark species are highly endangered. What was once a symbol of vanity, power, and wealth has had a devastating effect on marine ecosystems."

"But you said we're studying Chinese culture as well as language," the student had protested. "Shark fin soup sounds cool and it's like part of their culture."

"Many Chinese advocate against the barbaric practice of shark finning these days," Ruth remembered saying. "You can appreciate a great deal about a culture without leaving your judgment behind."

"What about Inuit being allowed to hunt whales?" The student's voice had been edged with challenge.

"Subsistence hunting by Indigenous people is another matter entirely," Ruth countered, swallowing her irritation at herself for once again climbing on her soapbox. She felt the tide of goodwill that had grown while students talked of their family and pets, and when she had allowed Esau Aoah to shoulder the burden of preparing their feasts, turn against her. She had strayed too far from how Mrs. Ling ran the class—vocabulary, grammar, repetition.

A bell rang somewhere down the hall and the students had stood, their relief evident on their faces. Most had never heard of shark fin soup, and Indigenous rights were always a touchy subject—they were embarrassed by their new teacher's passion and anxious to return home to the comfort of a life without the image of a bleeding animal dying for frivolity, or whales being harpooned by Inuit. They murmured their goodbyes as they filed out, except for Esau Aoah, who had remained in his seat, arms folded and legs stretched out before him.

"What do you think?" Ruth asked as she picked up the cardboard hatbox she had placed on the front table before the beginning of class. Now she was glad she hadn't had the time to share its contents. How was that for childish pique? "Am I too different from Mrs. Ling? Too political? Have I lost them?"

He nodded. "Probably a few, but I solemnly swear, no apex predators will be harmed during my food preparation."

"And for that, we thank you," Ruth said.

When she thought she might have seen a smile on that terribly ravaged face at her use of the pronoun 'we,' she added, "Not the royal use of 'we,' I assure you, Mr. Aoah, I merely refer to my sharky friends and I."

He chuckled. "Mr. Aoah would prefer you to call him Esau—" he got up "—and I'm wondering what's in the box."

"It's a teapot. Qing Dynasty, mid-nineteenth century. I meant to end class by showing it to everyone but the shark fins got in the way. If you come here, I'll show you."

Many would have resisted handling something so obviously valuable, but when Ruth handed the teapot to Esau, he had taken it without hesitation. Turquoise, apricot hues, greys, and green, the knob on the lid was gilt with gold. She watched him examine the figures of two men and a woman sitting cross-legged under a tree, sharing a pot of tea. They sat near the edge of a cliff. Across a steep chasm stood a temple, snowcapped mountains in the background. Esau carefully removed the lid and smiled at the tea stains inside. He had looked up at her and asked if she actually used the pot for tea.

"Indeed I do." Ruth took the teapot and nestled it back its box. "I believe objects only retain their true value if they are used for the purpose for which they were made." Remembering her audience, she added, "Of course I make exceptions for organic material—feathers, porcupine quills, some basketry."

He gave another chuckle. "Whew, had me worried there for a moment."

"Do you like tea, Esau?" She enjoyed the sound of his name. But had this Esau's parents chosen the biblical name without knowing it referred to the non-favored child of Rebekah and Isaac?

"Yeah, I drink quite a bit of it."

"When you come to Comfrey sometime, we will share a pot. It's an open invitation."

He had nodded and smiled politely the way people do when you've tried to be too friendly too fast. He told her to wait while he got his bike, which was locked to the rack down the hall. If she had parked in the faculty lot, it'd be pitch dark because all of the lights had been vandalized last week.

She had admired the sturdy bike as he walked it toward her. It was turquoise blue and made not a sound. He told her it was Bianchi, and since he didn't have a car, he could afford it. She said on their feast days she'd pick him up. No need, he said. A guy where he lived had a car and owed him some favors.

They had exited the building into a bone-chilling pitch black. He turned on his bike light and walked her to her truck. After her engine started, he swung effortlessly onto his bike and started to pedal off, his long hair whipped by the wind. Ruth rolled down her window.

"You need a helmet, Esau," she had shouted, her words swallowed by the night. She doubted he would wear one, but she knew she wouldn't be able to prevent herself from suggesting it several more times.

CHAPTER FIFTEEN

THE GORY DETAILS

"I mean it, Esau. I've got a nice fixer-upper, handyman's dream, gardener's delight, all the buzz words that mean it's affordable," Ruth said as she packed her Mandarin tapes and books into her briefcase on the last day of her second stint of subbing. "And I know of a job possibility—a talented German woman with two young kids is opening a restaurant. She's a first-class chef, the product of rigorous culinary training in Europe. Based on what you prepared for our feast days, I mentioned you to her last year when she was thinking of purchasing the restaurant. I knew I'd have to look outside Comfrey for someone who could keep up with her."

Esau stifled a sigh of irritation. After pushing it last semester, Ruth Creeley had given up trying to get him to wear a bike helmet, but she wasn't shy at getting in people's business in other ways. Ruth had been a little too effusive over his cooking last year and it had been almost a relief to have Mrs. Ling back.

"Plus my niece, Elizabeth, is looking for a handyman a day or so a week," Ruth continued. "I don't think you have to be particularly handy, but her husband's away a lot, road crew, and she's completely out of her element when it comes to anything practical. She owns a little enterprise called Toot's Lucky Thirteen, named after the founders of Comfrey. It has thirteen cabins and it's popular with hunters, hikers, and the like. Her little boy, Lucas, is a precocious one and will provide plenty of amusement. Anyway, this is all to say, Esau, we can keep you plenty busy. Added bonus, now that I've finished my stint here, I'm restarting my classes with Comfrey's little group of Mandarin learners. We've been going several years. We meet at the church hall after AA meetings Monday, Wednesday, and Friday. Everything you'll need, under one roof."

Esau looked at Ruth in surprise. Had he said anything about AA? He wasn't offended—it was just nothing he would have shared. He didn't get the sense Ruth had fought alcohol herself, but she had obviously seen the struggle within him and understood his need to keep busy.

"Thanks, maybe. I'll think on it," he said, wondering even as he said it what there was to think about. He'd been in his current digs too long, afraid to move on, afraid not to. He couldn't hang around at a halfway house in Rock Springs forever, putting in time until death's release. Ruth had said Comfrey backed into the Wind River Range. He had looked at the other side of those mountains every day when he lived in his uncle's house on the Wind River Reservation. A cabin with a garden, in a town probably filled with narrow-minded whites, a town that had produced this one adventurous, pushy little woman who had managed to rope in a German executive chef...but a chance at a full-time job, part-time work with Ruth's niece, and he wouldn't be more than four hours from his uncle's house.

Would there be enough to distract him in that small town to keep the cork in the bottle? Maybe. Yeah, maybe.

* * * * * *

A week later, Esau walked through the open front door of The Crow's Nest and looked around. Ruth had said the place was supposed to open in a few weeks, but it looked like there was still a lot to do. The booths had been installed along the plate glass window, but the floor still needed work, chairs and tables were pushed against a wall, the counter held shelves yet to be installed, light fixtures still in boxes. Was the menu planned, the kitchen stocked?

"Hello?" he called.

A trim, blonde woman came through the kitchen doors and asked if he was Ruth's friend. Then she looked at him more closely and flashed him such a brilliant smile, he looked around to see if he'd missed something.

"You do not recognize me?" she asked, her smile receding.

Did she look familiar? Esau wondered, before shaking his head.

"Emma Lazarus, the poem, you do not remember?" she asked. "At Saint Gemma's in Riverton. Not even two years ago, we talk about the painting on the wall of the dining room, the Statue of Liberty, and the next day you bring me ..." She stopped when he continued to shake his head.

He had lost years—maybe their paths had crossed. People remembered him because of the scars. Esau knew the poet, but not her connection to this woman. He had still been an automaton in those days, going through the motions, nothing inside.

The woman backed off and introduced herself formally as Heidi Crow. She spoke in lightly accented English. Ruth had said she was German, but he would have had her pegged as a European even without the accent. You could always tell; whites from Europe had a different way about them than American whites. He knew Luisa, his wife, would have argued, "You're kidding, you can't lump people into just two big groups like that, American whites, European whites. A Greek the same as a Swede?" And he would have said, "They do it to us, a Shoshone the same as a Ute?" Toward the end of their marriage they had argued just to argue, not remembering how much they used to be on the same side.

Heidi Crow directed him to one of the red upholstered booths and sat opposite him. Real leather, nice touch, risky—but if people liked her, they wouldn't cut into the seats. He watched her scan his application, her lips moving.

When she was done, she looked up with a small smile, then out the window to the mountains, before saying, "A beautiful view, in the rain, the snow, the sun."

He nodded. He wanted to add, like a little kid, "The Reservation on the other side is beautiful too."

She probably wouldn't think so—you had to wake up to it day after day to understand. The rolling hills, the smell of dirt and sage, the way the sun could pierce the clouds and light up the high prairie grasses. On ceremonial days, the odor of fry bread and meat, the sound of people beating on a big circular drum together, one rhythm, singers raising a single voice to the sky.

Esau was conscious of the German woman waiting for him to meet her eyes and when he did, she said, "You were an accountant for the federal government for over eight years and you want the job as a cook? Is the seven-year gap in your employment the reason why you go from the big numbers job to the kitchen?"

"Pretty much. You want the gory details?"

Esau watched as she examined him at length, a pretty woman with dark blue eyes who saw, he imagined, a generic Indian with a fucked-up face, looking like another Indian with a fucked-up face she'd met before. Or had they met? Those lost years were a price he was still paying. Maybe she did look a little familiar.

A Brooks Brother's suit had distracted from his acne scars during his white-collar years, but no suit could pull eyes away from the damage done in the accident that had killed the kid. Besides, you'd never wear a suit to an interview like this, something more casual but not shabby, clean, nothing ethnic. She would assume from the seven-year gap, he'd been locked up or in the gutter those years, maybe both. She wouldn't think he would be someone to take a chance on. Except Ruth Creeley had written a letter of recommendation for him. Anybody who knew Ruth would respect that.

"Yes, I think some gory details are necessary," said the woman who would determine whether or not he moved from the safety of Rock Springs to Comfrey. She said it in a business-like way and held her hand bent at the wrist, palm up, the way the choir director at his parents' church in Laramie had invited the choir to begin.

Esau took a deep breath, but instead of launching into *Gloria in excelsis Deo,* he said, "I'm a recovering alcoholic, one year, nine months, three weeks, two days, and," he looked at his watch, "... four hours sober."

She raised her eyebrows, her mouth gave a slight twitch, and she made a note on his application. She looked at him expectantly.

"I lost years, lost my job, lost my wife, shamed myself." He felt self-conscious, trotting out such a predictable, pathetic story. Was it really a disease? Some days it just felt like he was a weak, lost, lonely bastard. Take away bastard—his parents were strict Catholics.

"Before you think we all drink, I have six brothers and I'm the only one who drinks...drank." He gave a wry smile.

"Six brothers? Seven children, your family is Catholic?"

"Oh yes," he said.

He had always been different from his brothers, the raging acne of his teenage years having ravaged more than his skin—it had socially isolated him. Two of his brothers had been afflicted too, but not as badly, or at least it didn't seem to bother them as much.

His parents had determined their boys would become Catholic. They were a model middle-class Native family who lived in Laramie and attended a mostly white church. He was the only one in the family who refused to be Confirmed. It had been his first real act of rebellion. His second had come six years later, at fourteen, when he had come home drunk, one time drunk but an unpardonable sin. His parents had sent him to the Wind River Reservation to live with his father's brother. Had they sent him away to protect him, or to protect them and his brothers *from* him?

Living in his uncle's house, he grew his hair long, learned Shoshone from his uncle, Arapaho from his uncle's wife, discovered his gift for languages—the words became a rhythm, like music in his head. He grew to love the big sky and barren landscape that surrounded him, his acne scars didn't bother him as much, he felt an acceptance he'd never felt in Laramie. He discovered he had an affinity for numbers from a devoted teacher in a small reservation school. She had encouraged him to go to college, and not knowing what else to do, he had. His parents paid. Was it blood money for sending him away? The non-handsome, non-Catholic son, who had come home drunk one time, became a success.

An accounting degree, a government job, a wife looking for the security that kind of life afforded. The drink placed on the backseat tray as he dozed flying back from a business trip in Washington D.C. had been courtesy of his boss, who sat across the aisle. His boss had been a nice guy.

"Salute," they had said to each other, raising their glasses. Jack Daniel's neat, just the way he had liked it on his occasional binges in college. Meeting his wife had put a stop to his drinking and he had been dry for years until that sweet and oaky Tennessee whisky put a crack in his armour.

During his fall from grace, he'd crashed his car and killed his passenger, a young hitchhiker desperate enough to get into a car that must have reeked of booze. In the hospital, face wrapped in bandages, slits for mouth and eyes, Esau had lain on his back for days, counting the holes in the acoustic ceiling tiles and wondering why he had stopped the car. Maybe even in his drunken state he'd realized a dark road in the rain was no place for a skinny, pallid teenage boy.

Now he greeted those scars every day in the mirror and asked forgiveness from the spirit of that poor faceless kid. One of America's lost children, accepting a ride from a drunken stranger because anywhere would be better than where he had been. The police had never managed to identify the boy, but Esau felt him out there, waiting patiently, waiting to give him absolution when he passed over.

"I've been living in this halfway house for almost a year," Esau said. "My third, I flunked out of the first two of them, but in this one I've learned to cook from a chef who owned a three-star restaurant in Santa Fe, in recovery like me. He lost his restaurant, but not his ..."

"Passion for food?"

"That's right." He felt his face trying to smile, liking that she supplied the word 'passion' when he was about to say 'interest.' "He infected me with a passion for food too. Accounting compared to food?" Esau slowly shook his head.

She gave a nod of agreement. You couldn't accuse her of being overly friendly like a lot of white women were, trying to pretend they were at ease with him. He thought he had become good at reading people, but he was having a hard time reading her, and he wanted this job. Ruth had taken him up to Lake Cheynook and they'd hiked part of the trail to Toot's Peak. She introduced him to a couple of people, a blacksmith artist type who lived off the road up to the lake; the town doctor, who she introduced as an old flame that was in the process of rekindling. He could continue Mandarin classes with Ruth and she had shown him the small house he could afford. It was fine, a little off the beaten path, couldn't see the neighboring houses. Any free time he had he could put in working for Ruth's niece, Elizabeth Darcy, who owned cabins at the end of town. He met Elizabeth's little boy, Lucas, whose eyes were more yellow than a wolf's, sharp, lots of questions. He'd be a pest but he had made Esau laugh. Comfrey might work out—it all depended on his getting this job.

Into the silence that followed his last comment, he offered, "I'm working on the second half of this life."

She leaned back in her seat, met his eyes, and said, "This life? I also."

Watching him, listening to him, Heidi concluded Esau Aoah really didn't remember their previous meeting or the following day, when he had come back with Emma Lazarus's poem, *The New Colossus,* copied in a shaky hand and left for her. And later that day she'd received a call from the Highway Patrol—the twins and their mother had been in an accident. In all that followed, she had forgotten the man she had dubbed 'The Wounded Man of Dignity.' But they had connected that day and she recalled him so clearly now and he couldn't remember her. How awful for him.

She gathered herself and slid out of the booth, saying, "I forgot to offer but I have made coffee, Ruth said you drank it. You were on time, thank you. Black or white?"

"Excuse me?"

"Your coffee. Black or with cream?"

"Oh, black. Thank you."

Esau watched her go onto the kitchen. She looked tired— she probably needed the coffee more than he did. He bet she didn't smoke, certainly wouldn't eat store-bought cookies. Coffee, cigarettes, and cookies, the staples of any AA meeting he'd ever gone to. Ruth said the woman had two kids and another business, a shortbread company. How much could one person take on? Germans were known for their industry, or so he'd heard. Maybe she couldn't help herself. Most days he congratulated himself for taking a shower, cooking meals at the halfway house, biking five to ten miles to keep busy, and going to a meeting or a class.

But with those four quietly spoken words, 'This Life? I also,' she'd reached across a divide and he realized he liked her—he could be useful.

Heidi came back with two cups of coffee, black for him, white for her, and a plate of shortbread. From Hebeka, her other business, she said. They had been baking in Comfrey for a few weeks now. She had set up the bakery in a space behind the feed store before she'd closed her bakery in Riverton. She had orders to fill and couldn't shut down production, even for a few weeks.

He sampled the shortbread—crumbly, buttery, delicious.

"Hebeka. Is that a German name for something?" he asked, taking another piece.

"It is a German, Italian, German name. My partners, Beppe and Karl, we take the first two letters of each of our names."

"I can see why you sell a lot of these, but I'm wondering, have you ever considered raspberry preserves?"

"I have. The raspberry with the almond flavor, I agree, is very good. Maybe even to my taste, I prefer it. But Karl thinks the lingonberry is unusual enough to give us a special edge."

"He may be right, marketing is nine-tenths the battle."

"Your accounting is showing, Mr. Aoah," she said, with the hint of a smile in her very blue, very clear eyes. "We make a single product and we export almost all of it to the luxury markets on the coasts. A lingonberry shortbread made in a small town in Wyoming makes the people tickle." She smiled at him before looking at his application again.

Her twist of the idiom made him stifle a grin and he studied his hands until her next question had him look up.

"How similar are the Shoshone to the Arapaho?" she asked.

"How similar are the Germans to the Italians?" he

118

responded, not sure if the comparison was apt.

"My nephew and niece are Arapaho, they live with me, I was hoping ..."

Ruth hadn't mentioned that. Esau tried to hide his surprise. Maybe Ruth had thought he'd disapprove. He would have; a white woman—German, no less—raising two Arapaho kids. Nephew and niece, a family tie, so maybe it couldn't be helped, but people wouldn't see their white side. He batted back a cloud that hovered and schooled his face. He wanted this job.

"I speak Arapaho and Shoshone," he said. "I appear to have a gift for languages, I'm learning Mandarin now with Ruth Creeley."

"I have had to work very hard at English, so I would say I do not have this gift," Heidi said with a wry smile. "I have heard about Ruth's classes, she has not asked me to join. You will let Amadeus, my nephew, practice his language with you?"

"Why not? Your niece too, if she wants."

"Marcela says she is German, she likes to practice with me."

Esau looked away, hoping his irritation wouldn't show. Arapaho kids with German names, and the niece identifying as German in the land of her own people, that was just part of the problem with whites raising Native kids, or half-Native kids. Was she a blood aunt? Somehow he doubted it. But he didn't know her story, he really didn't know, and she hadn't taken the kids to Germany. And he wanted this job.

"Just to be clear, you are looking for a *cook*, am I right?" he said.

At that, she gave a laugh, her eyes lit up and years melted away. She grinned, saluted, and said, "Welcome on the board."

He puzzled at that—on *the* board? Was that a German thing? He asked who else was on the board.

"Two brothers, Armand and Tyree, perhaps Ruth's niece,

Elizabeth. I meet her one time and I am not so sure of her concentration."

Esau grinned. "I've done a little handyman work already for Elizabeth Darcy, and I know what you mean. Do you think people around here make the connection with her name to Jane Austen?"

"Perhaps not so many. But you make the connection and I make the connection, and we may not be so special."

Esau looked at Heidi and nodded. He liked her humility. It seemed genuine and not what you'd expect from a woman this white and this good-looking. She hadn't shown surprise when he had mentioned Jane Austen. Had they met before?

After Esau Aoah left, Heidi sat back and released a sigh of relief. When she had served him on the food line at Saint Gemma's Kitchen in Riverton, this man had told her he minored in English Literature in college. Now he couldn't even remember their meeting and so he wouldn't remember her sitting with him briefly as he ate his meal. He wouldn't remember her telling him she was looking for Nara Crow and her identical twins. And that would mean Marcela was safe.

CHAPTER SIXTEEN

ESAU SETTLES IN

His legs burning the last two miles, Esau made it up to Lake Cheynook's parking area and debated whether to lock the bike to the rack near the restrooms and jog up the trail to look down on the lake, maybe even take a dip. The cold would be welcome but dark would descend by the time he got home and his light had burned out on his bike—he gave a wry chuckle. For years he hadn't cared what happened to him, but something good floated in the wind and he was going to give this new life a try.

The only other time he'd been up to the lake, Ruth had taken him in her truck. Wild Horse Valley Road was an incredible workout. Parts of the road were so steep, he could smell his brakes burning as he descended. So that was going to be an expense—tires and brakes—but he wasn't going to give up this ride. He stopped at the metalworker's gate to pick a handful of comfrey from the thick mass growing there. Ruth had pointed it out, courtesy of Greta Magroot, an herbalist from Pennsylvania. The woman had settled the area in the 1850s with her husband and kids, and the orphaned kids of another family. She sowed seeds wherever she found a suitable place in homage to the powerful herb. Ruth had said the leaves added to bathwater soothed aches. They also made a healing tea that was toxic in large quantities and tasted like death warmed over.

He entered his cabin still redolent of the white sage smudging he'd done on the weekend. He put on the drumming tape his uncle had sent him, lifted some weights, and then took a hot shower, afraid he'd fall asleep in the bath. The comfrey leaves would have to wait.

After toweling off, Esau took Bill, the corn snake, out of her tank. With the snake around his neck, he put on the tea water and allowed his brain to wander. Bill, a constrictor, added a gentle pressure to his neck before heading down his shirt to the warmth of his waist. He enjoyed her trust and the intimacy of her contact. Normally he didn't approve of keeping animals in cages, but he had rescued Bill from a guy at the halfway house who found procuring mice from the pet store too much of a hassle, rarely fed her, and refused to heat her cage. Bill had shown her gratitude for being rescued by producing over a hundred orange-and-cream-colored, leathery eggs one weekend, thus leaving no doubt as to her sex. The pet store guy had said unfertilized eggs rarely hatched and if they did, the babies all would be female, clones of their mother. He told Esau the eggs would have to be kept warm and moist, but not wanting to be responsible for another generation of caged animals, Esau had put the eggs outside for the crows.

"Get some exercise, girl," Esau said as he placed Bill on a large branch in the corner that he'd brought in from outside. He waited for his tea to steep and watched the snake twist her way around the branch in a rapidly moving upward spiral. Once at the top, she peered down him, and he chuckled. "Yeah, I see you," he called up to her. "You're a Queen."

He sat on the futon couch Ruth said folded out to a bed—handy for guests. Unless his wife sought him out and they decided to take it slow, the only guest would be his uncle. Esau sipped his tea and pondered his current state of affairs. Here he was, working for a German woman with two Arapaho kids.

He had gone to college with a guy whose parents were

from Germany. Adolf Majewsky, not an Aryan for sure, black hair, dark complexion, narrow eyes. Adolph claimed to be a Hun—everybody had gotten a kick out of that. Heidi was a blond-haired, blue-eyed German, classic, Hitler's ideal. The twins weren't half Heidi's kind of white, even with the color of their eyes and skin being a little lighter than you might expect, if you were really looking for it. Amadeus was a handful, liked to climb anything, as high as he could, already almost fluent in the language of his people. The girl, Marcela, was not really shy—she was *guarded*, no other word for it. She could run like the wind or be as still as a fawn when a predator walked by. She was going to grow up to be a beauty, Heidi had better help her learn how to deal with it.

He experimented with different groupings. A white and three Natives, the most obvious, became two adults and two kids, then two females and two males. Finally he arrived at the three of them and an alcoholic who committed himself every day to staying sober.

"Fuck," he muttered, trying to work his way back into the group.

How about the four of them as survivors? He nodded his head and sipped his tea. Yeah, that worked. The Crow family had survived the death of the kids' mother, Nara—but there was more. The three of them were hiding something, he was sure of it. Heidi and the kids might need an ally, a soldier in their army. If he could make his peace with whatever their secret was, maybe he'd enlist.

He had just put Bill back in her cage when the phone rang. He looked at the phone. Heidi? His uncle? Please, God, not Elizabeth Darcy.

"Oh, thank you for picking up," said Elizabeth, breathy as always. Both Fred and Ruth were away, she said, and the Dubois brothers weren't answering their phone. A group of hunters had booked all her cabins and were arriving by noon tomorrow.

"And?" Esau said patiently.

And Fred had turned off the water to the lower three of the cabins because the sinks in the kitchenettes wouldn't stop dripping and he didn't know if he'd have time to fix it before his road crew went to repave that strip of Highway 191 in Sweet Water county. When she had tried to turn the water to those cabins on at the main, because even if Fred hadn't fixed the drips they had to have water, part of the handle broke off.

"And Tyree and Armand aren't answering their phone and Ruth's away," Elizabeth said again, sounding injured.

"The handle broke?"

"I used a wrench," she said proudly, before turning to plaintive. "Fred knew the hunters were coming and I don't know if he even fixed the drips, because he didn't turn the main back on."

"Okay. How bad were the drips?"

"We didn't think we would need those cabins, but the hunting party grew bigger."

"Okay, but how bad are the drips?"

"Drip, drip, drip, pretty bad, well maybe not so bad but I don't even know if Fred fixed them before he left."

"Can you check the toolbox and see if there's still that bag of washers in it?"

"Maybe, I'm not sure ... are those like the nut things that you put on the end of a screw?"

Esau swallowed his exasperation and asked if Lucas was up. The little boy was becoming a favorite of Esau's. He was such a strange kid, hair as blond as Heidi's, skinny as all get out, narrow ferrety face with those gold-yellow eyes.

"Lucas? He just went to bed, no wait ... here he is," said Elizabeth.

The four-year-old came on the phone. "Hi, Esau," he said, sounding very alert.

"Hey, Lucas, now listen, do you remember where we put the toolbox when I was there a couple of days ago?"

"Uh huh, in the garage by the door."

"Okay, can you go look in it and tell me if there's a bag of washers?"

"The rubbery things that are flat and round and there is a hole?"

"Sounds right. There was a bag there a few days ago, but your dad might have been using them to repair the taps before he left. There were more than dozen, if you can tell me how many are left, I'll know if he got to the repairs."

He waited, rolled his shoulders, and looked at his bed. Ruth had put a new mattress on it, and she hadn't scrimped. The small voice came back to the phone and informed him there were only seven washers left in the bag, three big ones and three little ones, so his daddy had fixed the taps.

"Good, but you said seven, and three and three is six," said Esau, unable to stop himself from correcting a four-year-old's math at nine o'clock at night.

"One looks funny so it doesn't count."

Esau allowed himself a grin—the kid was scary smart.

"Um, is Marcela, is she ... can you say Hi when you see her?" the small voice continued. "Say Lucas says Hi. Say Lucas *Darcy* says Hi so she knows it's me."

"Okay, will do." After finding out Esau worked for Heidi, it was a request Lucas frequently made, but Esau had given up passing on Lucas's salutations when   Marcela had wrinkled up her nose and said, "Why? He's just a little kid and he's weird. We don't even like him." Heidi had heard her say that and chewed her out, which had earned Esau a scowling look from Marcela, as if he were somehow at fault.

After Elizabeth came back on the phone, Esau asked her to put the wrench she had used next to the water main and he'd stop by to turn the water back on before he went to the restaurant in the morning.

She thanked him and asked again if he thought Heidi Crow would give her some work at The Crow's Nest when it opened.

She could almost drive now and she was ready. Esau gave his usual noncommittal answer.

"Even Ruth says her niece's mind wanders," Heidi had said the first time he had mentioned Elizabeth's request to her. "If we have to let her go, in a small town the hurt feelings will be many. You and I are the outsiders here."

CHAPTER SEVENTEEN

SPOTTING SCOPE

Ruth gave Booker McNabb updates every time she came by to drop off a meal, and today was no exception.

"Heidi's done with moving her shortbread baking business from Riverton to that space behind the feed store on Spruce Street," she said, moving some things around in Booker's fridge to accommodate a large serving of pot roast with all the trimmings.

"I know, I've seen the van the last few weeks." Booker put on coffee. If he'd been busy when she arrived, Ruth would have made it herself and carried two cups out to the shop.

"And now that Esau Aoah's here, she's moving ahead, guns ablazin', on renovating the restaurant," Ruth continued, opening the jar of molasses cookies she had given him a couple of days ago. One cookie remained. She broke it in half and put the two pieces on a plate.

"Why does a woman with two kids need both a restaurant and a bakery?" Booker asked after they had settled into the cushioned wicker chairs on his front porch.

"She says Hebeka can more or less run itself, once her people are trained. She just needs two bakers and a driver, so she may not be spread too thin when the restaurant opens. The bakery makes one product, lingonberry shortbread. She's made quite a name for herself in the luxury food market. On the coasts, people view shortbread from Wyoming as quite the novelty."

"So why's she need a restaurant too?" Booker dunked his cookie half in his coffee.

"So why are you asking, Mr. McNabb?" Ruth countered. "You afraid she won't have enough time for a restaurant, a bakery, two kids, a little dachshund with back problems, *and* you?"

"Two kids and a ridiculous dog? You got me, Ruth, can't wait for an overworked woman to try and involve me in all that."

"That? Did you really just objectify two children and a really very fine little dog as a 'that?'"

Booker narrowed his eyes at her. "Not fallin' for it, Ruth. Not apologizing for the 'that' and not interested in your new friends."

"Your lack of interest is duly noted," Ruth said, grabbing her bit of cookie when she saw Booker eyeing it. "Now tell me how the plans for your show in Jackson are progressing."

Booker chuckled. Ruth could be as annoying as hell, but she knew when to change the subject, when to back off. He didn't deserve her attention, but he now couldn't imagine his life without her intrusion.

As soon as they had finished their coffee, Ruth took off, saying she had to find an emergency foster for a dog on the Put-to-Sleep list at the Pinedale animal shelter and then she promised to help Vera make a batch of plum jam. Booker would get a couple of jars, of course.

Booker watched Ruth's truck bump down the road. Her shocks needed changing. She was up to the task, but he'd find a way to do it for her. He went to his shop to finish work on the last of the three ravens he was making out of scrap metal for a woman in Lander. She had sent over boxes of scrap from her late husband's garage and the medium suited the birds perfectly. Each was three times the size of a real raven, with plenty of attitude, mouths open, wings flared, angry.

He worked his sore shoulder as he returned to the cabin to make a late lunch. With a salami sandwich and a beer he walked out onto his deck and angled his spotting scope down into Comfrey. A beeline from his deck to the restaurant's front door wasn't much more than a mile. For the last few days this had been his lunchtime entertainment, watching the final transformation of the long-closed Taylor's Refresher on Main Street.

Yesterday, Heidi had hung The Crow's Nest sign. The Dubois brothers had done the heavy work while she'd stood on the sidewalk directing, and a lot of laughing seemed to go on. The kids had been there, dancing around with that little dog, pointing to their last name on a sign.

Today, a truck was parked in front of the long plate glass window. A large, flat object wrapped in moving blankets lay in the bed. He focused in on the license plate. New York. So the two Mexican-looking guys were New Yorkers. They walked with a New York swagger. Heidi came out of the restaurant with them, the taller one with his arm around her. Striped t-shirt and overalls, she had her hair up today. He did like a woman in overalls.

Abruptly, he pulled away from the scope, took a few bites of his sandwich, and looked toward a smear of clouds in the eastern sky. Rose, the girl who had become his brother's wife, had worn overalls most of time when they were growing up, and they'd teased her about it plenty. Two thousand miles away in Pennsylvania, she was battling cancer again. Should he pay a visit, one last time?

His mouthful of sandwich suddenly became impossible to swallow and he spit it over the side of the deck. He threw the remainder of the sandwich and it arced high in the air before spiraling downward toward Comfrey like a wounded bird. Rose ... he'd named his horse after her. He had chosen a chestnut because it reminded him of the color of her hair.

Finishing his beer, he watched a small plane approach the

airstrip, set down with a jolt, and bounce its way to a halt. With the spotting scope angled on the plane, he identified it as Cessna Skylark. Four passengers got off, all men, dark glasses, suits—they sure as hell weren't hunters. His deck was turning him into an observer, watching other people go about their lives. He felt a tinge of embarrassment; a hidden observer— next he'd be a goddamn Peeping Tom.

He trained the scope back on The Crow's Nest. Heidi had disappeared, but the New Yorkers were leaning against the truck. The Shoshone, Esau, emerged from the restaurant. Ruth had brought him by last month, just being friendly, trying to connect people, typical Ruth.

Esau climbed into the back of the truck. The three men struggled to tip the whatever-it-was on its edge, Esau began to shove, the other guys began to pull from the opposite end. Booker whistled as the object's corner came down heavily on the cement. They'd better be more careful than that, he'd already pegged it as a mirror.

Booker grinned as the kids came out of the restaurant and climbed into the bed of the truck. They were probably happy to be taller than everybody else. The men rocked the mirror, pivoting it corner-to-corner across the sidewalk, leaning it against the wall near the entrance. The New Yorkers began to pull the blankets off. Why are they unwrapping a mirror outside? Heidi arrived with a tray and put it in the bed of the truck. Esau stood back to watch the unveiling, and damn! Not a mirror but a big, carved wooden door. Heidi clapped and hugged the New Yorkers. Yeah, she looked like a physical kind of woman.

He watched Esau inspect the door up close. The Shoshone ran his hands over the wood and turned to look at the others. He said something that had them laughing. They got drinks from the truck and stood around, one of the New Yorkers leaning against the truck, again with his arm around Heidi.

A wooden door like that in Wyoming couldn't be an

outside door, not with that amount of carved detail. Maybe tomorrow he would go down and sign the papers Raul Diaz said were ready. Raul's law office was a few hundred yards from The Crow's Nest. He could take a closer look at the door then. Rosie was owed some exercise, he'd been thinking of riding her up to the lake but he could just as easily ride her down into Comfrey. There was an empty lot behind the restaurant, he'd ask Ruth if she thought it'd be okay to tie Rosie up there.

"Why don't you ask Heidi yourself?" said Ruth impatiently when he phoned. "She owns the lot, I'll give you her number."
"Ruth, c'mon, just ask her. I'm busy."
"That better not be a whine I hear in your voice," Ruth warned.
"It's not, I swear on all that is Holy."
Ruth gave a snort.

Ruth phoned Booker back that evening. "She said what's wrong with a man who can't make a call himself."
"*What?*"
"Oh settle yourself. What she actually said was sure, tie the horse up in the lot, it's clean back there, no glass, etcetera. Little Amadeus has offered to watch the horse for you."
Booker gave a short bark of laughter. "Like in a big city, you pay a kid so no one steals your tires?"
"I think what the boy really wants is to be around a horse, Booker," Ruth said evenly, "and you can do that for him."
"Yeah, well maybe. I'm not sure if tomorrow's going to be convenient. I've got some pieces to finish for the Jackson show. Now that I'm thinking about it, I might have to delay my lawyer visit until next week."
"Oh that's right, I'd forgotten this was about a lawyer visit. Now this poor kid is going to be disappointed, but children get their hopes dashed all the time, so nothing new there."

Booker gave an exasperated sigh and said maybe he could be down around ten.

"Maybe could or definitely will?" Ruth demanded.

CHAPTER EIGHTEEN

TO COMFREY AND BACK ON A ROAN HORSE

If he had taken his truck, he could have been in Comfrey in a matter of fifteen minutes, but at the moment Booker wasn't regretting the ride. He concentrated on the creak of the saddle and let Rosie pick her way along the steep dirt path that zigzagged down the back of his property toward town. It was a crisp June day, just a few gusts of wind. The temperatures would hit the high 70s on their way home, hotter in the sheltered areas. Insects hummed, wildflowers bobbed on their spindly stalks, the resinous scent of sage and tough mountain conifers, red and yellow dirt, Rosie's methodical steps ... Booker tried to block thoughts of his agent and the amount of work he still had to do for the upcoming show. This jaunt today could have waited, but signing the papers at Raul's wouldn't take long. He could be home in a couple of hours, tops.

His nephew, Philip, the only one of Rose and Simon's kids he had any contact with, had alerted him to Rose's reoccurrence of cancer and he had done the only thing he could think of to honor her struggle. He had asked Raul Diaz to draw up the Trust papers necessary to leave his ever-increasing assets to his nieces and nephews. Raul had applauded him for being so forward-thinking. He said single men in their late thirties rarely planned so far ahead, but Booker knew your number could be up anytime. The Army had taught him that.

Sign the papers, let the boy get on Rosie for a bit, girl too maybe, walk them down the block, like a carnival ride, take a look at that wooden door from New York, give a nod to Esau, maybe say hello to Heidi Crow if she was around, and then head back up the hill. He'd be home for lunch. He'd attach the saxophone to the Billy goat sculpture this afternoon, the Dubois brothers could drop the goat off for electroplating when they picked up the elk and the moose statues tomorrow in Rock Springs. That would free him up a bit, but he'd still have to work late. He sighed—life was getting a little too full.

Long-stemmed, silvery pink calypso orchids lined the banks of the stream at the bottom of the cliff. Their lightly striped petals and delicate slipper-shaped buckets were a luxury to see after the rough, herbaceous plants along the trail. The water ran clear and burbling under the wooden bridge. Something about the hollow sound of Rosie's hooves on the wood made him realize he hadn't really planned out this thing with the kid. Big horse, little boy who apparently hadn't been around horses, would Amadeus just be waiting at the lot? Would there be anywhere to tie Rosie up while he went to sign papers? He should have checked everything out ahead of time. Damn Ruth, he wouldn't be doing this today if it weren't for her.

Both children and the little dachshund were waiting when Booker and Rosie trotted into the lot. They jumped off chairs that had been placed on either side of the restaurant's backdoor and ran over, squinting up at him, the sun and their grins lighting up their faces. The dachshund stood at their feet, his lips drawn forward into a low menacing growl. The girl picked up the dog and attempted to shush it.

From the odors wafting through the restaurant's backdoor, some kind of meat was cooking. The children looked tiny from where he sat and Booker quickly dismounted. They

COMFREY, WYOMING: MARCELA'S ARMY

still looked small, they'd looked bigger through the spotting scope. He hadn't really noticed how similar they were when they'd come to his house last fall. They were almost identical, except for the clothing, same height, same straight, long black hair, same skin tone, same scrawny little bodies, except one was a girl.

"Hi Booker, remember Gering?" Amadeus asked, pointing to the dog in his sister's arms. "He was with us when we came to your house and ..."

Marcela interrupted, "Ruth told us your horse's name, because you didn't tell us her name when we came to your house. Rosie, that's her name and we have water and snacks for her." She pointed at a galvanized pail filled with water and a plate that held four carrots neatly lined up next to two green apples.

The dog's eyes rolled in alarm as the girl held him up to Rosie's large, round velvety nose. The horse flared her nostrils and gave a soft, moist huff, which somehow had the effect of calming the little dachshund.

"Apples and carrots, that's great. Thank you," said Booker.

"They're for Rosie," Marcela emphasized.

Booker bit back a grin. "I understand that."

"Do you see us waving at you?" Amadeus asked. "Ruth says you look at us all the time with your big periscope."

Jesus, *Ruth*, somebody had got to rein that woman in. She had walked onto his deck the other day when she'd been delivering him a blackberry pie, looked through the spotting scope down into Comfrey, and chortled, "See anything you like, Booker?"

Ruth—in another life she must have been a gypsy matchmaker.

"Spotting scope, not periscope, and I mainly use it to look at birds," Booker said, not entirely untrue, but from the look the boy exchanged with his sister, he could tell the kids weren't buying it. Why would somebody be looking at birds when they could be looking at them?

Apparently, Amadeus didn't consider Booker's spying on them worth any more discussion, because he pointed to the wooden hitching post Esau had helped him make that morning and said, "You can't just hold a horse for a really long time and lawyers can take a really long time, so you can tie her up there."

Booker assured the boy he just had to sign a few papers, and he was thinking he might delay that for a couple of weeks anyway, because his time was pretty short at the moment.

"Then why'd you come?" Amadeus demanded. "Ruth said you had to see your lawyer. Did you come just to see us and so that we can ride on Rosie?"

Esau saved Booker from having to reply by coming out the back door. "Don't worry, I got you," he called. "We'll hitch up the horse, I'll keep the backdoor open. You go do your lawyer business."

"She's not 'the horse,' she's 'Rosie,'" Marcela called back, pushing her lips out and frowning.

Esau corrected himself, gave what passed for a grin, and said if Booker had time, he should stay for the lamb stew. He and Heidi were still working out their menu, it was his aunt's recipe and Heidi wanted to give it a try. Booker thanked him and said maybe next time, it smelled great, but he had a lot of work waiting for him up the hill.

"Hi, Cousin," said Raul Diaz, looking up from placing files in a box when Booker came in the door.

Raul's mother had been a McNabb and he had inherited the iconic hair passed down through the descendants of Cora and Faolin McNabb, a negress and red-haired Scott who had died crossing the North Platt River. Their orphaned children had been absorbed into the Magroot family, who had founded Comfrey in 1852. Raul wore his bounty of wavy, greying red tresses pulled back in a ponytail while he was at work, loose when he was riding his motorcycle. He looked over his bifocals at Booker and beamed.

Booker found this whole cousin business tedious. How many generations did it take to sever a family connection? But he liked Raul well enough, and he was a decent lawyer.

"Looks like you're moving," Booker said, stating the obvious.

"I am indeed. I'm taking both of the office spaces over The Crow's Nest, next to the apartment up there. Nobody's used that upper floor for years. Heidi has spruced it up great. I've got more space and a view for not much more than the rent I pay here, plus a lady landlord I could look at all night and day. She and the kids are staying in the apartment for now, until Ruth finds them a house close to the school. Have you met her?"

"Who, Heidi Crow?"

"Yes, Heidi Crow," said Raul with a grin. "Good looking woman, you expect German women to be stocky, but what a figure. She's tougher than she looks."

"Yeah, I met her last year," Booker said abruptly, feeling unaccountably annoyed.

"And you've been watching her, right? Through that spotting scope on your deck?"

"That's for bird watching. I've been too busy to do anything much but work."

"Bird watching, uh huh, well, Ruth says you can look right down onto Main Street. If I had your set up, I'd be looking, you know, just for interest, nothing intrusive. Heidi's hired a Shoshone cook, you seen him? I mean the scars, damn." Raul shook his head.

"Esau Aoah, yeah, we've met. Listen Raul, I have a lot of work to get back to. Time's pretty tight right now, I have a ..."

"Show coming up, busy man, so you've said," Raul interrupted. He selected a file with Booker's papers from a stack and slapped them on the desk with a grin and a flourish.

"Can we ride Rosie now?" chorused the twins when he returned.

Booker put his legal papers in his saddlebag and said, "Okay, short ride because I've got work to do. Who's first?"

Esau poked his head out the backdoor. "I know you're busy, but you have to eat, right? How 'bout an eat-and-run? I'll set up a card table back here for lunch, whole restaurant smells like latex paint and floor polish. Heidi's stuck at Hebeka, her other business, something to do with an oven. She says thanks for bringing the horse."

Amadeus wanted to ride first but he didn't want to be led on a rope—he wanted to be up in the saddle with Booker.

"It will be more real," he insisted, and Booker understood. Being led on a rope was for little kids. He swung into the saddle, reached down, and, with Esau's help, hauled Amadeus up in front of him. The kid was surprisingly light, couldn't be more than forty pounds.

"Can I hold the reins?" Amadeus asked, tipping his head back to look up at Booker.

"No, not yet. You can hold onto the horn if you want," said Booker, but Amadeus shook his head and held onto Booker's wrists instead. Booker brought his arms in tight to his body to clamp the kid in place and Amadeus sat absolutely still, his hair whipping about in the wind as they crossed the road into the field. As they picked up the pace and circled the field at a slow canter, Booker could feel the kid grinning. He was amazed at how natural it felt and Amadeus was doing a good job of hugging the saddle with his skinny little thighs, leaning back so their bodies moved as one.

They did several rotations around the field and took a little detour to the stream so Amadeus could see the orchids and Rosie could get her hooves wet. Just across the stream, a little dust devil suddenly picked up and flung pebbles and dried leaves their way. Rosie shook her head and sneezed.

Booker said, "Interesting, there's not even any loose soil over there." Amadeus looked up at him. "She likes Rosie," he whispered, eyes dancing.

"Who? Your sister?" asked Booker, puzzled at the change in subject.

Amadeus shrugged a shoulder and looked down at their hands holding the reins together.

By the time they got back to the lot, Booker realized with a shock they'd been gone for most of an hour and Marcela was nowhere to be seen.

"Doesn't she want a ride?" Booker asked. "It'll have to be short, but I have time."

"She's not going to ride. She doesn't really know you."

"You said back there she liked Rosie. I could put you both in the saddle together and lead you."

"That's okay," said Amadeus. "You probably shouldn't talk about it, she'll tell you if she wants to ride."

The card table had been set up with utensils, a pitcher of water, and rolls. Marcela walked out the backdoor with butter, Esau brought out a couple more chairs, then went back inside to get four steaming bowls of stew. When the four of them were seated, Esau and the kids closed their eyes and Esau said, "We thank the spirit of the animal that gave its life for our meal."

"*Hotoobe!*" said Amadeus, raising his spoon.

"*Auffessen!*" said Marcela, wagging her spoon at her brother.

"They're telling you to eat up in Arapaho and German," said Esau, and Booker thought he detected a hint of pride in his voice.

"So you're cook, nanny, and working on your day off for Elizabeth Darcy at Toot's. Busy man," Booker remarked, unable to think of what to say to the kids.

Esau shrugged. "Takes a village, man, and this place may be the end of the road for me. I may be home." He locked eyes with Booker. "I need to keep busy."

Busy. Booker nodded, understanding the need for work to occupy the mind and keep demons at bay. To end the pause that ensued, Booker decided it was about time he remark on the excellence of the stew when Amadeus got there before him.

"This is good stew," said Amadeus. "Right, Booker?"

Booker nodded. "I was just going to ..."

"And if you come down tomorrow so I can ride again," the boy broke in earnestly, "you can have some more because Esau always makes extra."

Booker met the bright, mischievous eyes, exhaled, and said, "The thing is, I got some deadlines coming up. I have to finish a few things and get some work to Jackson."

"Can Amadeus ride the day after tomorrow?" asked Marcela, putting her fork down and giving Booker a look that was older than six years. There was challenge there and something fiercely protective.

Somehow the girl asking for her brother made Booker feel even more like a jerk. He could imagine Ruth glaring at him too.

"Tell you what, these deadlines are a big deal. I can't make them go away, but if I work really hard, maybe toward the end of next week. The day after I return from Jackson, I can do that."

The kids looked at each other. Amadeus blinked rapidly. "That's too long," said Marcela.

Esau stepped in. "Enough, guys, clear the table. Bring out the jar of peanut butter cookies, you can each have two."

"Three," said Marcela.

"Okay, four," said Esau, and succeeded in getting a grin from both twins as they gathered up the bowls.

"Sorry about that, Amadeus has been talking nonstop about riding since Ruth called yesterday." Esau shrugged. "Ever hopeful, I guess."

"No, I get it," said Booker. "I'll make it a priority, but I've got a show coming up."

"No problem. Ruth was showing us some pictures of your work a few days ago. Pretty incredible. We'll try and make it up to your show in Jackson at some point, but there's a shit load of stuff to finish before we open. Talk about deadlines."

Booker narrowed his eyes at Esau. 'We'll try?' Was that just the Shoshone and Heidi having a nice little time with art and a meal in Jackson? Or were the kids included?

"Amadeus is a tough kid, he's six, but then, you know, he's *only* six," continued Esau. "When you have a date, I'll put it on the calendar. That'll hold him."

Booker squinted upward at faded blue sky without even a wisp of cloud. He was trying not to like this guy. What had he expected? A man and a woman working together side by side, perfecting their damn menu, both taking care of the kids. He caught Esau watching him. Was that amusement he saw? Difficult to read a face that scarred up.

"You're pretty good at the kid thing. Kid management," said Booker, remembering how this whole social give-and-take was supposed to go.

"Oh yeah, I surprise myself sometimes. Notice how I held the line on the cookies?" They both laughed at that.

Marcela came out of the kitchen and offered the cookie jar around. Esau told her to leave it on the table, and to take two each for her and her brother.

"You said four each," the little girl protested.

"I did, but by the crumbs on your shirt and around your mouth, I'd say you got a head start."

Frowning, Marcela took four cookies out of the jar and went to Amadeus, who was sitting on the ground next to Rosie.

"That animal must weigh a ton. Are they safe next to those big horse feet?" asked Esau.

"Rosie weighs about 1200 pounds and she's a pussy cat," said Booker with a grin. A Native nervous around horses, imagine that.

Esau nodded dubiously and picked up Gering. He settled the dog on his lap, raised his eyebrows at Booker, and said, "Never thought I'd like a wiener dog."

"Not much of a dog for Wyoming. Did the kids' aunt get it because she's German?"

"From what I understand, he came with the house she rented in Riverton. You'll have to ask her about it sometime, Heidi's got quite a story."

Booker shrugged; everybody had quite a story, but yeah, someday maybe he'd ask her about hers.

Esau asked Booker about his work. Sculpture, what was it, iron? Bronze? "Mostly steel these days," said Booker, settling back. He had a lot to do, but Heidi Crow hadn't shown up yet and he was reluctant to go before seeing her up close, one more time. He'd check out her greeting to Esau, a hand on the shoulder? Peck on the cheek?

Esau held up a hand. "Hang on a sec', I'd like to hear more about your work, but do you want a quick cup of coffee to go with the cookies?"

"Sounds good."

"Cream, sugar?" asked Esau, getting up.

Booker shook his head. "Black. Thanks." He'd better load up on the caffeine, he'd be pushing midnight.

"Coffee's great, strong. What is it?" asked Booker, taking another appreciative sip from the mug Esau had handed him.

"A French Roast from a place in Riverton. Two people Heidi used to work with at Saint Gemma's brought ten pounds over when they came to check out how the restaurant is coming together."

"Man and woman, youngish, big, she's probably Native, he's more Samoan looking?" asked Booker without thinking.

Esau let out a bark of laughter. "Ruth's right, you *are* spying on us."

Booker back-pedaled rapidly. He said he'd been watching a red-tailed hawk but the guy had caught his attention because looked like someone he'd worked with once.

"Uh huh," said Esau with a grin. "Anyway, Heidi's thinking of making French Roast our house coffee but it may be a little strong for some around here. If I tell her you like it, though, she'll keep some on hand."

"Why?" said Booker bluntly.

"Why do you think? Ruth likes you, the kids like you. You have a horse."

Booker gave him an inscrutable look, except Esau was good at inscrutable. He grinned to himself—Ruth was right, Booker McNabb was definitely interested in the boss.

"Tell me more about these steel sculptures of yours," Esau said as they drank their coffee.

Booker talked about his transition from bronze to steel. He didn't want to cast pieces anymore. He wanted to make individual items out of steel. It was cheaper and he could do more of it alone, except for the galvanizing. But he still did a little bit of wrought-iron work. There was something about working with a pure element that tied him to the earth.

Esau nodded at that. Ruth had said this guy had seen two tours of duty, Army Ranger or Special Ops, either way quick, strong, maybe lethal. Esau could see how a man like that could be attracted to the power of iron.

The phone rang inside and Esau got up to answer it. He returned with the news that Heidi was stuck at Hebeka waiting for the oven repairman to finish. It would be another hour or two.

"She said she's sorry she's not here to thank you herself for giving Amadeus his ride," said Esau. "She's probably darting around, cleaning, organizing, peppering the guy with all sorts of questions about equipment. She still has to decide on some of the appliances for this place. She has a hard time delegating. Last week her cousin Karl phoned from Germany. It was his dime, so I was happy to talk. When I told him Heidi wasn't here, he said how she's always been like this, work, work, work. He's a nice guy, if you don't mind the Teutonic stick-up-your-butt way of talking. He had all kinds of questions, trying to check me out, that kind of thing." Esau shrugged and offered Booker a second cup of coffee.

So even Heidi's cousin thousands of miles away thought something was up between Heidi and Esau. Booker let out a long exhalation—what a waste of time. He refused the offer of more coffee and said he really must get going.

Esau stood up and said, as he gathered the mugs, "In case you're wondering, and I'm not saying you *are* wondering, I'm getting my wife back some day."

"Where is she?"

"She's waiting for me to get it together. Originally she gave me five years, but she's extended it to ten. After that, she's done."

"You believe her?" asked Booker, surprised at himself for asking the question.

Esau shrugged. "I tell myself we're like prairie voles and mated for life, but who knows who'll come her way."

The parts of the trail with no shade and shelter from the wind were uncomfortably hot. Rosie took her time climbing as Booker replayed his day. It had been longer and more interesting than he'd anticipated. The trust the boy had shown him was humbling, the distrust from the girl likewise. He'd forgotten to ask about taking a look at the door from New York. Esau's words reverberated, 'Need to keep busy,' so Esau was a recovering addict and 'Getting my wife back some day'…was that Esau's way of saying his journey did not include a romantic interest in Heidi Crow?

"Fair enough," said Booker to a Rocky Mountain Juniper. "Fair enough," he said, leaning forward to pat Rosie on her sweat-dampened neck.

The horse was in a lather when they turned off the trail. He let her have a short drink, pulled her away to cool down, took off the saddle, the blanket, more water, rubbed her down.

"Girlfriend's back," he said to the Billy goat, who ambled over to nibble at the horse's legs. Rosie stamped, flared her nostrils, and flicked her tail and the goat backed off, watching her placidly, chewing whatever he seemed to be constantly chewing. Booker left them to work it out and walked into the house to check his message machine.

The Dubois brothers had left a message saying they couldn't come tomorrow because their Uncle Smitty had just broken a hip. The old man was in the hospital and they had to help out. Booker wasn't sure what kind of helping the brothers could do at the hospital. The sculpture they were going to take to Rock Springs would be an inside piece so it wouldn't need a hot dip, but he'd now have to be the one taking it to be electroplated. Then he'd have to pick up the two elk sculptures and the moose that had been hot galvanized, bring them home, and carefully grind off any drips. Maybe when the Dubois boys were done with performing hip surgery on Uncle Smitty they could give him a hand the day after tomorrow with making the bases for the elk and moose.

He got a glass of ice-cold water and walked out to his shop. He had to get up to Jackson in the next few days, check on how they were planning to display the last of his bronze work. He'd like to get rid of all of it. Too many people were involved in the process, although you could cast multiple pieces from the same mold and really make some money. His agent was pressing for more bronze work—he'd have to deal with her—and the other thing, extricate himself from their romantic entanglement.

He turned the radio on loud. He'd have to work late tonight and put in some really long days. He wheeled the Billy goat sculpture to the bench that held his welding supplies. It was made of hammered sheet metal but still weighed over a hundred pounds. The animal lay semi-reclined with its hind legs crossed, waiting for the saxophone he'd formed yesterday to be attached.

Just before midnight, he closed up the shop. Too much to do, and at the back of his mind he heard that little girl speaking up for her brother, saying the end of next week was a long time for Amadeus to have to wait to ride again.

"Thanks, guys," he called to the horse and the goat when he saw they had put themselves back in their open stalls. He closed the barn doors. Trudging back to the house, he massaged his reconstructed left shoulder. Walter Reed Hospital had done a decent job of healing the wounds they could see, but days he worked too long reminded him of things he'd rather forget.

In a steaming hot shower, his aching muscles began to relax. He forced all thoughts of metal sculpture from his mind and pondered instead whether he should get a second horse. He'd been considering it before today, so this had nothing to do with the kid. Last week he'd gone so far as to write down the number for a quarter horse gelding listed on a card on the bulletin board at the feed store. A big horse, almost sixteen hands, five years old, needed an experienced rider. But there were a number of other cards. He recalled one with a small thoroughbred-quarter horse-cross, just over fourteen hands, ten years old, easy temperament. Better for a scrawny little six-year-old.

Booker groaned and turned off the hot water. What the *hell* was he thinking?

CHAPTER NINETEEN

A FRIEND FOR ROSIE

When Booker declined his agent's invitation to return to her house as they left the first night of his show in Jackson, he realized he had seriously misread the extent of her feelings for him. He had thought they were having a casual dalliance. She was good at her job and had connections at galleries all over the west. He appreciated how she ran interference for him at showings, rescuing him from fawning women or the occasional fawning man, but she had become increasingly proprietorial as of late and he was beginning to feel hemmed in. To his shock, her cool, professional persona dissolved before his eyes when he suggested they stop mixing pleasure and business.

She cried, mascara running down her cheeks, grey splashes landing on her ivory silk blouse. She said over the last year she thought they had been coming to an understanding but she had never pressured him. She accused him of having another woman, he said no, that wasn't it, he just needed space. How much space? she demanded. They spent one or two nights together each month, how much more space could a man want?

He had no good answer, and they stood looking at each other hopelessly, both realizing that *he* had changed the equation and there would be no going back.

If he was firing her as a lover, was he firing her as an agent as well? she asked after coming back from the bathroom, having reapplied her make-up. Not if she would still consider having him for a client, he said. She shrugged, maybe, probably, but she'd need to increase her fee.

The following day he drove home, hoping his agent would choose business over hurt, relieved to have said his piece, depressed he had allowed the affair to start in the first place. The next day he spent taking down a tree that threatened the barn and chopping it up into firewood. He spent another day riding Rosie up to the lake, then along the steep trail to Toot's Peak. They stopped before the snow line, in an area sheltered by twisted scrubby trees and shrubs. He dismounted, retrieved his sandwich from his saddlebag, and positioned himself with his back against a warm granite boulder. A small stream of snowmelt attracted insect life and Rosie. She took a long drink, but the sparse vegetation offered little forage, so he left her bridle on. She nibbled at whatever she could find, her strong upper lip pushing debris aside. She nodded her head up and down when she found something edible, which made him chuckle. He crossed his arms, drew his hat down to shade his face, and remained inclined, not wanting to fall asleep in the warmth radiating from the rocks. He listened to Rosie's determined jaws, like boots crunching through snow, the hoarse screech of a red-tailed hawk, the loud buzz of an insect flying by very fast, bits dropping from trees, the sudden interludes of total silence.

As he rode home he remembered he should phone Ruth and see if she could set something up with Heidi Crow regarding taking Amadeus for a ride. It might be a reason for Heidi to come up and have another coffee on his deck. He'd been thinking about getting Rosie another companion, *two* horses and a goat, not too much to handle.

"Ruth," he said into the phone.

"Booker McNabb," Ruth said flatly.

After a moment's silence, he asked, "Everything okay?"

"I was wondering that myself," Ruth replied coolly.

"Okay, well, sounds like maybe you're busy so a question and I'll let you go. Can you tell Amadeus Crow, or ask Heidi first maybe, that I'll come down next week and we can ride over to the airstrip. Think his aunt would let him be away for a couple of hours?" His question was followed by a prolonged pause. "Ruth?"

"That was the sound of me rolling my eyes," Ruth said with an exasperated huff. "For heaven's sake Booker, I've come to accept you are as you are, that you put up all this defense, for reasons I can't begin to imagine, but let me tell you something. When I went by to see how the restaurant was coming along this morning, Esau Aoah told me that child waited for you to come by all day yesterday. Amadeus seemed convinced that you were going to honor your promise to take him riding again as soon as you'd finished setting up your show. He heard you say the day after you returned from Jackson you would be by and Esau heard something similar. I saw it written on that calendar they have hanging in the kitchen. When the sun set yesterday, that little boy finally agreed to come inside and eat his supper."

Booker protested, he'd never promised a specific day.

"Oh, no?" asked Ruth.

"Okay, I can't remember precisely what I said. You know, with a kid pushing at you, it's easy to say whatever."

"Really? Is that how we teach young people to honor their promises? All of us know you finished setting up in Jackson *two* days ago. Tyree Dubois saw you driving home up Wild Horse Valley Road and you waved at him. Amadeus is a six-year-old boy, Booker. You have to see things from his perspective. I'll phone and say you'll take him tomorrow, if you can't phone yourself but ... are you sitting down?"

"Just tell me," said Booker, a feeling of dread beginning to settle.

"If you'd gone yesterday, as Amadeus was expecting, a couple of hours would have worked out but tomorrow Esau, Heidi, and the kids are taking a trip to Riverton to pick out glasses and dishes for the restaurant. If you take Amadeus, you'll be saving that boy from a tedious shopping trip. Marcela will be fine, she and Heidi are wedded at the hip but Amadeus needs to be out and about."

"I can't babysit for a *day*," sputtered Booker. "What am I going to do with him for what, *eight* hours?"

"Maybe more if they don't find what they need in Riverton, ten, twelve if they have to go further afield."

Ruth then pointed out he was doing a lot of moaning and groaning for an adult. Take Amadeus somewhere, she suggested. Don't forget to feed him, do some horse-related chores, and at the end of the day, Booker could congratulate himself for doing his part.

His part—he didn't have a part, Booker protested feebly.

"Sure you do, Booker, all good people have a part."

"Anybody tell you that you have a really irritating way of inserting yourself in other people's business?"

"Excuse me? I believe *you* phoned me," said Ruth, hanging up the phone.

The words were spoken in the careful cadence of a nonnative speaker. "Hello, Booker, this is Heidi Crow. How are you?"

"Doing well, and you?"

She gave a soft laugh before saying she had been sorry to miss him when he had stayed to lunch with Esau and the twins. She had a problem at her other business. She thanked him for taking Amadeus for a ride on the horse. He had liked it very much.

She paused and Booker realized she was waiting for him to say something like, great kid, looking forward to spending more time with him, a whole day together tomorrow, can't wait.

Instead, he said, "No problem. Esau said there was an oven issue at your bakery. Hope it's taken care of."

"The problem has been solved, thank you. Ruth Creeley ..."

"Ruth, yeah, about tomorrow," Booker interrupted. "It's fine."

Heidi laughed, a warm sound, light and young. He'd seen her laughing through the spotting scope and thought she would sound like this.

"Ruth said you were *schroff*," she said.

"Ruth said I was what?"

"Gruff, I think. That is a word? Curt, brusque."

"Gruff's a word," he said. What was Heidi doing, thumbing through a thesaurus?

She laughed again. "Ruth said also, that you are a good and a safe man, so I am very happy for Amadeus to be with you tomorrow, but I would like for you to tell me that this long, long day is acceptable with you. You understand how Ruth can be, she wants the best for her friends and sometimes she goes over the boards. Amadeus can come with us tomorrow, it is not a problem."

She was offering him an out—he should grab it. He was about to suggest a couple of hours another day might be more convenient, but stopped when he realized Ruth would be merciless. And he caught a flash of Amadeus tipping his head back to look up at him as they cantered around the field, that skinny little body vibrating with excitement.

"No, tomorrow's okay, I can work around him if he wants to help me take care of some things," he said, trying not to release a sigh.

"Work around?" she asked carefully.

"Work around?" he repeated, confused.

"You said you can work around Amadeus, and so now I think a shorter time another day will be better for you," she said.

"I didn't mean work around, wait, did I say that? It's not a problem."

"Amadeus thinks there will be a horse ..." She left that dangling, no doubt wanting to establish the expectation.

"Sure, yes, there will be horse-related events tomorrow." Booker ran a hand over his face.

Heidi thanked him warmly and said she was looking forward to seeing him again soon. He hung up, went to the sink, and took a long glass of water. What was that? He'd been, nervous, no, not nervous exactly ... uneasy, that was it, *uneasy*. During that whole conversation he'd been uneasy about how much this woman he'd seen once face-to-face last fall and a bunch of times through his spotting scope, was getting under his skin.

At eight the next morning, Booker stood on his porch with his second cup of coffee and watched the white van come up the driveway. The moment it stopped, the twins tumbled out. They waved hello and ran to the paddock, climbed on a fence railing, and called to Rosie to come over. The horse looked up with mild interest.

Esau emerged from behind the wheel and reached back into the van to retrieve a backpack. "Just droppin' and runnin'," he called. "Heidi had to get a couple of things taken care of at Hebeka. She says thanks and she'll comp you some meals when she opens."

"Ah," said Booker, "busy woman." He squinted at the design on the backpack Esau held up to him. Four large green turtles stood with arms crossed, looking very tough. "Are those *ninja* turtles?" he asked.

"Yes, they are *mutant teenaged* ninja turtles, to be exact," said Esau. "We've got snacks, sunscreen, two changes of clothes, because, you know, anything can happen."

"No, I don't know. Why's he need *two* changes of clothes?"

152

"Stuff happens, he's a kid." Esau grinned, shook his head. "Heidi, Ruth, they got you good, man, a whole day with a six-year-old. This will be good for him, he's around his aunt and his sister too much. Hanging out with a horse and a macho blacksmith—" he looked around "—yeah, this will be real good for him."

"*Marcela*," he yelled to the little girl. "Let's go."

Marcela came running over. Her yellow Keds had purple laces that coiled like old-fashioned telephone cords. "I have new shoes, they're not even dirty yet," she said, grinning up at Booker.

"Me too," said Booker, sticking out a scuffed black boot.

She giggled. "We're going out to lunch in Riverton. We're going to a sushi restaurant," she said, eyes dancing. "Are you and Amadeus going out to lunch?"

Booker looked over at Amadeus. Rosie had walked to the fence and was allowing her ears to be scratched. "Maybe."

"Where are you guys going?"

"Not to a sushi restaurant," said Booker.

Marcela made a face at him and ran to the van. Booker watched as Esau walked after her, a confident, slightly bow-legged stride, long hair hanging loose, khaki pants, white button-down shirt, physically fit. Ruth said he biked everywhere, always on the move. Could a woman get used to those scars? Would a woman like Heidi Crow find Esau attractive? Was Esau really waiting for his wife?

Booker left the backpack on the porch and walked over to the boy perched on the paddock fence. They didn't say anything for a few minutes. The Billy goat had come out of the barn and was coming their way. The goat stopped, lifted his tail, and exposed his considerable testes as he released a stream of urine.

Amadeus looked at Booker, eyes wide with delight. "He's got big balls," he said in a loud whisper. "Like bigger than anybody."

"Some goats do have them big," Booker agreed.

"Aren't you supposed to cut them off? Like with dogs they cut them off."

Booker shrugged. "Never saw the need for it in a goat, but not everybody would agree."

"Why do some people see the need for it?" Amadeus grabbed the railing with both hands and leaned back to look up at Booker.

Booker grinned to himself, and he'd been wondering what they'd have to talk about. "Well, some people eat goats and the meat's supposed to taste better if the males are ... you know ... cut, so the testes, the balls, are cut off when the animal is young. And some animals are more aggressive and it helps with that. Male adult goats can smell pretty strong if they're left intact."

"Intact means they still have their balls," said Amadeus knowledgeably.

Booker bit back a smile—kid was smart, he'd give him that.

Amadeus wrinkled his nose and sniffed the air experimentally. "He doesn't smell that bad, so you don't have to cut them off."

Booker agreed that had been his thinking. Now he had to make a couple of calls so Amadeus should probably come in the cabin.

"Why?" asked Amadeus.

"Because I have to keep an eye on you."

"Why? I'm six."

"You're six, I'm aware of that. I'd be more comfortable with you inside while I'm inside, you outside when I'm outside. Until we've spent more time together."

"But you know me. We rode Rosie."

Booker regarded the stubborn little face, aware he was being tested. Shouldn't somebody have given him a list, like what to feed the kid, what the boundaries were? Amadeus looked up at him expectantly.

Without even thinking about it, Booker scooped the boy off the fence and flung him over his shoulder, the child squealing with excitement. They started toward the cabin, Booker grabbing with one hand the little feet that were trying to kick. Suddenly Amadeus went completely limp. Booker's chest tightened in alarm. Oh God, now what?

He carefully laid the boy down on the porch, looking at the motionless figure that barely seemed to be breathing. "Hey," he said, kneeling down to look more closely at the prostrate form.

Amadeus slowly opened an eye a slit, then closed it.

"Hey, Amadeus," Booker repeated, his hand on Amadeus's shoulder, shaking it gently. He started back when the child suddenly leapt up, grinning. "Fooled you," the boy chortled as he darted through the screen door and into the cabin.

Booker let out a long exhalation. *Jesus Fucking Christ*, this was going to be a hell of a long day. He picked up the mutant ninja turtle backpack and went inside.

Amadeus stood in the middle of the cabin, looking around, beaming. He opened his mouth to say something, but stopped when Booker said, "Here, take your pack and sit down. Stay there, while I make my calls."

Amadeus's smile faded. "It was funny," he said tentatively.

"No, not funny. I almost had a heart attack. Do something like that again and I'll..." Booker stopped, at a loss for a suitable punishment.

"What are you going to do?" asked Amadeus, his face too solemn for a kid who a moment ago had pulled a prank that, Booker had to admit, was pretty genius.

"Not have you back up here."

"Ever?" Amadeus's mouth made a tight little line.

"Just behave and you won't have to find out."

"Like, never have any fun?" Amadeus persisted.

"Look, I have to make a couple of calls, then we'll get going.

155

I'm having another cup of coffee. Want something to drink while you wait? Milk?"

"I'll have coffee too," said Amadeus.

"No, you won't, but I'll get you water or milk. I don't have any juice."

"Do you have special milk like Aunt Heidi buys?"

"It's probably special," said Booker.

"Because I'm lactose intolerant. So is Esau, so is Marcela, so are a bunch of Indians and a bunch of other people. If it's not special milk, my tummy will hurt. I'll have poop a lot and that's going to hurt too."

Booker pinched the bridge of his nose. Why had nobody told him Amadeus couldn't drink milk? Sure the kid had told him but what if he hadn't? A lot of poop wasn't going to fit into their day.

Amadeus leaned over and ferreted in his backpack. He brought out a bottle of some kind of amber liquid, probably apple juice, and attempted to open it.

"Need a hand?" asked Booker. Amadeus wordlessly handed him the bottle, avoiding his eyes, not saying thank you when Booker handed it back.

He'd bet Heidi Crow had drummed plenty of manners into those two kids. Amadeus was trying to exert whatever control he had over this situation. Not surprising.

Esau phoned just as Booker was about to make his calls. "Sorry, forgot to tell you, no milk."

"Amadeus made that clear."

Esau laughed. "I told Heidi he would, but you know, she made me phone, just in case."

Booker left a message for his agent, phoned the guy in Eden, the woman in Boulder, then went into the sitting room to find Amadeus had barely moved an inch.

"Ready?" Booker asked.

Amadeus gave him an inscrutable look. "Are we going to

ride Rosie?" he asked, barely audibly.

Booker laughed, inexplicitly feeling his spirits lift.

"Patience my man, this is going to be good," he said, whistling as he left the house without waiting for the boy.

He heard Amadeus thunder down the wooden steps behind him. The little boy, backpack slung over his shoulder, dashed around him and ran full bore to the truck. Booker turned to see the cabin door wide open and walked back to close it. He remembered how important it had been to get to the truck before his dad or his brother.

"Your road is bumpy," said Amadeus as the truck shuddered slowly down the drive.

"Just the way I like it," said Booker, who had actually been thinking of having it graded and more gravel laid down before winter.

"Why?"

"Why do I like it bumpy? Because, it means the only people who come to visit don't mind a bumpy road."

Amadeus nodded. "Where are we going?" he asked.

"We're looking for a friend for Rosie."

"Another Billy goat?"

"Nope."

"A cow?"

Booker shook his head.

"An elephant?" Amadeus asked.

"A giraffe or a horse, I haven't decided." Booker looked over to catch the little boy's broad grin.

"Rosie said she wanted a horse," Amadeus said.

"She told you that? And what are you, the horse whisperer?"

Amadeus leaned over and whispered very loudly indeed, "I am the horse whisperer."

Partway down Wild Horse Valley Road, Booker slammed on the brakes, putting a hand out in front of Amadeus as the seat belt strained to hold him. A fawn stood frozen on one side of the road while its mother watched from the other. You never could tell with deer if they'd stay where they were or if they would make a mad dash into the road.

As they waited, Amadeus asked, "What's a 'horse whisperer?'"

"Someone who talks to a horse and listens when the horse talks back."

"You have to whisper?"

"Sometimes it helps. And thank you, Mama," Booker said as the doe finally decided the truck was going to remain stopped and walked slowly in front of it, studiously not looking their way, her ears tracking them.

One of the Dubois brothers was removing a ladder from the bed of Ruth Creeley's old green Chevy, which was parked alongside the Toot's Lucky Thirteen office. Her big wheel Jeep had blown a gasket, as he'd known it would. The other brother, surrounded by paint cans, looked up and lifted a hand.

They drove through town, where a red 'FOR RENT' sign was pressed to the window of Raul Diaz's old office. The lawyer must have already moved into his new digs above The Crow's Nest. With Heidi and Esau gone, the restaurant presented a long, blank window to the road. For weeks the building had been a hub of activity, now the final touches—going to Riverton or wherever to choose the china and utensils—had left it dark, and Booker found the absence of life disturbing. He imagined Heidi, Esau, and Marcela enjoying their day away, laughing over raw fish at lunch, relaxed, having fun.

Booker pulled onto the highway, heading south on 191 to a ranch just outside of Eden. Amadeus sat quietly, every now and then casting Booker a look, biting his lips, trying to control his excitement. They turned onto a gravel road and in a few hundred yards they stopped in front of a doublewide trailer.

A lean, lantern-jawed man came out the screen door with

a trembling white poodle under his arm. He assured them the dog belonged to his missus and offered a nicotine-stained hand. He took them around back and, in a paddock, stood an Appaloosa colt, a beautiful animal, roan with a spotted white rump. Amadeus ran to the fence and it rolled an eye, snorted, pawed at the ground. The little poodle gave a series of shrill yips and rolled its eyes in return.

Booker frowned and narrowed his eyes at the horse. "Thought you said you had seven-year-old gelding, good with kids. This is a nice-looking horse, but I'm not interested in breaking a colt. I have way too much on my plate right now."

"Indian pony for an Indian kid," said the man. "Soon as I saw the boy, I knew you'd be hooked. The gelding went yesterday. A kid could grow up with a horse like this."

"Yeah, well I phoned a couple of hours ago."

Booker called to Amadeus and when the boy turned around, he pointed to the truck. Back on the highway, they headed north toward Boulder. Booker was conscious the little boy kept glancing at him.

"What's up?" he asked, but Amadeus just shrugged.

"That horse wasn't what I was looking for, Amadeus. That's why we didn't spend time there. We need to find the right horse and maybe that won't happen today."

"Because that was a horse for an Indian kid and not for Rosie," said Amadeus.

Booker looked at the solemn little face. Kid wasn't a whiner, Ruth would appreciate that. "This Indian pony, Indian kid business, the poodle guy was just trying to make a sale," he said.

"Poodle guy," Amadeus said with a smirk.

"Yeah, I know. What kinda dog is that for a guy trying to sell a horse?"

They both snickered. Amadeus sat up a little straighter.

"Anyway, an Indian kid can ride any damn horse he wants to," Booker continued. "In fact, I'm thinking whatever we get for Rosie, is going to be ridden by you sometimes, maybe."

"But it's still going to be Rosie's horse. We're not buying me a horse. And you say 'maybe' a lot."

"Maybe because I'm hedging my bets. Maybe because I..."

"Maybe because you want people to just let you alone," said Amadeus.

"Maybe. Maybe I'm getting hungry. Maybe we'll get a burger at that ice cream place in Farson before looking at horse number two," Booker said, waiting for the kid to smile.

"Maybe I don't have any money," Amadeus said.

"Well, maybe I do."

"Maybe we'll have ice cream too," said Amadeus, setting his trap.

"Maybe we will," said Booker. "Strawberry or maybe they have blackberry."

"You forgot," said Amadeus, victoriously. "I'm lactose intolerant and..."

Booker cut him off, "Yeah, I know, lots of poop. Thanks for the reminder. Maybe they have something different, like a snow cone. Can you eat one of those?"

Amadeus nodded. "You can still have ice cream if you want," he said generously.

Over burgers and cokes, Booker said, "I still want to take a look at the big door those guys brought from New York a few weeks ago. Is it inside the restaurant somewhere?"

"Yup, in the front part," asked Amadeus. "Did you see it through your scope?"

"Guess I did at that."

"It's Peter's door," said Amadeus.

Booker felt himself relaxing—four or five more hours until he handed the kid back. This was an okay conversation. "Yeah? Is Peter the guy who made it or one of the guys who brought it out from New York?"

Amadeus shook his head. "Peter's a dead baby. Aunt

Heidi's dead baby."

Booker sat back, shaken; he could think of absolutely no response to that.

Amadeus looked up, the challenge in his eyes not matching the casualness of his tone. "Mama's dead too, but she and Peter aren't all the way dead."

"Maybe not." Booker looked out the window. He'd witnessed the 'not all the way dead' in one Middle Eastern village in particular. He closed his eyes and forced the image away.

"Maybe not," whispered Amadeus.

The waitress came over and offered to refill their sodas but Booker waved her away with a 'thanks, we'll stick to water.'

"Aunt Heidi lets me drink as much coke as I want," Amadeus said, smiling angelically.

"Oh, I am sure she doesn't."

Amadeus pushed his plate away. "Can I still have a snow cone if I don't finish my hamburger? Because I'm tired of eating it but I'm not tired of a snow cone."

"Yeah, just give me a moment to finish mine," said Booker, then couldn't stop himself from asking, "What did you mean when you said Peter and your mom aren't all the way dead?"

Amadeus gave a soft sigh, and Booker was about to tell him to forget it when the boy said, "Peter is in ashes in Aunt Heidi's pocket sometimes, in a little round ball. And she holds him like this," he cupped his hands to illustrate, "but only when she thinks we can't see her. Sometimes she puts him in the wooden box by her bed. And my moooom..." Amadeus put his head down on the table and looked at Booker sideways, "she talks Arapaho to me, like in secret. Like in the wind."

At that, the boy closed his eyes and used his index finger to trace a circle round and round in a little spill of water. Booker took this to mean the child was done, no more questions. Ashes, the wind, there was a lot going on in the Crow family. He signaled the waitress for their check.

After using the bathroom, Booker and Amadeus stopped at the ice cream fountain by the door and ordered a red snow cone, supposed to taste like cherry, and purple one, supposed to taste like grape. They sampled each other's and agreed they both tasted the same, and they both were great, way better than ice cream.

Their next stop was at a small ranch on the road out of Boulder, leading to Big Sandy. A twelve-year-old buckskin gelding, good with children, the woman on the phone had assured him. Both of her kids had learned to ride on him, they were off at college and she really didn't need the extra horse.

The woman was expecting them and had the horse saddled and ready to go.

The gelding, named Cochise, was under fifteen hands, one-quarter Arab, the rest Quarter Horse, light tan, black points. Booker ran his hands down the animal's legs, checked each hoof. The horse remained calm, chewed at his bit, flicked his tail. Nice solid animal.

Amadeus whispered, "His hair's like mine."

The woman heard him and laughed. She lifted the horse's black mane, looked at Amadeus, and said, "Can't hardly tell you boys apart."

She assessed Booker and Amadeus and pronounced no problem with two of them in the saddle, Cochise wouldn't balk at 220 pounds or so. If they took the trail next to the road to the bottom of the hill, then along the stream, they could get a good sense of whether they'd all make a good match.

The horse cost more than Booker wanted to pay for a twelve-year-old, but he was an easy ride, sure-footed, and didn't shy when a Dusky Grouse flushed out of the bush in front of them. As before, the boy was quiet, held Booker's wrists, leaned back against him so they rode as one. This was only the second time Booker had ridden with a kid in the same saddle and he had a feeling they wouldn't all be this easy. On the way back, he gave Amadeus the reins and held his hands over the boy's.

Another truck was waiting as they rode up the driveway. A middle-aged man with a crew cut was talking animatedly to the woman, who held up her hand. She walked over, gripped the bridle, looked up at them, and said, "You interested? You willing to pay my asking price?"

Booker looked over at the man. "He our competition?"

She nodded. "He's been haggling with me for a couple of days."

"Got the cash in my truck. I'll pay you half now, pay you rest tomorrow when I come back with my trailer."

"Deal," she said. She turned to walk toward the other man, but he'd already gotten in his truck and was backing down the drive.

Booker dismounted and reached up for Amadeus. The boy shook his head and asked, "Can I stay up here while you give the lady the money?"

"Then I'll have to tie him to the rail, he's not ours yet. There's paperwork and it'll take a few minutes. You heard we're not taking him today, right?"

"That's okay," Amadeus said, looking pretty darn small—his feet didn't come close to reaching the stirrups. "We're coming back with the trailer tomorrow."

Booker looked up at the little face, so sure of itself, just assuming that 'coming back tomorrow' included him. Jesus, he was actually buying a horse for a kid he'd met two times before today. No, not for the kid, he reminded himself, a horse that a kid—or anybody—could ride. And it didn't feel like the wrong thing to do.

He went to the truck, opened the locked box attached to the floor behind the seat, and withdrew thirty-five hundred dollars. He had more than enough money, but no sense handing it all over if they weren't taking the horse until tomorrow. He sat with the woman on her porch. As she recounted the money, he looked through the file she had given him. The horse had been well taken care of. She asked if he was interested in a kid's saddle and they went to a shed to check out a small western saddle. He shelled out another two hundred dollars and put the saddle in the back of his truck.

Booker offered to take the tack off the horse and rub him down, but the woman said no, she'd take him out for one last ride to say good-bye. They shook hands and he said they'd be back at ten tomorrow. Booker walked to the horse and reached up for the boy, but Amadeus shook his head, brought his knees up so he was crouching on the saddle like a frog, and jumped soundlessly to the ground. Nibbling on his bit, Cochise turned his head and bobbed it with a loud, moist snort.

By the time Booker got to the truck, Amadeus was buckled in his seat.

"Is that my saddle?" he asked looking over his shoulder.

"Maybe."

Amadeus gave a look of pure satisfaction. "Maybe thank you," the boy said.

Booker stopped at The Crow's Nest as they drove down Comfrey's Main Street. The restaurant remained shut up tight. The door that led to the upstairs office and apartment was locked, so they drove home.

Amadeus had been asleep for most of the ride, but Booker couldn't tell if he was still asleep or pretending. No movement, so he picked the child up and carried him into the cabin, deposited him on the couch, and covered him with a blanket.

Four messages on his answering machine: Esau saying they'd be late because they were heading to Casper; his agent asking him to phone her—all but one of his pieces had already sold, how long before he could get her some more? Another from Esau, to say he'd try to retrieve Amadeus before midnight. The last call was from Ruth saying Heidi had phoned to ask her to pick up Amadeus if Booker needed a break.

Before he could call Ruth back, the phone rang. "How are you doing, Booker?" Ruth asked, friendly as a circus clown. "You and Amadeus enjoy yourselves today?"

"Fine. Had hamburgers, bought a horse," said Booker shortly.

Ruth gave a hoot.

"The horse is a companion for Rosie," he said.

"Sure, sure, but now listen, Heidi's asked me to come up get Amadeus. They won't be back until tomorrow afternoon."

"Esau left a message saying he'd get him before midnight," said Booker.

"The latest intel is that they're moteling it in Casper, something to do with waiting for a delivery of something. I'll come and get the boy."

Booker let out sigh. He said he might as well keep Amadeus since they were going back to Boulder with the trailer in the morning to pick up the horse anyway. There were extra clothes in Amadeus's backpack, should he wake the boy up? Make him pee? Leave a light on?

"All of the above," said Ruth. "Now, did you say horse? You bought another horse?"

Booker said impatiently it had been in the works for a while and like he said before, he wanted a companion for Rosie.

After a moment of barely stifled laughter, Ruth managed, "This is very good of you, Booker. We're all very grateful."

Booker squeezed his eyes shut with a grimace. 'We're all very grateful.' Here was Ruth, sticking her nose in again, part of everything.

"Yeah, well I can keep him tonight but this can't be a regular thing, I'm way too ..."

Ruth broke in, "I'll have a lasagna waiting in your fridge when you return with Rosie's new friend tomorrow. Now, from one busy individual to another, I'll bid you goodnight."

Booker hung up, opened the kitchen's back door, and looked toward the corral. It would have an additional occupant tomorrow, a really great horse that neither he nor Rosie needed. He had Rosie and she had the Billy goat, they had all been just fine. He clenched his fists hard, forced them open and cracked his knuckles.

Heidi called before ten, apologizing for phoning so late. Booker was surprised at his visceral reaction to her voice. Jesus, it was like being a horny teenager again.

She spoke quietly, thanking Booker very much for spending a day and a night with Amadeus. She confessed this would be their first night apart since they became a family and she missed Amadeus very much. When Booker asked her to speak up a little, she said Esau and Marcela were sleeping—the motel had only one vacancy, so they were all crowded into one room. Booker made some kind of sound that elicited a quiet chuckle from her.

Would he please make sure Amadeus visited the toilet before going to sleep? she asked, and she hoped Amadeus was being a good, polite boy. Very good, very polite, Booker assured her.

After a prolonged pause, she said, "Ruth says today you and Amadeus bought a horse, a horse for your horse, but Rosie has a goat friend already."

"Rosie sometimes finds the goat annoying."

Heidi laughed again. "I have a question for you. Do you know Ruth's niece, Elizabeth Darcy?"

"I do. Ruth tried to ... well, never mind. Yeah. I've met her a few times. Why?"

"She has asked me for a job in the kitchen. She can work in the evening when her husband is home to take care of the little boy and I can use evening help. But Esau works sometimes at Toot's Lucky Thirteen and tells me she has her head in the cloud most of the time. Is this how you see her?"

Esau had nailed it. When Booker had first arrived in Comfrey, Ruth had brought Elizabeth by several times. She was very pretty, if you liked that kind of delicate, pouty look, but she never seemed one hundred percent there. He'd finally told Ruth he definitely wasn't interested and he hadn't been particularly polite. It had been a relief when Fred Darcy took her on.

"I've met her a few times," Booker said slowly. "She's ... she appeared distracted a lot, I guess. Esau will know her better."

"I ask you because my cousin, Karl, tells me to always try to get the opinion of someone who does not have the dog in the game when I hire."

"Dog?"

"Yes, and Esau and I agree this is most especially important in a small town, where a person's hurt feelings can spread very far. I will offer Elizabeth something, but perhaps I keep the responsibility low. There are many jobs in a restaurant."

"I would think so." This was more of a conversation than he would have expected, given their limited contact. He wanted it to continue. He heard her yawn.

"I will say goodbye now, Booker. Marcela has our bed warm like toast," she said, her voice low, soft. "You are a good friend to us. *Gute Nacht.*"

"What? Oh, good night." Booker looked at the phone, but she had already hung up.

PART TWO:
QUANTUM LEAPS

CHAPTER TWENTY

GETTING READY FOR SCHOOL

When Heidi had enrolled the children in kindergarten in Riverton, she asked for Marcela to be registered as a girl, but the district and the school refused, stating enrollment papers had to match a child's birth certificate. Although the principal had assured Heidi that his office staff would keep Marcela's confidence, the little girl had been betrayed. The experience had been devastating for Marcela and also for Amadeus. He had made friends easily and loved school, but he refused to return when his sister was bullied.

Opening The Crow's Nest had distracted her from getting a new birth certificate for Marcela, and enrollment in Comfrey Elementary would be closing soon. Heidi prayed she hadn't left things too late when she phoned Richard Gayle, the transgender brother of the social worker who had helped arrange Heidi's guardianship of the twins. Richard had been Nara's nurse and had accompanied Heidi to Nara's cremation.

"I've been waiting for your call," said Richard, his voice businesslike. "I heard from my sister what happened when you enrolled Marcela in kindergarten. I was glad to hear you had moved. You can't trust people will accept that Marcela is who she says she is."

He reiterated what Heidi already knew; a legal petition could be filed when Marcela turned eighteen, but because she was so young, changing gender on her birth certificate through official channels would not be possible. He said there were people in Cheyenne who could modify a birth certificate for the purpose of elementary school enrollment. He'd give them a call and Heidi could expect a postcard with a number to call in a few days.

"They're very cautious," said Richard. "They'll tell you what to do to be recognized and they're fast—you'll have what you need within an hour or two. I recommend you bring the twins with you. They're young, but they're complicit and this will help them not let their guard down."

"I understand. Thank you."

"I'm glad you phoned, Heidi," said Richard, his voice warming. "You need our help now. People like you have never had to look over your shoulder."

And perhaps because he couldn't help himself, he went on to remark on the easy life of a heterosexual, educated, white woman, protected from fear and prejudice ... but Heidi had stopped listening. Instead, she remembered how often she had looked over her shoulder in New York, dreading a glimpse of the angel of death that finally moved to steal her baby after one hundred and eighty-two days. To be so helpless—oh, she had known fear.

A postcard of the Grand Tetons arrived several days later with the name Felix and a phone number on the back. When Heidi called and asked for Felix, the voice on the other end chuckled and said, "We're all Felix."

The transaction would occur at a public library near the Cheyenne courthouse at 9:15 A.M. She would need to bring a manila envelope with the original birth certificate and a hundred dollars in twenties.

"A hundred dollars seems inexpensive," said Heidi.

"We help each other," said Felix. "We do what we can to

keep children safe."

The trip from Comfrey to Cheyenne would take a little over five hours, so Heidi and the twins spent the night in a hotel near the courthouse and walked to the library after breakfast. With the children sitting at their own table nearby, Heidi placed the envelope containing the money and the birth certificate on the corner of her desk against the west wall across from the mystery section, and sat with a magazine turned upside down, as directed. A few minutes later a young man walked by and, without breaking his stride, picked up the envelope and disappeared down the nearest aisle.

Heidi looked over at the children, who had paused in their coloring to watch. Marcela clamped her hand over her mouth to stifle a giggle and Amadeus hissed at her. They looked at Heidi guiltily and she felt a pang. She had promised them lunch and a trolley ride when their mission had been accomplished, something to assuage the lies and deceit that had become part of their lives.

A librarian came by and spoke to the twins. They pointed to Heidi, and the woman walked over.

"Children must be accompanied by an adult at all times. They say they are yours." The woman pursed her mouth, as if sucking on a straw.

Heidi looked from the librarian to the twins. "Yes, and I have my eyes on them like the hawk. We are practicing good library manners and I am very proud of how well they behave."

"It's just that I didn't see an adult that looked like them and sometimes children are just left, as if we're here to babysit."

"It must make your job very difficult when this happens," said Heidi, smiling up at her.

"Just so you understand," said the woman, sounding

somewhat mollified at the recognition her job was not an easy one.

An hour later, the young man reappeared and left the manila envelope in his wake. Conscious of the children's eyes locked upon her, Heidi opened the envelope and withdrew the contents. She looked up and beckoned. She pointed to the 'a' at the end of Marcel, and to the 'F' that proclaimed Marcela a female. The children, who had been giggling together just minutes ago, now looked solemn.

"Can they change it back if they want to?" asked Amadeus.

"Can the people in the office at the school change it?" asked Heidi.

At his nod, she said, "I will hand in the certificate that is like all the other students' certificates. No one will know we had to make this correction."

"And you said we can get me special underpants before school starts," said Marcela.

Richard had given Heidi the name of a woman in Rock Springs who had a transgender child and now made underwear for little girls to wear before their physical transition. Are there so many? Heidi had asked the woman. No, not really, she had replied. Most families were still in denial, but still, she had quite a following.

"We have an appointment to see the underpants lady next week," said Heidi. "Now I am hungry and I have heard of a restaurant that has fish you may feed."

Fish—Nara, with her fascination of all things aquatic, would have approved.

The maître d' at the bistro in Historic Cheyenne seated them on the patio alongside a koi pond. He brought over a small bowl with koi food pellets.

"Make sure they scatter the pellets so the fish fan out," said the maître d' to Heidi.

The fish gathered, roiling the water, their bodies mottled red, black, and white, one all yellow. They gazed up with large, expectant eyes.

"Aunt Heidi, what are those wiggly things by their mouth?" asked Marcela.

Heidi, distracted by a thin blond boy talking animatedly with his family at a nearby table, didn't answer immediately. The boy had a pale, intelligent face with bright eyes. He looked to be about twelve. This was Peter's birthday month, and he too would have been twelve. He too would have been thin and pale—children with cystic fibrosis usually were—but this child radiated health. His mother leaned over and whispered something to him ... did the woman realize how lucky she was?

"So what are those whisker things called?" Marcela's voice intruded and Heidi dragged her attention back to the twins.

"Your mother once tells me they are called barbels," she said. "Some fish have their taste buds there."

"Mama knows everything," said Amadeus, scattering his fish food pellets wide.

Marcela opened her mouth but Heidi touched the little girl's arm and shook her head. Now was not the time to say dead people are dead so they can't know anything. Heidi ordered a flute of champagne and a salad niçoise. Amadeus and Marcela ordered sparkling cider, hamburgers, and fries made from sweet potatoes, since the bistro didn't have the regular kind.

"They're floppy," said Marcela, her nose wrinkled in distaste. "They smell funny." She waggled a fry at Heidi.

"I'll eat yours," Amadeus offered, and Heidi helped Marcela transfer the fries to his plate.

As she watched the twins tucking into their food, she gave a silent toast to her mother, who had often said, "*Gott gibt uns nicht mehr, als wir tragen können.*" 'God does not give us more than we can bear.'

But there had been days after Peter's death when emptiness engulfed her so completely, it truly did seem God had handed her more than she could bear. She also raised her glass to Nara. After they became estranged, their bond had remained strong enough for Nara to write 'Aunt Heidi' and Saint Gemma's phone number on Amadeus's forearm. Heidi knew social worker Lily Brown would not have been able to award her the twin's guardianship if their mother hadn't claimed her as kin.

CHAPTER TWENTY-ONE

COFFEE AT THE CROW'S NEST

It had been three months since Booker first trained his spotting scope on the activities at The Crow's Nest, two months since he'd bought Cochise. Esau had been dropping Amadeus off twice a week for riding lessons but, except for the day Ruth had brought the Crows by in the fall, Booker had not met Heidi face-to-face again.

Esau kept urging him to come to The Crow's Nest for coffee, insisting the invitation came from Heidi herself. He did finally stop by, only to find Heidi had taken the kids to Cheyenne to get some kind of document related to enrolling them in school.

"She had to drive over ten hours round trip for something Sublette county needs for school enrollment?" Booker asked. "Bet she could have gotten what she needed at the county offices in Pinedale."

Esau thought the same thing, but had let it go, figuring the trip had something to do with whatever Heidi and the kids were hiding. He shrugged and said Heidi had planned for her absence. Elizabeth Darcy was getting better at waitressing with help from Tyree, and was now working most lunches and the occasional dinner. A couple of high school kids came by to do dishes. Heidi had enlisted Armand to help in the kitchen and he was turning out to be pretty damn good.

Ignoring most of this, Booker demanded, "So when's she

coming back?"

"Tonight or tomorrow. You object to her going away?"

Booker shook his head in frustration. "God dammit, small towns can be a pain in the ass."

"Sometimes," Esau said with a chuckle, "but now that you're here, want some coffee with little ol' me?"

The following week, Booker phoned the restaurant to suggest he and Amadeus take a ride up to the lake. He had to talk to Esau of course, Heidi being out and about.

"Hey, thanks," said Esau. "He'll be pumped."

"Don't you have to check with Heidi? I haven't taken him off the property before, the trail to the lake's pretty steep in parts."

"Now don't sound all pissed off, my man," Esau said. "You've offered the kid something nice. If you thought it wasn't safe, you wouldn't be doing it. I'm saying yes for Heidi because I'm saying yes for Heidi."

Esau arrived with a beaming Amadeus, who tumbled out of the van and ran immediately into the tack room. Camera in hand, Esau gave Rosie—already saddled and tied to a hitch—a wide berth and came to stand next to Booker. He asked how long it was going to be before they headed out, because Heidi wanted pictures.

Booker nodded at Cochise in the paddock. "Amadeus has to saddle up first."

Esau checked his watch and muttered he had bread dough proofing. Booker pointed out that no one was standing in his way, and suggested Esau give him the camera and he'd take the shots.

Esau shook his head. "She wants both of you heading out together."

"Oh, does she now?" Booker frowned at his boot to control a smile.

The men stood, each with a foot on the lowest railing of the paddock fence, forearms on the upper rail, in the classic stance of men watching someone else saddle a horse.

"Just wondering if this is some kind of game Heidi is playing that I don't recognize. Unless I do recognize it, in which case I'll back off," said Booker as they watched Amadeus carry the saddle out of the tack room, holding it high to avoid trailing the cinch on the ground.

"There you go, talking your riddles again," said Esau. "If you're talking about Heidi being busy, we're all busy. You're busy."

"Not that busy, nobody's that busy."

Amadeus dropped the saddle as he tried to heft it onto a horse considerably taller than he. Cochise swung his head around and bobbed his head.

"Aren't you going to help him?" asked Esau. "Look, the horse agrees with me, he's saying help the kid."

"Nope, he's saying let the kid alone." Booker stretched and adjusted his hat. The horse gave a whicker but stood still.

"A pony might be more Amadeus's size." Esau batted a fly away. "A Shetland or something."

Booker snorted. "Not buying a toy horse," he said. "Cochise is not a big horse, he's under fifteen hands. Do you not know *anything* about horses?"

"Not all Indigenous folk know horses," Esau grunted.

"Not if you're anything to go by."

Amadeus rested the saddle against the fence and marched to the shed, coming back with a wooden box.

"Atta boy," said Booker, quietly enough so Amadeus couldn't hear.

When Amadeus climbed on the box with the saddle, Cochise did a little sidestep and the boy and saddle tumbled. Amadeus dusted himself off and yelled over, "I'm okay."

"Kid breaks an arm, Heidi will be pissed," Esau muttered to Booker. To Amadeus, he called, "You're doing great, let's go,

I've got to take pictures and get going."

When Amadeus swatted the air in Esau's direction, Booker chuckled and said, "You can't rush a man when he's saddling a horse."

"So how much longer do you think?"

"Long enough for you to tell me about this wooden door those guys trucked out from New York a while back. Amadeus called it Peter's door. What's that about?"

Esau sighed. He'd just have to hope Heidi would be back from Hebeka in time to deal with the bread dough.

"Peter is Heidi's son," he said. "He died of cystic fibrosis. You know what that is?"

"Something genetic, hard to breathe?"

"Yeah, and then some. It's the most common serious genetic disease in whites—Heidi's cousin Karl told me about it. He's got a cousin on the other side of his family who has it, but she just turned thirty. She works for him and although she gets pretty sick at times, she's mostly okay. Since the condition is recessive, each parent has to contribute a gene, so I'd say whites shouldn't get it on with whites. Or let me broaden the playing field a bit for them—*European* whites shouldn't marry *European* whites."

Booker flicked a look at the Esau. He was beginning to think the guy spent too much time in his own head unless ... was the Shoshone saying *he* was a better bet for Heidi than a white guy?

"Got you, man," Esau broke into his thoughts with a chuckle. "I don't care who gets it on with who, or whom, just leave kids and animals out of it."

Booker muttered a mild expletive under his breath and asked about the door again.

Esau told him that according to Karl, the door was a challenge Heidi set her German ex-father-in-law, Emmett Vogel, before Peter was born—like if you're as powerful as you say you are, see if you can have a door carved of black forest oak, inlaid with a light wood for edelweiss flowers. She had laid out really specific parameters, including the exact positioning of a specific breed of hunting dog.

"Vogel is as rich and controlling as hell," continued Esau. "He thought he could control Heidi the way he controlled his own gutless kids. When he found out the baby was going to be a boy, a future heir to his dynasty, he called Heidi and told her he'd send her whatever she wanted from the homeland, like for a reward. She thought she had set him an impossible task, but he met it—when you see the door up close, you'll see what I mean."

"You know ..." Booker gave Esau a long look, which Esau returned, "...when Ruth brought you by the first time, you didn't seem like the chatty type, but here you are, buddying up to cousin Karl and dishing out the family dirt."

Esau chuckled. "Just getting you caught up."

"Okay." Booker watched Amadeus a moment. "So what else?"

Esau looked up at the sky. What else? Heidi had said if Booker asked questions about her, to give him answers. "Well, I'll tell you, with the baby dying, Heidi's got all these superstitions, or not that exactly, but rituals I guess," he said. "She's pulling out the stops to keep the twins safe. Next week she's getting them baptized so the *Will-o'-the-Wisp* won't get them."

"The *what*?"

"Yeah, I too am just getting used to the primitive beliefs of Europeans." Esau stopped a moment when Rosie stamped her feet and whickered. "What's she want?"

"To get going, but continue, still got some time."

Esau cast him a sour look and continued, "Okay, well when you look at some of the old lore, it'll blow your mind. The *Will-o'-the-Wisp* is a kind of apparition that comes out of the mist and takes unbaptized kids. She's careful not to scare the twins—she just has her little ways. Heidi's a practical person, she's just hedging her bets."

Booker stepped away from the fence and cracked his knuckles. "Sounds like you're pretty cozy with her."

"Real cozy because we let each other be. Come by the restaurant for coffee and you can cozy up to her too."

"Christ, you and Ruth are like a couple of old yentas. Anyway, I'm pretty..."

"Yeah, busy, I know," Esau interrupted. "But listen, if you and Heidi don't hit it off, you can't let this thing with Amadeus drop. That's separate."

"Obviously."

"And about the superstition thing—she doesn't believe a lot of weird fairy stuff, nothing like that. You know, she's rooted in reality."

"No, I don't know. I've rarely talked to the woman."

"Then come by for coffee and talk to her. You want an engraved invitation?"

"Yeah, engrave one for me."

"You know who doesn't need an engraved invitation? Wyatt Beauclaire, the Fire Captain—he's there almost every day."

Booker shook his head and looked over at Amadeus, who now had the saddle on the horse.

"Good job," called Esau.

"He's not done yet," said Booker tersely.

"Right, well, how much longer?"

"He's getting there."

"What's he doing now?" asked Esau. Still on the box, Amadeus was pressing his knee into the side of the horse as he tightened the cinch.

"Cochise has a habit of trying to inflate his belly while being girthed."

"So horse un-bloats himself and then the saddle's too loose, then you're on like a steep part of the trail and the saddle slides back?"

"Pretty much, and we're not going to let that happen," said Booker. "I'm attaching a three-point breastplate and security straps, all nice and secure, nothin' slidin' nowhere. No need to worry your pretty little head about Heidi's boy."

At the 'pretty little head' comment, Esau raised his ravaged face and let out a howl of laugher. He punched Booker playfully on the arm.

Booker got the breastplate and straps out of the barn, stopping by his truck on his way back to get a cowboy hat that was similar to his, but in a size the saleslady thought would fit a six-year-old. He wouldn't mind Esau taking a picture of Amadeus in the hat for Heidi.

When he went into the paddock and placed the hat on Amadeus, he whispered, "Keep cool or Esau will want one too."

The delighted boy bit his lips and nodded. He could keep cool.

Esau yelled, "Hey, I want a hat too."

Amadeus gave Booker a grin and whispered, "Then he gotta stop being so scaredy of horses."

"You got that right," Booker whispered back.

Booker showed Amadeus how to attach the breastplate. He checked the cinch, tightened it a little, and boosted Amadeus into the saddle.

Esau took his pictures, held up a hand, and jogged to his truck.

Bought the kid a hat—Heidi would love it. Esau chuckled as he headed down the drive. Booker was a strange guy, but he had his moves.

* * * * * *

When Booker stopped by The Crow's Nest on the way home from picking up welding supplies in Pinedale a few days later, the lunch crowd had already cleared out and, except for

183

Wyatt Beauclaire at the counter, the place was empty. Heidi sat at the booth furthest from the door. Several books were stacked on the table, another lay open, and she was industriously scribbling in a notebook.

"Here goes," Booker said under his breath as he walked toward her.

Heidi looked up when he slid into the booth. Her eyes widened in surprise before she smiled.

"Hello, Booker," she said, as if they were old friends.

"Hello, Heidi," he replied. He had thought of blue eyes as hard and cold, maybe because his high school girlfriend had them, but Heidi's weren't. They smiled when her mouth smiled.

"Do you like caraway seed?" she asked.

"Not particularly," Booker replied, amused.

"Neither do I."

She closed the book and he tipped his head to read the title, *The Bible of Artesian Bread*. Food as religion, he knew some people thought of it that way. The other books on the table were bread cookbooks too.

"I am considering using blue fenugreek in our rye instead. What do you think of that?"

"Are there other colors available?" He hadn't a clue what fenugreek was.

She laughed and didn't bother to enlighten him. "You have come for coffee and plum kuchen?" she asked, sliding out of the booth before he could answer.

He watched Heidi go behind the counter and make new pot of coffee. She said something that made Wyatt Beauclaire laugh. She got a plate and cut a slice of what must be the plum thing.

Good God, she was a pretty woman. What color were those eyes? Kyanite, the blue found in aluminum silicate formed under high pressure, low temperature, came pretty close. Swiss blue topaz? He had bought a piece at a flea market in

Landers because he liked the color. He found out later the color was formed when colorless topaz was irradiated. It remained slightly radioactive, not dangerous but false, manmade. He didn't know where he'd put it.

He watched Wyatt turn and examine Heidi as she walked back to the booth. He and Wyatt locked eyes and exchanged a nod. Wyatt gave him a little salute. Like what? Good luck or let the better man win?

Heidi smiled down at Booker. She had brought one large piece of cake and two forks.

"I bring the extra big piece so I may have some too. *Zwetschgenkuchen,*" she said with satisfaction, sliding into the booth. "It is German plum cake. I use Italian plums. They are firm enough and have a good flavor. Ruth's friend Vera has a tree with too many plums, so..." she reached over and took a forkful, "I make out like the bandit."

There was something so intimate in her assumption she could eat off his plate, he could feel himself grinning. Grinning and winning. He met Wyatt's eyes in the mirror that spanned the wall behind the counter.

Her hair was piled on top of her head today, some silky long strands had come loose. Heidi studied her forkful, eyes narrowed as if assessing its appeal. She put it in her mouth and chewed slowly.

She gave a small nod and pronounced, "It is very good. Esau suggested a hint of ground black pepper. He has more imagination than I have and I am glad I listened."

She raised her eyes to Booker and caught him staring at her. He drew the plate back toward him and concentrated on his next bites.

He had assumed they'd talk about Amadeus, she'd thank him for giving the boy all his free time, he'd tell her it wasn't a problem, Amadeus was a good kid. She might ask him about his work, he'd try to make it sound interesting. He could ask her about Germany.

She did thank him for Amadeus's hat, but then the talk turned to fruit trees. Ruth had been looking for houses for them. Heidi said she wanted something near the school with a big backyard, big enough to plant some fruit trees if it didn't already have some. She had been researching cold hardy plants and asked about his property—did he have fruit trees?

He did and she was welcome to the fruit. He, the birds, opossums, and raccoons couldn't keep up with it. He told her he'd been raised in rural Pennsylvania and he and his brother had worked at a nursery during summer vacations. It was probably why he'd planted one too many fruit trees on his property.

As soon as Booker had said it, he knew he had made a mistake and, sure enough, she wanted to know about Pennsylvania and his brother.

"I went military, Simon went nursery," he said shortly, and looked at his watch.

He said he had work to get back to and thanked her for the coffee and cake. He didn't insult her by offering to pay.

Through the window, Heidi watched him walk out to his truck parked along the curb. An attractive man with a powerful body and a confident walk, who was so good to Amadeus. He had the kind of awkwardness she liked in a man, shy but not meek. He acted tough—but did he know how funny he was? Ruth said he had been in the military, but not to ask him about it. A question about Pennsylvania and his brother should have been safe enough.

"What did you say?" asked Esau when he came to remind Heidi she had promised him an hour in the kitchen before she and Marcela went to watch Amadeus's basketball game.

"A question about Pennsylvania and the brother."

"Yeah, that could get him heading for home," said Esau, gathering up the cookbooks and herding her into the kitchen. "Strange guy, definitely not one to reminisce about the past."

"He was the one to mention Pennsylvania first."

186

"Must have let his guard down. Let's get to work, woman."

"Do not be my bully," said Heidi, putting on her apron.

"No Boss, sorry Boss," said Esau, watching her start to chop onions with incredible speed. "Your Indian name shall be 'Lightening Onion Chopper Woman.'"

She stopped for an instant to bow her head, as if so anointed.

CHAPTER TWENTY-TWO

LET'S TRY THIS AGAIN

Booker heard the white van come up the drive and came out of the barn. When Heidi emerged, he called, "How'd Esau get off the hook?"

She smiled and walked toward him, saying nothing as she passed close enough he could smell a light floral perfume. She stood peering into the barn where Amadeus was attempting to open a hay bale with a pair of wire cutters.

The boy looked up and called, "I have to feed Rosie and Cochise and put saddle soap on my saddle before I can go."

"You do not need to hurry," she called back. "I have a few things to say to Booker."

Booker came up behind her. "Things to say to me?" he said quietly.

She turned to look up at him. "Oh yes, quite some things to say to you."

"Want to sit? Porch? Deck?"

"Porch," she said, marching around him toward the cabin and leaving him to follow.

She took a seat in a chair with a cushion patterned in red, blue, and green curved teardrops. Paisley—her cousin Karl would have approved. Instead of taking the matching chair, Booker lowered himself to the top step. He sat sideways, one knee bent, and leaned back against a porch support.

"These are very pretty cushions," she said, running her

hands over the fabric.

"Ruth. I told her no flowers."

"Ah yes, of course, Ruth," said Heidi, flashing a smile that made his pulse quicken.

He looked away and she waited, saying nothing until he returned his eyes to hers. He raised a questioning eyebrow, inviting her to start.

"I came to pick up Amadeus, because I need to tell you I am not someone who asks questions if I understand what a person does not want to talk about." She looked composed but he heard a slight tremor in her voice.

"Okay," he said slowly.

"And I would like to know you a little better because you are Amadeus's friend and I approve of this friendship very much. And I think the other day I walked into some territory you want to keep private and I have some of these territories also, so I understand."

"Uh huh," he said after a moment, looking down at the porch step with a grin. She was sounding particularly Germanic today. He had acted like an idiot the other day, but he was over it.

"Do you understand what I am saying?" she demanded.

"Yes ma'am. I believe I do."

Her lips twitched at the *ma'am*. "The Crow's Nest is closed on Sundays as I believe you may know from Esau," she said. "I would like you to have lunch with me and the children at our apartment on this Sunday."

He looked at her a long moment before saying, "Lunch? *This* Sunday you say. Hmmm, let me see." He stroked his chin and looked at the ground, deep in thought. He could feel her eyes upon him, he knew exactly how blue those eyes were.

He looked up at her and asked politely, "Before I commit to giving up a Sunday, would you please tell me the food options?"

He could tell she was struggling not to laugh by the way

she bit her bottom lip. Once composed, she rattled off a long list—fewer than half were terms he knew.

"How about the second German-sounding thing you said," he suggested.

"If you like, unless you would you prefer breakfast, brunch, or perhaps dinner."

"May I choose more than one?"

"Not until we are better acquainted," she said with a dimpled smile.

"Oh, Heidi Crow," he said, shaking his head. "You're breaking my heart."

She put her hand over her heart, patted her breast, and gave him a smile so ridiculously flirtatious, he laughed out loud.

They decided on lunch so Booker could be back in plenty of time to pack up some artwork he had to deliver to a gallery in Lander the next morning. Amadeus came out of the barn and yelled he was too tired to walk over and Heidi had to come to him.

She stood up, looked down at Booker, and asked, "You are the troll? Do I have to pay you to cross your bridge?"

He swung his legs aside and watched her walk away, as pretty from the back as from the front. Amadeus waited by the van and put his arms around Heidi's waist when she got to him. He looked up into her face. She kissed his forehead and said something that made him laugh.

"You're coming to lunch, you're coming to lunch," he taunted in that classic children's sing-song way, dancing up and down and pointing at Booker.

Booker watched them drive off, and muttered, "Are you out of your *goddamn mind*? Breaking my heart?"

Had he actually said that?

CHAPTER TWENTY-THREE

HEARTS GO PITTER PATTER

Sunday morning at ten o'clock, Booker rolled his 1965 BMW motorcycle out of its storage shed. He had bought it from the mother of a young soldier with the unlucky birthday of September 14, 1947, and the unlucky initials JJJ. Private John Jasper Johnson had scored a series of firsts. First place in the first Viet Nam draft lottery, first in their neighborhood to go to Nam, first to come back in a body bag. His mother had stored the motorcycle in her garage for years before she could bring herself to sell it. The BMW had less than a thousand miles on it when Private Johnson left for war, and had almost two hundred thousand on it now. It was a beautiful motorcycle, a smooth ride, zero to sixty miles per hour in ten-point-three seconds. Booker hadn't ridden it in weeks, but he needed it today.

"Looking good enough to make every heart in Comfrey go pitter-patter, and don't go giving me that scowl, or I swear I'll swoon," Ruth said with a grin when Booker stopped by to pick the brownies she'd made. She had heard about the lunch from Esau and had insisted Booker bring what she called 'a bread and butter' gift.

"Those kids will be pestering you for a ride on your bike," Ruth warned. "You probably should have thought of that and come down in your truck, although I understand your desire to work off all that pent-up energy and frustration."

"What the hell are you talking about, Ruth?" Booker muttered, knowing exactly what she meant.

"I'm making meatloaf this afternoon, one for me, one for my niece's family, one for you. I'll bring it by tomorrow and you can tell me how the brownies went down."

Booker groaned. "I'm allergic to meatloaf."

"You love my meatloaf and how else am I going to find out how your little lunch went?" Ruth waggled her eyebrows suggestively.

Amadeus came thundering down the stairs when Booker rang the bell. He took in Booker's leather jacket, the helmet under his arm. and darted around him onto the sidewalk.

He walked to the curb and circled the motorcycle, his eyes alight with excitement. "I want a ride," he said. "C'mon Booker, *pleeease!*"

"Your sister first," said Booker.

"She won't want to," Amadeus protested.

"Ask her and before a ride, your aunt has to give her okay. My helmet will be too big, but you guys will have to wear it anyway, so we'll just be going real slow."

Amadeus tore back upstairs and returned with Heidi and Marcela in tow, wearing matching denim overalls and red turtlenecks.

"Aunt Heidi and I match," said Marcela. "Even our hair."

Both Marcela and Heidi turned around so Booker could see their ponytails were tied back with identical purple ribbons.

"Booker's getting me a leather jacket," said Amadeus. "Hurry up, Marcela, and take your ride so I can have mine."

"Booker, have you heard a please or thank you from either Marcela or Amadeus?" asked Heidi.

"Not yet, no ma'am."

"And I think a leather jacket for a boy who just turns seven and who will soon outgrow it is foolish."

"Didn't get my first one until I was sixteen."

"I must say you look very masculine and appealing," said Heidi, trying to control her grin.

"And you look very ... ah, practical," he returned. "Think I could do with a pair of overalls myself."

"And a red turtle neck," said Marcela.

"Can we, *please-thank you*, stop talking about clothes, so Marcela, *please-thank you,* can hurry up and get her ride so I can too?" moaned Amadeus.

"*Maultaschen,*" said Heidi, placing a round dish with very large German raviolis on the table. The large white squares were bathed in a white sauce and surrounded by sliced hardboiled eggs.

Booker inhaled deeply. So apparently this was what he had selected from the list of potential offerings the other day. "Smells great, what's in them?"

"You put bacon and onion and chunks of wet..." Amadeus started.

"Sautéed sweet onions," Marcela interjected.

"Yeah, sautéed, then chunks of wet stale bread and you mix that into a bunch of spinach and ground meat, but not veal."

"Because veal is mean," said Marcela, nodding emphatically. "They stick the baby cows in crates so they can't move."

"Then you put sausage and sour cream and you mix it all together with your hands." Amadeus illustrated by moving his curled fingers energetically.

"And what spices?" asked Heidi.

"Nutmeg, salt, and *pepper,*" chorused the twins.

"And it's good!" whispered Amadeus in a dramatic stage whisper.

It was pretty good, Booker admitted to himself. Different— he was a traditional red sauce, Italian ravioli guy—but he managed to ask for one extra of these, which seemed to please Heidi.

After lunch, they walked through town, pulling Gering in his wagon. The little dog wore a black and white checkered jacket Marcela recently bought him with her own money. Heidi explained Gering's disc degeneration was slowly getting worse and walking more than a few blocks was hard on him.

"You know what Gertrude Stein said about little dogs?" Booker asked Marcela and Heidi. Amadeus had run ahead and was on a porch talking to a couple of kids.

"Gertrude, that's a weird name," said Marcela, wrinkling her nose.

"Gertrude Stein was a famous poet," said Heidi. "Booker will tell us what she said about dogs. Gering wants to know too."

Hearing his name, the dachshund looked at them soulfully.

"She said, 'I am I because my little dog knows me.' One of my teachers in high school made us memorize quotes from famous people. Think that's the only one I can remember accurately. There's more to it, but the rest escapes me." Here he was, out with a woman, two kids, and a dog, quoting poetry. He remembered the rest of the poem, but enough was enough.

Heidi laughed. "Esau probably knows the rest, he studied the lesbian poets in college."

"He *what*?" asked Booker incredulously.

"He did very well in college," said Heidi with a grin. "He is a most interesting person."

"Of course he is," muttered Booker, earning an amused look from Heidi.

On their way home, they stopped at a playground with basketball hoops and played a little ball. Marcela was as quick as her brother and made as many baskets.

Booker asked, "Don't they have girls' teams, or can't she be on her brother's? They're seven, why are they separating them at this age?"

"They have a team for girls under ten and there is a mixed team but she is not interested. It is her choice. Marcela is not fond of team sports. Did your parents force you to be on a team?"

"Didn't have to, I was competitive. I loved sports," Booker said. Both he and Simon, his younger brother, had been star athletes in high school. Those had been easy times.

He said no thanks to tea when they got back, saying he'd planned to be home by five to start loading his truck for tomorrow. Heidi told the kids to take Gering upstairs for his supper, and yes they could each have another brownie.

Booker stood by his motorcycle and looked at Heidi, wondering how much of a goodbye he was going to get.

"Thank you for giving us so much of your valuable time, Mr. McNabb," said Heidi, putting a hand on his arm to steady herself as she stood on her toes to give him a kiss on the cheek.

"I have more valuable time to give next Sunday, Miss Crow," he said, grabbing her wrist when she stepped back and pulling her to him for a light kiss on the lips. And a second one. Her lips parted just enough to give him a rush of heat.

He put on his helmet, straddled the bike, and rocked it off its kickstand. She stood on the sidewalk smiling at him, the pink in her cheeks hinting she'd felt the heat too.

"See ya," he said.

"See ya," she responded with a grin.

Lunch was ... well, amusing, he thought as he accelerated down the road. What had they eaten? Those huge ravioli things, he couldn't remember their name. Not something he would have eaten as a kid, but the twins scarfed it down and asked for more. And that kiss she'd accepted—he bit his bottom lip, revved the engine, and approached Wild Horse

Valley hill a little faster than was perhaps wise. That kiss hadn't been amusing at all. That had been the start of something, but how the hell was it going to go further in a little apartment with two seven-year-old kids?

It was a relief to be back on his property. He parked the motorcycle outside its storage shed, he'd wax it this evening. He listened for a moment to sounds he understood—the clinking of metal as the bike's engine and exhaust pipes cooled, the wind rustling the conifers behind his shop, a gentle high-pitched neigh from Rosie, calling him over to the paddock. Cochise was still keeping his emotions to himself. He promised the animals he'd feed them after he'd checked his answering machine. The Billy goat gave him a glare.

"Yeah, I know, but work's work," he said to the goat. "Somebody's got to provide for all this."

Mountain spring water, always cold, always crisp, with a slight mineral taste. The water was one of the major reasons he'd made a bid for this property. He drank a long glass as he listened to his messages. His agent wanted to talk about a potential client in Santa Fe, Raul Diaz needed something signed, Ruth said she wouldn't be coming up with a meatloaf tomorrow, her grandson had arrived and needed her help.

Ruth's grandson? Booker put down his glass. He was stunned. Ruth was the closest friend he had in Comfrey and he hadn't even known she had a kid—let alone the kid had a kid.

CHAPTER TWENTY-FOUR

MINKIE

"Ocean Rain? Really, Debbie? That's a mouthful, is there a nickname?" Ruth Creeley asked the daughter she hadn't seen for almost ten years.

"I prefer Ocean Rain, Mom, but if it's too much for you," Ocean Rain rolled her eyes, "you can call me Ocie. Minkie came up with that, but you know, as he's a kid, I've had to make allowances."

"Well, thank you, D ... I mean Ocie. I'll be an allowance too, generous of you to make an allowance for the young and the old," said Ruth. She eyed her grandson, who did not look well. "Come sit on the porch, I can't stand here looking down on you."

"Then come down. Knox and me got to get going, Mom, and I have a favor to ask."

Ruth walked down the porch steps and looked over at the man who stared straight out the window of the battered truck. He hadn't bothered to turn off the engine. "Knox?"

"Knox, Fort Knox, he's good with money," said Ocean Rain defensively. "Anyway, so, I mean I need to drop Minkie off with you for maybe a few weeks. Some school might be good. I think he's behind in reading and stuff, but we've noticed he's got this really creative side. I don't want a school to squash that right out of him."

"I don't think you just drop a child at school for a few

weeks, honey. Where's he been going to school?"

Ocean Rain released an impatient snort. "Mom, look at all the uncreative, unhappy kids that graduate from school. That's what I had to escape from. If I had stayed, who knows how limiting that would've been? I might have been stuck in a job, florescent lights, eat not when you're hungry but when they give you time. Freedom from all that shit has allowed me to become who I truly am, I feel the rhythm of life, the pulse of the earth. I actually feel nature's energy fields."

She chewed on a hangnail and put her finger in her mouth to suck off the tiny bead of blood that gathered. She knew she was talking too fast but holy shit, they didn't have all day to just chat. Sit and chat, *Jesus.* She flicked a glance at her mother and tried to take a calming breath or two.

"So Ocie, honey, has he been going to school anywhere?" Ruth tried again.

Minkie had taken a seat on the lowest porch step and stroked one of the bolder feral cats that he had enticed onto his lap. He knew he smelled bad. His mom smelled bad, but his grandmother hadn't remarked on it. She hadn't backed away or wrinkled her nose the way people in stores did. He hoped his grandmother would take him in for a while. Forever, maybe.

Ocean Rain picked at one of several scabs on her forearm. Her eyes darted from her mother to her son to the truck in the driveway. It wouldn't do to let Knox get mad.

"We've got to get going, Mom," she said. "This isn't going to be for that long. Minkie can help out, do stuff. Look, he's good with that cat. You can maybe work on reading, but let's not give him just anything to read. You know, not the European 'white man is king' crap. Give him something nourishing, creative. And Mom, he's not a Creeley anymore, he's a Birdsong. Minkie Birdsong, sounds beautiful, doesn't it?"

Ruth looked at her daughter, vibrating with nervous energy, anxious to bolt. A free spirit enslaved by any feel-good, reckless, exciting opportunity that presented itself. And here was her grandson, a constellation of freckles dominating his pale, thin face. She couldn't recall anyone in the family sporting freckles like that before.

She hadn't seen him in close to ten years. He had been called Cricket back then; she thought the last name might still have been Creeley unless Debbie had already severed all family ties at that point. Debbie had left him on the doorstep, refusing to come in, and returned the following week to claim her son and disappear. Heading north, she'd said.

Minkie leaned against the banister, stroking the grey cat, who was drooling in rapture, and looked up at his grandmother with tired eyes.

No, he did not look well to Ruth, and she asked, without thinking, "He looks sick, Debbie—Ocie—has he been to a doctor? Do you have any vaccination records? Anything you're leaving with me?"

"Mom, *stop*! You always ... *Jesus!*" Ocean Rain sputtered and bit off a piece of thumbnail, which she picked off her tongue before continuing, "He's good, maybe needs some rest. This happens to him sometimes and then he gets better. It's a part of growing up. Hormones or something. You know all the damage vaccines do. I'm lucky I didn't get sick from all those checkups, shots you subjected me to, all the time, Mom, like *all* the time."

Ocean Rain looked at her son—he'd just have to deal with this. In some cultures, a twelve-year-old was a man. "I've *got* to get going Mom, stop making such a big deal about everything. You're always trying to control everybody's life. I'm giving you the opportunity to get to know your grandson."

She examined her son a long moment before turning anguished eyes to her mother. She closed them tight and muttered, "Well, shit."

Steadying herself with a hand on the banister, Ocean Rain held out her other hand to her son, as one would to a dog, and he leaned his head into her caress.

"Minkie, you be good for your grandma," she whispered.

The truck started to move and Ocean Rain ran to catch it. It stopped abruptly, but began to move again while she still had one leg out the door.

* * * * * *

"Pretty sure it's Crypto. Cryptosporidium," said Doctor Tom, looking down at Minkie's prostrate form on the examining table. "We'll know definitively when we get the test results from Riverton. Diarrhea, cramping, fever, weight loss, vomiting, lifestyle all point to that."

"Debbie said he's had this before."

"Yeah, repeated infections are fairly common. It's a water-borne parasite, so he's been swimming or ingesting contaminated water. People who are otherwise healthy can rid themselves of the parasite in a few weeks, some never even have symptoms, 'though they can transmit it."

Minkie watched his grandmother talk to the doctor. Tall guy in jeans with shaggy hair and the biggest mustache he'd had ever seen, but his white coat said doctor. Minkie was unused to adults focusing on his welfare, and if he weren't so tired, he'd try and join in.

"I'm mostly worried about his overall health, Ruth. Did she leave any records with you?"

"Debbie? Oh, come on Tom, you know she's incapable of ... well, you remember Debbie."

"Yeah, I get it. How long do you think you'll get to keep him?"

"I'm staying," moaned Minkie, "and I'm gonna puke."

After Ruth tended to her grandson, Tom Magroot

continued his conversation. He wanted to get Minkie healthy before they vaccinated him for the obvious communicable diseases. The over-the-counter lice medication Ruth had bought at the pharmacy was fine, but she'd have to be meticulous with the laundry for some time. And there were two teeth that needed to be pulled.

"They must hurt like hell, don't they son?" asked the doctor, laying a cool, bony hand on Minkie's forehead. "We'll have to get him to Pinedale for the extraction. He'll need an oral surgeon, the rot's so deep. There's a new guy up there who I hear is real good. I'll set up the appointment for you but we've got to get rid of the Crypto first."

For now, Minkie would be prescribed an antiemetic and rehydration therapy. When test results came in verifying Crypto, there was an additional medication to be prescribed if he was still experiencing the same degree of diarrhea.

"Trucks still not working, Ruth?" asked Doctor Tom.

"No, two down, and Betty Ann's car needs a battery. Heidi brought us. She said to phone when we're done and Esau will collect us."

"Not necessary. One more patient and I'm done. I'll take you back and help you get Minkie settled and we can have some tea on that front porch of yours."

He pointed to a refrigerator in the corner. "Ginger Ale in there, give him small sips. Stay in here and I'll use the other exam room. Give me half an hour."

They restored Minkie to his grandmother's cool cotton sheets, and he silently vowed that if his mother ever returned for him, he'd run and hide and return when it was safe. He heard Doctor Tom and his grandmother talking about him in the kitchen. They laughed a few times—he could tell they were friends.

Outside his window, the gray cat sat by the screen, cleaning her face, licking her paw, over her ear, lick, over her other ear, lick, lick. She took care of herself, she was beautiful, and he loved her. The cat turned her head to look at him with large golden eyes, opened her mouth, and made a rough noise that sounded like *Mow yowp.*

He tried to say it back at her a couple of times and she rubbed her head against the screen before stretching out on the sill and going to sleep in a patch of sun. He'd never had a pet before.

Minkie rubbed his face on his pillow—*his* pillow, with a blue cotton pillowcase that smelled of nothing but clean.

"Grandma, I'm home now," he whispered before descending into a deep, dreamless sleep.

CHAPTER TWENTY-FIVE

UNDOCUMENTED

Raul put on his lawyer hat and Ruth put on her client hat. They greeted each other formally, and Ruth sat down in front of his desk, the Wind River Mountains out the window behind her.

"You're not sure of the state, the month, or day, but you're pretty sure he was born in 1985?" asked Raul, trying not to sound incredulous.

Ruth took a moment to respond, reviewing the math in her head. "Debbie said, well she goes by Ocean Rain now, she said he was two when she left him with me for several weeks in March of '87. He seemed about two at the time, hard to tell, but he talked a little, wasn't potty trained, but during his time with me, he got a good start. Might have been born sometime in the fall of 1984, I guess, but I'm more comfortable with 1985."

A solemn little boy, he'd been then, but they'd had fun. Big brown eyes, freckles, and curly hair. She'd cleaned him up, and after washing his hair, discovered that what she thought of as a dull brown had very attractive ginger tones. She bought him a little dump truck, she still had it. Debbie wouldn't let him take it when she returned for him—too much plastic, she said. Ruth remembered how he'd cried and clung to her. She managed to hold her tears until their car disappeared down the road.

He'd used that little truck to help her move dirt from one flowerbed to the other. His little dump truck and her shovel, they'd both been very proud of themselves. She taught him a song. What was it? *Clean Up, Clean Up, Everybody do your share?* That was it. He learned to sing it too.

"Ruth?" Ruth blinked and looked at Raul. "Did you say she goes by Ocean Rain now? That's her name? Ocean Rain—Rain is the last name?"

"No, I think it's all the first name. The last name might be Birdsong, or maybe that's just for Minkie. She threw Creeley out the window years ago. Minkie says he likes Birdsong and wants to keep it. He may have come up with that himself and she might have agreed to just let him have it."

"Was she still using Creeley when she dropped him off the first time?"

Ruth shrugged. "She called him 'Cricket' at the time and I assumed he was Cricket Creeley. I'll admit I liked the sound of that. Cricket Creeley, very alliterative. Now I'm not so sure what last name they were using then."

Raul tapped the eraser of his pencil on his legal pad. Thus far he had written very little. "Where he was born? Can we narrow down the states or was a hospital ever mentioned?"

Ruth shook her head. "I can't guarantee it's even a state, she spent time in Canada and Mexico, and I'd bet good money she didn't have a passport, so she snuck back and forth somehow. A hospital? Debbie? More like a cave or backroom somewhere."

This was going to be much more difficult than Ruth had described over the phone. For the first time, Raul truly came to realize that someone could exist in the United States and have absolutely no paper attesting to his or her existence. The battle for recognition would be no easy task.

He looked at Ruth's anxious brown eyes and the lines of

worry etched across her brow and asked, "How did he get into school?"

"Well Raul, I don't believe he has *ever* been to school," Ruth's voice was husky with frustration, "and he's twelve. He won't talk about it. Says he can't remember anything about life with his mother, although he's of normal intelligence, smart even, so he just doesn't want to." Ruth's eyes filled and Raul handed her one of the several boxes of tissue placed strategically around his office.

"If you had a daughter like my Debbie, you wouldn't judge me. And I'd ask that you not judge my grandson either." Ruth dabbed at her eyes. "People cry in here a lot?"

"When things are really tough they do. People usually come to me when they have problems, so crying's not uncommon."

"As you know, I'm not a wet rag kind of person, Raul, so you don't have to worry I'll dissolve here on the spot. It's just that I think this boy has been through so much, he's suffered, and I never managed to tame his mother."

Raul looked down at his legal pad. He had added *Mexico? Canada?* and doodled a passable little bird, beak open in song. That was about it.

"Ruth, I'll have to do some research on this. It's a new one for me so it'll take a little time. School may let him attend classes as we work on a birth certificate."

Ruth shook her head. "Minkie and I are waiting until next semester for school, summer's almost here. He says he won't go if he can't read, says they'll think he's a dummy. And he's right."

Ruth dabbed her eyes some more, blew her nose, and got up to throw the tissue away. Raul's Labrador, Amicus, raised his large, black head and huffed as she passed by.

"Hello, my sweet. Lovely boy, aren't you?" she said as she stopped to give him a pat. "That lip looks funny Raul, hanging down like that. Is that where he got bitten?"

"Yup. Up by the lake. A yelp, two little beads of blood, and then his whole face began to swell, got a swelling in his throat big as a grapefruit. We never heard a rattle. Booker McNabb was riding his horse and stopped and helped me carry Amicus down the path to my truck. Think Booker will ever go back to Pennsylvania?"

"He's a Comfrey McNabb now, I can't see him leaving us, business is good for him out here, he belongs," said Ruth firmly. She looked down at Amicus again. "Well now, the lip doesn't take away from his handsome looks, does it?"

Once she had resumed her seat, she said, "I hope we're not breaking the law, keeping a twelve-year-old out of school for now, but I understand my grandson's point. Once you're labeled a dummy, it'll follow you. I'll get the boy reading in the next few months. Heidi gave us some of the twins' old books. They're little kid books but Minkie's enjoying the stories and he's anxious to learn. I understand he will need to go to school when we work all this out."

"Didn't Debbie say she was just leaving him for a few weeks?"

Ruth looked at Raul, stunned. Obviously Minkie couldn't return to the life that was. She hadn't considered that her daughter would actually come back and try to take Minkie. But who could predict what Debbie would do?

"He asks me almost every day if he can stay at home. After only three weeks, that's what he calls it, home. He says he'll run away if he sees her coming."

"But the first time she left him, when he was two or three, you said she was back in, what, a couple of weeks? Why do you think this stint away will be longer, or permanent?"

Why had it seemed a *last* goodbye? Her bright, beautiful girl was being consumed by hunger, there was so little of her left now. Minkie might be the best part of her. Don't let the tears start again, woman, Ruth said to herself sternly.

Raul watched Ruth's struggle; he was so uncomfortable

when a woman of his own age cried. It reminded him of his ex-wife.

He waited while Ruth regained her composure before he said, "She's still his mother, Ruth, documented or undocumented."

"Yes, she is. But my Debbie, Miss Ocean Rain Whatever, was different this time, wilder, eyes darting all over, anxious to get away, picking at this and that. And Minkie's not a baby, he's more work now. He says, 'No' plenty, believe me, he knows his own mind. Maybe she loves him enough to leave him with me now." Ruth locked eyes with Raul. "Anyway, I'm keepin' him."

"Are you saying you want to sue for custody?"

Ruth gave a snort of laugher. "I can't sue my own daughter, Raul. For heaven's sakes, I can't imagine suing Debbie. And she'd never stand still long enough to sign a paper, or meet with an authority figure, anyway."

"Forget I used the term 'sue,' but we may want to have a plan if she does return. I'd like to talk to Minkie, with you there of course. His words will carry weight."

Ruth considered. "Yes, alright, but I can't guarantee he'll have much to say. He's scared but he's a nice young man."

"And you said Tom Magroot saw him? Can you authorize him to send those medical records over?"

Ruth nodded. Oh, the gifts and destruction her daughter left in her wake.

Raul went downstairs to The Crow's Nest for a late lunch. As he'd hoped, the usual crowd had thinned and Heidi joined him in a booth by the window with a cup of coffee, as she occasionally did.

Raul asked how the kids were doing in school, that kind of thing. Heidi inquired after Amicus's health. Had he recovered fully from his rattlesnake bite? He had, except the droop to his lip made drinking a messier business. Heidi got up to refill their coffee cups and sat back down.

"So, Raul, you have a question for me. I can see that." Heidi smiled and tilted her head to the side in the way that charmed her customers.

"I want to ask you a question, as they say, 'off the record.' For Ruth Creeley."

"Okay. I deny we ever speak about this." Heidi drew her thumb and forefinger across her lips to seal them shut.

Raul grinned and nodded. "Thank you. You know she has her grandson staying with her?"

Heidi nodded. "Minkie, yes."

"As it so happens, he's completely undocumented, no birth certificate, no nothing. Her daughter's disappeared, neglected the boy, Ruth said. Ruth doesn't want authorities involved, she doesn't want them trying to track down her daughter, none of that, but she needs a birth certificate to enroll Minkie in school. We're just Comfrey, whatever we give the school secretary or whomever will be good enough, for the time being at least, so I'm wondering how you got Marcela's new birth certificate."

"I didn't tell you I did this," protested Heidi, her eyes wide with alarm.

"You didn't, the twins did. You left them with me when both you and Esau had to deal with the power failure at Hebeka, remember? I told the kids not to spread it around about the birth certificate and they looked scared that I'd heard anything. It's not like they told me outright, they were whispering real loud while they were working on that jigsaw you gave them, at the desk in the corner. And you know, Heidi, this was when I had the yen for you, anytime I heard something with your name in it, I paid attention."

Heidi closed her eyes and let out a deep breath. "*Mein Gott.* It is so hard to be the parent."

"They understood, Heidi. I don't even want to know if what you did was illegal, or if they misunderstood what you were doing, but they know how to keep their mouths shut."

"So young they know to keep secrets, and this is what I have taught them," said Heidi bitterly.

"It was *me*, Heidi, and this a while back. They were excited about going to school together. I just heard them talk about a guy in a library in Cheyenne and how they were pretending they didn't know you, sitting at a different table, and something about Marcela's birth certificate. I don't think they really knew what was going on, I mean what kid knows anything about a birth certificate? They were giggling that you were like a spy, and that you looked cool with an upside-down magazine, or something like that. So, I paid attention, filed it away in my Heidi file."

He read the unease on her face and hastened to say, "Not a real file Heidi, just in my brain, in the old days. I'm over you now." He gave her a smile and was relieved to receive a small smile in return. But there was a hint of sadness there. Christ, he hoped she wasn't feeling *pity* for him.

Heidi stared out the window at the Wind River Range, dwarfing them all and their secrets and their struggles. The problems humans make for others. Marcela should have just been allowed to be who she was. How would her enrollment in school as a girl, despite what her birth certificate had said, have *possibly* harmed anyone? Survival for a human was so much more than food, shelter, and a nesting place. Survival for her family relied on subterfuge.

Raul traced the rim of his coffee cup with his finger and wondered for the umpteenth time why Heidi wasn't interested in him. He was a lawyer. By Comfrey standard, he was rich. He rode a motorcycle to work, for God's sake. She had turned him down nicely, but it had been a disappointment. What did Booker McNabb have that he didn't? At least they were past the awkward stage now. And what was she thinking about, biting her lip with her even white teeth and frowning?

He reminded her gently again, Ruth would not be able to

afford a prolonged exchange with the state of Wyoming, and Minkie needed to partake in the normal, functional life that his grandmother was determined to provide. If Heidi truly had managed to skirt bureaucracy with this birth certificate thing, she might consider helping Ruth.

He added carefully, "Legally I can't know the particulars, but do you have a contact who can come up with a birth certificate in a situation where there are no records of any kind?"

"Our case was different, we had the records but they needed a little change that the state would not make. I cannot give you details."

"Okay, I respect that. But the person that did this for you, can you see if it's possible to get a birth certificate when we don't have a *single* record?"

Heidi considered. "This may be easier than trying to alter a few letters on a document that already exists. A completely new birth certificate. Would Minkie need a new name? Something more formal like, perhaps, Michael Creeley?"

Minkie had been adamant about this and Raul shook his head. "He made up his own name, Minkie Birdsong. He'd like to keep it."

"Then I will try to contact this man who helped me, I will see if he will do this and if yes, I will drive to Cheyenne for Ruth." She reached across the table and took Raul's hand. "This I do because she is *eine sehr geschätzte Freundin*, our treasured friend."

Raul squeezed her hand back. 'A treasured friend.' Man oh man, what he wouldn't give.

CHAPTER TWENTY-SIX

WEST POINT GRADUATION

As Heidi and Esau were making the week's pie dough and puff pastry, they dissected Booker's most recent Sunday visit. As usual, after lunch, they had walked to the schoolyard to play basketball, pulling Gering in his wagon. As usual, before Booker roared off on his motorcycle, Heidi sent the children upstairs so she and Booker could say goodbye properly.

"Properly means agony for Booker too, I think," said Heidi.

"Of course for Booker too," said Esau, exasperated. "You're both adults, figure this out. All this sexual tension is not good for either of you."

"And you are now the counselor for couples?"

"No, I'm a man who lives with sexual hunger not being satisfied until Luisa comes back. You guys are making barriers that don't need to be there."

"You have no word from Luisa?"

"She checked in with my uncle a while back." Esau rolled out the puff pastry with more force than perhaps necessary. "I should say she checked on *me* with my uncle a while back."

A delivery truck arrived at the backdoor and Esau went to greet it. Heidi stacked the piecrusts in the freezer.

"Booker lets something slip about his past yesterday," Heidi said when Esau returned.

"Do tell," said Esau shortly. A mention of Luisa always had its effect.

"He says he has a nephew named Philip, who is graduating from West Point Military Academy next week. He is going to go to the ceremony. He says he went to West Point also and because of this, Philip went there too."

"Booker went to West Point?" Esau whistled. He'd known Booker was an Army Ranger, but not that he'd gone to West Point. That meant stellar grades in high school, AP classes, the lot. It also meant marching in lockstep, taking orders—not the Booker McNabb he thought he'd come to know.

"I tell Booker how nice it will be for him to see his family, and he gives a big shrug and says his sister-in-law is sick. Her breast cancer has come back and she probably will not be there at the graduation and maybe not his brother either."

"She must be pretty sick to miss her son's graduation," said Esau.

"I say this too. Booker says he does not know how sick she is, but she beat the cancer once, so she can do it again. I ask if there are family members who can tell him how sick she is and he says his knowing won't change her odds. Then he shuts down all the way so I can ask no more questions."

* * * * * *

When Booker told Amadeus there wouldn't be any riding for a bit because he was flying back east for his nephew's graduation, Amadeus didn't ask how long a bit was. As soon as Booker said there were three other kids in that family, he knew a bit could be a very long time. Booker was going be with his real family and they wouldn't want him to leave.

Amadeus refused to go to Rock Springs to get more of the underwear that stopped Marcela's penis from showing. He was tired of worrying about people finding out about Marcela, he was tired of the restaurant, he was tired about how many times Esau and Aunt Heidi stopped talking when he came into the room. He was tired of not living his own life—but he had a

COMFREY, WYOMING: MARCELA'S ARMY

plan.

He told Esau he was going to shoot hoops in the lot and Esau said okay, but to leave the back door open. Esau said he'd come out and shoot a few hoops too after he'd talked to Uncle Karl, who was supposed to be phoning from Germany any minute.

When the phone rang and he heard Esau say, "Hey Karl," Amadeus put the basketball down and quietly walked off the lot. He ran down to Main Street, waited for a car to pass, and crossed the road to the field. He looked back at The Crow's Nest. No one was coming.

He didn't walk on the path, but through the high grasses so he would be harder to see if someone—if *Esau*—came after him. He planned to cross the wooden bridge, climb the trail to Booker's, get Cochise, and ride up to the lake. Then they would keep going. Booker said there were trails through the mountains that led to the Reservation. Amadeus knew if he just kept on riding, he'd find the blue house by the river. The house would be empty because Grandpa was gone. He and Cochise could stay there and fish in the river and eat apples from the tree.

But before he got even halfway across the field, Mama came. She whirled and she whirled and whipped at his hair. She picked up dirt and leaves and threw them at him. She pushed him back and made so much dust, he bent over coughing until he gave up and simply fell to the ground.

Esau hung up the phone and looked out the back door. He swore to see the lot empty and the basketball placed so carefully under the basket. How long had he talked to Karl— ten minutes? He ran through the restaurant, unlocked the front door, and stood on the sidewalk facing the field. He could just make out the head of a small figure pushing through the grasses, long black hair whipping in the wind. A dust devil had kicked up, not along the path where the loose dirt lay, but in front of the boy.

Esau ran at a low crouch—if Amadeus saw him and took off, he wouldn't be able to catch the kid before he hid somewhere. He heard the boy yelling in Arapaho, "Stop, leave me alone." Then the boy's head sank from sight.

The devil died as he approached the spot where he had seen Amadeus disappear. He found the boy lying on his back, eyes closed, face filthy, snot running from his nose. Quietly Esau lay down, closed his eyes, and turned his face to the sun. Had he left the door to the restaurant wide open? Armand was due in at ten—Tyree and Elizabeth an hour later. He didn't know how long this was going to take, so he'd just have to hope Armand would take the roast beef out of the oven while it still had some pink in the middle.

But it didn't take long. He rolled his head to the side when he felt Amadeus watching him.

"Me and Cochise want to find Grandpa's house but Mama won't let us," said Amadeus, his voice flattened with resignation.

After a moment, Esau said, "Your mom probably thinks your basketball team will fall apart if you're not there. Booker will be home tomorrow, by the way."

"Mama threw so much stuff," Amadeus said, sitting up in indignation. "I yelled at her to stop and she didn't."

"Are you saying you're so hurt I'm going to have to carry you?" asked Esau. "Because if I have to carry you, I might not have enough energy left to make you a roast beef sandwich, mayo, steak sauce, no mustard."

"And no lettuce," said Amadeus, his mouth twisting into a half-smile.

"No rabbit food? Not one piece?"

Amadeus shook his head vigorously. Esau pushed himself to his feet and reached down for the boy. To his surprise, Amadeus held onto his hand until they reached the road.

* * * * * *

Booker flew into La Guardia Airport, picked up a rental car, and made it to West Point with half an hour to spare. His nephew had told him where to sit, and he found the row. The seat on the aisle must be his. Sitting next to it, he recognized the smooth blond hair of his niece, Samantha, a little darker than when she was a child. Next, Martin, dark wavy hair like his mother's, and next to Martin sat the youngest McNabb— Melissa, the child he had never met. Beyond her were two empty seats. So Rose must be very ill.

He put his hand on Samantha's shoulder and she looked up and smiled. He sat down and Martin leaned over, grinning, and shook his hand. Melissa peered around her brother with curious, intelligent eyes. She gave him a nod, which he returned. Booker knew she was twelve but thought she looked younger.

"Your mom?" he whispered to Samantha.

"A new chemo, so you know ... Dad's at home with a damp cloth and a bucket. She said to thank you for coming."

"I've got to fly out right after I congratulate Philip."

Samantha nodded. "No one expected you'd come back to the house."

As they had waited for the band to start, he asked Samantha about Rose's treatment. His niece was careful in her response—the new chemo protocol was promising, but the side effects were the most brutal yet. He asked about college and she said was majoring in herpetology. Her professor had written a paper on the Midget Faded Rattler. She asked if he was aware of the snake and he nodded.

"Most are found further south than Comfrey," he said, "but there is a colony by the lake a few miles up the road from my cabin."

Her eyes lit up. "They're pretty rare. Have you actually seen one?" she asked.

"Several—on the trails, basking in the sun."

At her grin of delight, he could tell he'd scored points. Martin leaned over to mention a car he and a buddy were working on. Melissa leaned over too, fixing her eyes on him. Booker smiled at her and again she nodded. Then the West Point Band began to play and almost a thousand grey-clad cadets marched onto the Plain from opposite sides, the sun glinting off their brass buttons. It seemed a lifetime ago, but it had only been sixteen years since he had been one of them.

After the hat toss, Booker managed to fight his way through the crowd to congratulate Philip, then jogged to his car, hoping to avoid the gridlock in the parking lot. He needn't have worried. Families were taking pictures amidst the sounds of laugher, shouts, and the occasional air horn. Many parents had no doubt bonded during family days and banquets, sharing their pride in their child, their fears of unrest in foreign lands. Rose had been sick most of those four years—he doubted she and Simon had joined in.

On the airplane, he had a row to himself. The peanuts were complementary, the whiskey was not. He smiled at the steward and waved off a second whiskey. Above the clouds he watched as the plane chased the sun, then closed his eyes and thought about his brother's family.

At last he'd met Rose's youngest child. They had stood when the hats were tossed, Martin behind Melissa with his hands on her shoulders. Rose had said, in her once-yearly communication, a letter tucked inside a Christmas card, they were all protective of Melissa.

"She struggles with speech," Rose wrote when Melissa was four. "Samantha adores her and insists they share a room. I hear them practicing words and phrases at night, giggling most of the time. Simon takes her everywhere—I really think she has become his favorite child."

Three years later, Rose had written, "Melissa is brilliant. She is artistic like you, and a dancer. But she refuses to participate in ballet recitals. With therapy and Samantha's ministrations, she is improving." There had been no clarification if 'improving' referred just to speech or other challenges too.

The following year, there had been little about Melissa. Philip was considering West Point. Rose said she knew he and Booker had remained in contact. Would he please try to talk Philip out of a military career?

For Rose he had tried, but obviously not hard enough.

Seeing Samantha and Martin again had been surprisingly easy. Not seeing Rose had been a relief, but oh so very hard. After the surgeries, the radiation, and chemical assaults she might not be able to beat back her cancer this time.

He had accepted an honorable discharge after injuries had almost taken his life. His release from Walter Reed had coincided with Simon entering yet another alcohol treatment program after almost losing his nursery business. Booker had stayed with Rose and the children to help keep the nursery going and for a while, they had become his family.

His flight arrived in Denver early and Booker got home before midnight. Ruth had fed the horses and left a plate of pork chops, corn, and mashed potatoes in his fridge. Why the meal almost brought him to tears, he couldn't fathom.

"Get a grip, you pathetic piece of crap," he muttered, sitting down with the meal, not bothering to heat it up.

After he ate, he checked his phone messages. His agent wanted him to consider a show in Salt Lake City. Tyree had picked up the supplies Booker had ordered from Lander and stored them in the workshop.

No message from Heidi. Good. He was too raw right now.

He phoned The Crow's Nest the next morning, and as he had hoped, Heidi had gone to Hebeka to check on the shortbread orders. He told Esau a big show had come up in

Utah and for a while he'd be too busy to drop by the restaurant. Maybe let Heidi know he'd have to cancel Sunday lunch and tell Amadeus there'd be no riding this week, but he'd make it up to him.

At Esau's lack of response, Booker said, "So, we good?"

"Sure," said Esau abruptly. "We're not going anywhere, so whenever you're ready."

Esau hung up before Booker could say, "Ready for what?" As if Esau would know. As if a Shoshone *chef*—Heidi had said don't call Esau a cook—would know. We're not going anywhere—Booker stared out the window. He was suffocating.

He had phoned his agent first thing in the morning and left a message saying no to the show in Salt Lake City, but it could be an excuse for a while. He saddled Rosie for a day's ride. Cochise's plaintive whickering from the paddock followed as he rode off the property.

The wind blew sporadically, the air scented with pine; he could smell Rosie's sweat as they climbed. Her feet sounded hollow as they crossed Lake Cheynook's asphalt parking lot, not a single vehicle in the sight. Light flickered off the ripples on the lake's surface, and he could make out dragonflies hovering along the shore of the marshy area to the left. The granite cliffs across the lake loomed large.

Not long after he had taken possession of his property, a teenage girl had died jumping off those cliffs into the water with her friends. Ruth, still almost a stranger, had come up to tell him. They'd sat on his porch, drinking coffee, Ruth filling him in about the girl, her family, and friends. He hadn't really minded Ruth trying to include him from the get-go in the lives of Comfrey's denizens; he'd recognized that trait in her the first time they'd met. For the most part, she hadn't succeeded.

Before he turned onto the trail to Toot's Peak, he paused by the immense slab of granite that extended into the water from the shore. This was where he'd first laid eyes on Heidi.

He and Rosie had watched her from the shadows until Rosie's snort had alerted the little dog. He remembered the dachshund growling, and Heidi's scowl as she had clutched the flannel shirt she'd picked up to hide the fact she'd been swimming in her underwear.

He rode the trail further than he ever had before, wiping his mind of Rose, her children, Heidi, and her children. He concentrated on the heat radiating off the rocks, the sudden burst of wind that lifted his hat, the salty scent of the horse, the creak of his saddle. He stopped at a vantage point and gazed over a vast expanse of few people and the Green River Basin, Sweetwater County, and Colorado beyond.

Three days later, Esau saw Booker's truck pull up in front of the restaurant. He continued to wipe the counter and waited a good five minutes before Booker emerged.

"Boyfriend's back," Esau said, pushing through the swinging doors into the kitchen. "Get out there, I'll finish your basting." The relief Esau saw on Heidi's face hit him deep. If Booker was backing off, Heidi and Amadeus were in for a whole lot of hurt.

Heidi surprised Booker by sitting next to him, not opposite. She had brought coffee, rhubarb pie—two slices on separate plates.

"Where'd you get the rhubarb?" he asked, smiling at her.

"The man across the street from Ruth has too much."

"Good thing," he said.

"The very good thing."

She congratulated him on his big show in Utah. He shrugged and said he'd decided against it. When she gave him an assessing look, he wasn't sure the fact he'd come for pie would be enough. They finished their pie in silence. She asked no questions about the graduation, shared nothing of Amadeus or Marcela, no mention of anything she'd done the last few days.

She stood up the moment they were done and said she had to get back to the kitchen. When she reached to take his plate, he grabbed her wrist and looked up at her.

"Amadeus..." she began.

"Yeah, about Amadeus," Booker said. "If he can miss basketball practice, maybe I can come get him and bring him up the hill for bit. I have a frozen pizza, I can return him by eight-thirty."

He hadn't known how much he needed that smile and couldn't restrain a chuckle when she said, "A frozen pizza? This is a very great treat indeed."

CHAPTER TWENTY-SEVEN

ESAU KNOWS

Sunday lunches continued, Booker stopped by the restaurant two or three days a week for coffee or a meal, gratis in exchange for Amadeus's riding lessons. Comfrey's citizens continued their pressure on Heidi to open for breakfast, and after consultation with Esau, she decided she would.

"So we hire a couple more people for the kitchen and two more for out front?" asked Esau.

Heidi nodded. "I think that will be enough."

"Enough if we stop accepting weekly orders from Saint Gemma's for five dozen frozen pie crusts."

Heidi shook her head. "I will not tell them no, this will not interfere with our routine. Tomorrow I come in at super duper early, Massimo will pick them up in the late afternoon."

"What's super duper early?"

"I think four will be early enough." She gave him a small smile.

After a long moment, Esau said, "How about you be the super and I be the duper and we both come in at five? You make the dough and I roll it out."

"Okay and someday I do you the very big favor also," she said without missing a beat.

"Yeah, the list of favors you owe me is getting pretty damn long." The grin she flashed him made the thought of getting up at four-fifteen almost worth it.

Esau returned home after his ride up to the lake in the dark—there would be no time for a ride in the morning. He lifted weights, had his tea, and put the snake back in her cage before going to take his shower. He stripped down and examined himself in the mirror. He was in the best shape of his life, his muscles defined and hard. He rode his bike up Wild Horse Valley Road to the lake every single day. No exceptions. Where would he be if Ruth Creeley hadn't enticed him to this nowhere town with its alpine lake? he thought as he stepped into the shower. Where would he be if he hadn't been hired by this talented German woman? This German woman—something traced through his brain. He tried to snag it, but couldn't.

After lathering and rinsing, he switched the water from hot to freezing for a full sixty seconds—he counted each one. It was all about control. His sponsor, Leif, a huge red-haired, part-Norwegian-part-Navajo, had recommended the hot-cold technique. Ideally it'd be a steaming sauna then a plunge into the snow, but this was small-town Wyoming.

"The shock to your body before bed will remind you who you are," Leif had said. "It will numb the desire to drink and help you get through the dark hours until morning."

This time, however, the ice-cold didn't numb him. Instead, it caused a dam to break and memories flooded through. Despite the hour, he phoned Leif—sponsors were used to late night calls.

"You said during blackouts short-term memories aren't laid down," Esau said. "You said they were irretrievable."

"So you're an exception to the rule. You're an unusual guy, Esau, what can I say? Obviously this particular memory was laid somewhere." Leif yawned. "This German woman you say you now remember meeting a couple of years ago, she and her kids mean something to you now. What wasn't worth retrieving before has managed to dredge itself up. Are these bad memories? Can you handle them?"

"Not bad memories, but disturbing. Big. I'm not sure what to do with them."

"Let them lie? You've buried them for a few years, so I'm thinking ..." Leif went on with encouraging words. They both knew any change in the underpinnings of a carefully reconstructed life could bring it down.

"Since you haven't shared the details, Esau, I'm not sure what to say here," Leif said. "You Shoshone have good instincts. If they're telling you to let her know you've remembered this thing about her family ... well, I'm just saying respect this relationship you have going. Respect her grace to let you into her life."

"Hah, respect, grace, spoken like a true Navajo."

Leif chuckled and after a pause added words of caution, "If you do decide to tell her, even with all the grace, respect, and instinct talk, this may go south. Are you prepared for a change in your relationship with this family?"

"Honestly? I don't know."

"Phone me, come see me, check in with me tomorrow," said Leif. "Don't let this be the straw."

After they hung up, Esau paced. He'd heard the worry in Leif's voice. He had a lot to lose if Heidi retreated. At last he understood her extreme vigilance around the children. He'd thought it was about the death of her baby, but that hadn't explained the way she and Amadeus guarded Marcela. Would Heidi trust him or would she fear him? Maybe he'd hide what he knew, tamp it down and it'd go away. What business was it of his anyway? But she was an astute woman, she would feel it lying there between them. He wouldn't be able to hide it deeply enough. Small things would change. Their ease with each other would be tempered.

He decided he would get to work and see what happened. It'd be so early, Heidi would be focused on getting those damn pie shells ready before dashing upstairs and getting the twins out the door to school. There was never enough time in the mornings. Maybe nothing would happen, maybe she wouldn't feel something was different about him. Then he'd bury it, just carry on as usual. Just carry on ....

Heidi set two alarm clocks and put one by each twin's bed. They were to get up, get dressed, eat the cereal she had put out and she would come upstairs at 7:30 to take them to school.

She got into the kitchen at 4:30 and made the pie dough five at a time in the big Hobart mixer, then wrapped them in plastic for Esau to roll out.

Esau arrived twenty minutes later and Heidi unlocked the backdoor to his knock. She stepped back as he rolled in his bike, and felt it immediately—something was different with Esau. Her hello stuck in her throat. Esau gave her an expressionless look, no hint of a greeting.

"What?" she whispered.

"Give me a minute," he said, going in the storeroom to park his bike, pull his hair back into a ponytail, and get an apron.

"What?" Heidi said when Esau came out of the storeroom and stood before her with a rolling pin, gently tapping it on his palm. The action might have seemed menacing if she didn't know him. She turned her back to counter and folded her arms. "Esau, you tell me what."

He reached behind her, grabbed a pie dough, unwrapped it, and stared at it on the counter. He stood motionless until she repeated, "Esau, you tell me what."

"Last night ..." He paused as the refrigerator's motor started and the overhead lights flickered, as they always did in their first response to sharing their electricity. "Last night," he began again, "I remembered everything, Heidi. Every detail of our conversation at Saint Gemma's—women poets, Emma Lazarus, the *Rouladen* you carried to my table."

"And the Statue of Liberty poem you dropped off the next day," said Heidi softly, dreading what was to come.

"That, and I remember you saying Nara's name and how you said it, Nara De'Nae Crow. I remember you asking if I knew of her on the Reservation. Nara and her identical twin boys."

Heidi forced herself to meet his eyes.

"*Boys*," he repeated.

Heidi felt a grip of almost paralyzing fear. Someone had breached the walls of the fortress she and the twins had constructed. She was unable to voice any kind of denial—unable to protest she had not used the word *identical*, that she had just said twins. Her friend now looked a stranger. Numbly, she went out to unlock the front door and start the coffee.

They spoke very little after that, focusing on their tasks. In the afternoon she went to pick up the twins from school and stopped by the high school to pick up the girl who stayed with the children upstairs, so Heidi could work the dinner crowd.

"Can you stay an extra hour tonight?" she asked as the girl got in the car. "Esau and I have business to discuss."

At the end of the evening, when everyone had gone and the night blanketed the Wind River Range and the entrance to Wild Horse Valley, they sat at the booth in the corner, lights out except behind the counter. In the shadows, Esau's dark, scarred face looked like a *Wiedergänger*, a zombie or ghost who prowled the night. He had released his hair from the ponytail he wore in the kitchen and it flowed over his shoulders, a black fall of terrible beauty. After a moment, he reached out his hand and she took it. Her eyes filled with tears as she felt his warmth, his strength, his comfort.

He sat quietly as she told him all of it—her relationship with Nara, the birth of the twins, Nara's death, Marcela claiming she was a girl and Amadeus claiming it too. When she was done, he sat back, brought his narrow dark eyes to hers, his face still. But he was not a *Wiedergänger* at all—he was Esau.

"Do you think I should tell Marcela that now you know?" she asked.

He leaned back, folded his arms and shook his head. "No. I think Marcela should tell me if and when she wants me to know. Otherwise, what's the point? You're asking her to trust me with something huge, and my sense is, she's not there yet. All that crap in Riverton must have scared her to death. To doubt your worth when you're five years old? And what's with this *goddamn* bathroom obsession these schools have? Who's she gonna hurt? Makes me want to ..." He shook his head in disgust when he could think of nothing even remotely polite.

She walked back into the kitchen with him so he could get his bike and she could lock up after him. As he wheeled his bike into the lot, she reminded him she would bring him the articles she had mentioned tomorrow.

"I'll read whatever information you've got," he said, swinging onto his bike. "Knowledge is power, and you know me, I'm all about power, white lady."

* * * * * *

When Esau got home the following evening, he took Bill out of her cage, placed her on her branch, and stretched out on the sofa, taking a few minutes before he looked at the articles Heidi had put in his backpack. He was tired from a day on his feet and his bicycle ride down from the lake in the dark. His headlight had reflected off eyes, some low to the ground, some higher. It had been stupid to ride in the dark, but he'd needed it. The sound of native drums and flutes from a tape he'd bought at a powwow in Fort Washakie surrounded him. Next year, he'd take Amadeus, and Marcela if she'd come.

The first article was about puberty blockers, substances

that delayed puberty in order to buy time before parents started on a path that would allow no retreat. Three articles advocated for their use. Certain changes, like the enlargement of the voice box and deepening of the voice in adolescent males, couldn't be fully reversed. Two articles cautioned against use of the drugs, arguing that interfering with the hormones of a healthy child might have a number of unforeseen consequences down the line. The experts couldn't agree. Great. Esau swore under his breath.

According to the articles, for some children the window into puberty opened before they were ten. If Heidi chose to expose Marcela to puberty blockers, it looked like the girl would have to start some initial assessments pretty soon. And if Heidi did choose to delay Marcela's puberty, the next steps would be to supplement the girl with estrogen and progesterone and remove her testes.

Castration. "*Holy Fucking Mother of God,*" muttered Esau, getting up and stretching. He dropped to the floor for a couple dozen rapid pushups before going into the kitchen to make tea.

As he waited for the water to boil, he thought of Amadeus, maturing like every other boy. He thought of the twins diverging. How the hell was a boy that young able to keep his sister's secret? Luisa would have said, for that kind of loyalty, they must have connected in the spirit world. Who knows? His wife had been right about many things.

Esau returned to the sofa with his cup and scanned a couple of articles detailing the surgery that would be required to transition Marcela's genitalia to female, if that's what she wanted to do at age eighteen. At least some decisions could wait until the girl was at an age where she could sign the consent forms herself. Now the consent had to be given by Heidi, and he could see that was a terrifying responsibility.

Whenever they were alone in the kitchen the next day,

227

Heidi and Esau talked about the research papers. She knew them by heart; he had absorbed what he could in a single evening.

"I have no doubt she is a girl. Do you?" she asked as she cut up a ham hock for the split pea soup.

"Nope, not a doubt in the world," said Esau, throwing the garlic he'd minced into a pan of olive oil. "How much does she know, about the whole process, I mean?"

"She has made me read all the papers to her, again and again. She has learned some big new words. She knows what she wants—to have a girl body to go with who she is. I am not sure she truly understands it all. I have been in contact with a clinic in San Francisco that works with transgender children. If they accept us, one of the things they do is explain again to the child the whole process. She will meet other children like herself. Marcela wants to go there now, but they tell us to wait until she is nine. The clinic wants to see Amadeus too. It is extremely unusual for identical twins to be so different in this way."

"I'll bet that's a massive understatement," said Esau. "You said Ruth doesn't know. Does Booker?"

"No, I don't know how to ..."

Esau interrupted. "If you don't tell him, the deeper you get into this, the further you'll be from him."

"He has his secret past." Heidi stirred the peas—they smelled dreary, depressing, their color drab and unappealing.

"I'm thinking Booker's refusal to open up about his past is so different from what you've got going here with Marcela, I'm not sure why you're even bringing it up," said Esau. "I don't know what happened that made him high-tail it from Pennsylvania, but if his not sharing that with you is your reason for not including him in this, I'd say that's bullshit. He has a relationship with you and the kids. We're talking about the here and now." Esau looked around. "Did we get that order of celery and carrots?"

"By the backdoor," said Heidi.

Esau came back with the box and emptied the vegetables into the sink for a thorough washing.

"I know Booker has become a good friend to Amadeus," Heidi said to Esau's back. "He comes for our Sunday lunches, he stops for coffee as he passes through town. He watches me with that look that makes my heart..." She stopped and Esau turned around and gave a grin. She flushed and continued, "He listens, he talks about what he is making in his shop, he talks about Amadeus's hijinks." She frowned. "Hijinks, this is an expression?"

"Sure it is, and Amadeus has 'em in spades," said Esau.

"In spades?"

"He's a mischievous kid."

Heidi nodded. "The point I am telling you is that with Booker, he does not share his heart and I do not share mine. Our talk is about impersonal things. When he leaves, I cannot remember what we talk about except that it is easy. You hear us laugh. But I need more time before I trust him with Marcela."

"Fair enough, but if you go to San Francisco and you haven't told him the real reason you're going, he'll know you're lying. And what do you expect Amadeus to do? You want him to lie to Booker too, tell him that you're just going on vacation? Booker's not much of a talker, but if you're in San Francisco and he doesn't know the real reason why, he'll keep showing up here, asking questions, and I'll have to deal with him."

Heidi stirred the soup, ballooned her cheeks, and let out a long sigh. If Booker couldn't accept Marcela, she would have to excise him from their lives. What would that do to Amadeus? What would that do to her?

"Give Booker a chance to get behind this, Heidi," Esau said. "And now I'll shut up about it." He peered into the soup pot. "What's wrong with the peas? We need to put in a whole lot more carrots to give it some color."

"We have a new supplier, if the carrots do not help, we make the soup compost."

Elizabeth Darcy pushed her way through the kitchen doors and said, "It's really slow out front and Tyree says he's fine by himself. I have to pick up Lucas from Aunt Ruth's and get back to Toots. There's a group of Canadians checking in this evening. Do you mind if I go?"

Heidi smiled at the young woman and told her to go. Elizabeth had part of her wavy, blond hair pulled back with a velvet ribbon and the rest fell in contrived ringlets to her shoulders. So very Jane Austen.

"How is little Lucas?" Heidi asked Esau after Elizabeth had left. "Does he still pine after Marcela?"

"And then some. He draws pictures of her all the time. He says he knows he has to wait, but some day she will love him."

"Love him?"

"He says he's going to marry her. He's a very determined kid, but let's figure this Booker thing out before we talk about the remarkable little Mr. Darcy."

Heidi looked at Esau in surprise. "You say you shut up now about this Booker thing."

"I just want to know what hoops Booker has to jump through before you tell him aboutn Marcela. He's pretty much a friend of mine by now."

Heidi sighed and said, "You are the badgering badger."

"Okay, I'll take that. Now if you'd said wolverine, I'd be insulted. Wolverine has a lot of negative energy to the Shoshone. Badger is cautious, hardworking, some say, a good parent." Esau dumped another bowl of chopped carrots in the soup and Heidi put on the lid and turned down the heat.

Heidi said wearily, "I do not know of Booker's hoops, but *my* hoop will be for Marcela to give me her permission before I tell him her story. She does not even know that you know."

"And we're keeping it that way for now. I don't want her

treating me any differently."

Heidi gave him such a tender smile, he would have blushed if his face had the capability.

"If Booker does not fall in love with my family, and if you find Luisa and you are no longer in love with each other, will you marry me?" she asked.

"What, and spoil a perfect friendship?" Esau didn't let his thoughts stray to setting up a life with Heidi. The heat when she and Booker were in the same room was palpable and, luckily, Luisa still had his heart.

"If I tell him, Esau, how do you think he is going to react?" Heidi asked, already feeling dread.

"React to what?" Tyree Dubois came into the kitchen, his large, pink innocent face breaking into a smile. He thought Heidi was just about the prettiest lady he'd ever seen, and when she laughed, he could hardly stand it. "You're talking about Booker, right? What's he gotta react to?"

"React to..." Heidi stopped. Tyree was so gullible he'd believe almost anything, but she was unable to finish her sentence.

"React to us putting way too many carrots in the pea soup," supplied Esau.

"He'll be okay with it," said Tyree, who liked carrots.

"Did you need something, Tyree?" Heidi asked.

"Oh, yeah, I just wanted to tell you Armand broke it off with the...ah, person, in Pinedale. The...ah, person..."

"Just say *guy*, Tyree, or asshole or doofus...whatever," said Esau. Tyree's attempt to keep his brother's sexual orientation under wraps was painful.

At Tyree's look of discomfiture, Heidi took pity. "Does this mean Armand can help us more in the kitchen, Tyree? Because this would be very good news."

At the young man's nod, Heidi gave a sigh of relief. Armand had a natural talent with food, and Esau would need help when she and the twins went to San Francisco. Unlike his brother, Armand worked quickly, efficiently, and quietly. Tyree, however, was a hit working the front. He was as friendly as a puppy and genuinely interested in what patrons had to say. He had managed to memorize the dietary restrictions of many of the locals. He wasn't hesitant at steering someone prone to heartburn away from a particular dish. "Try the stew instead of the chili." High cholesterol? "Let's have turkey bacon in your BLT."

When Heidi had remarked to Ruth how different the two young men were, Ruth had said enigmatically, "Different fathers. We've all made our peace with that now."

CHAPTER TWENTY-EIGHT

EVERYBODY GOT THEIR PART TO PLAY

The day warmed. The sky faded to white where it met the horizon. Shadows momentarily darkened the Reservation hills as a flock of puffy windblown clouds blocked the sun. Esau parked next to his uncle's house and opened the van door to the scent of meat cooking.

He hadn't been around during his aunt's decline, hadn't stood by his uncle and cousins at her funeral, but when he had called from the halfway house in Rock Springs, Frank Aoah had picked up the phone and welcomed him home. This place, this man had once more become his salvation.

Esau found his uncle grilling steaks on the barbecue. His uncle had cut his hair when his wife passed. Ten years regrowth in two neat braids, interwoven with white, now spilled part way down his back— a symbol of the life after. It also reminded Esau of the years he had lost.

Frank cut into the thinnest of the steaks. "Another coupla minutes, corn needs a little longer too," he pronounced, putting the cover back on the Weber. He watched two vultures ride the thermals above the expanse of dry grass stretching toward the Wind River and nodded his head slowly as he considered what his nephew had just told him about Marcela Crow.

"So you're saying this girl is Two-Spirit," he said, eventually. "Some of our people celebrate the Two-Spirit as having the best of both worlds. It's too bad this child can't make peace with her body."

"No, I'm not saying she's Two-Spirit. I don't see two spirits in that one body," said Esau. "I just see a girl trapped in a body identical to her brother's. She wants a full physical transition when she's old enough."

Frank whistled and shook his head. "Hard to imagine the extent of all that."

And Esau waited, knowing what was going to come next, because he'd heard his uncle say it for years, and he loved the man for it.

"But everybody different," said Frank. "Everybody got their part to play."

They each selected a steak and a couple of ears of corn, roasted in their husks, and took their plates to a picnic table under a chokecherry that had been pruned into a sizable tree. Its long creamy white blossoms had become green, pea-sized fruit. When they were dark purple and ripe enough, Esau told his uncle he'd pick some and bring them back to Comfrey to make jelly.

"Jelly? No, make pemmican," said Frank. "You teach those kids."

"What, you going to dry the elk meat for me?"

"Bison better," said Frank, without offering to dry either. As they ate, Frank asked about the other twin—the boy.

"He's big into basketball and horses," said Esau. "Booker, this guy Heidi is involved with, has a couple of horses. Rumor has it he bought one of them for Amadeus, but he won't admit it, says he bought the horse as a friend for his other horse."

"Sure he did. And what, no horse for you?" asked Frank innocently. When his nephew gave him a sour look, Frank chuckled. They had gone riding when Esau, a teen full of attitude, first came to live on the Reservation. It had not gone well, the boy had displayed no feel for horses.

His uncle was particular about his Weber, so at the end of

the meal Esau went into the house to make coffee while Frank cleaned the grill. When they had settled into two white plastic lounge chairs with their coffee and slices of Hebeka shortbread, Frank asked if Booker was standing behind the little Crow girl.

"I think he will," said Esau, "but he doesn't know about her yet. Heidi says she has to get Marcela's permission before she tells him."

Frank grunted his approval. "Only right the girl should call the shots on this one, but Heidi Crow gotta tell her fella and see what he's made of. You think he's a good guy?"

"I'd say he's good. Ex-military, now he does black smithy work and metal sculpture He's pretty shut down but he's got manners."

"That's alright then, everybody different, everybody got their part to play," said Frank. He rolled his head to the side and cast his nephew a long look. "And how does this Booker feel about your friendship with his lady?"

Esau chuckled. "He's not much of a talker but he's always eyeing me, like, "Does she like the Shoshone more than me? Could a woman like her find a man with a face like that attractive? It's clear as day in thought bubbles above his head."

Frank let out a bark of laughter, spilling part of his coffee in the process. With his wife at rest, a daughter in the Air Force and a son working in Gillette, he was grateful to have his nephew back.

* * * * * *

Heidi stirred raisins and a chopped apple into a pot of steel cut oats. Esau was right, she admitted to herself. If she wanted to move forward in her relationship with Booker, she needed to tell him about Marcela.

Up before her brother, even on a Saturday, Marcela came into the kitchen, peered into the pot and heaved a sigh.

"On TV they show oatmeal that you just have to add hot water to," she said, sitting down in front of her orange juice. "It's instant and it already has all the brown sugar in it so it saves you lots of time and it has tiny little candy dinosaurs in it and dinosaur eggs."

"Eggs are nutritious but I would say the other ingredients are not." Heidi gave the oatmeal another stir and put on the lid. "Armand has taken over my Saturday morning shifts, so I have lots of time."

"They're not eggs, they're dinosaur eggs, and they're real little. You're not the fun kind of aunt." Marcela scowled at her orange juice. "There's a boy in my class who says his aunt is way more fun than anybody else in his whole family."

"This is a very lucky boy to have such an aunt and I have been thinking about our own family this morning, " said Heidi, sitting down opposite Marcela and smiling. She ignored Marcela's wary look and continued, "Because Booker has become our very good friend, I think it is time to tell him how our family is different than perhaps any other family he has met before."

She felt the little girl stiffen. The lid of the pot gave a lift and Heidi rose to turn down the heat.

"No, you want to tell him *I'm* different," said Marcela flatly, when Heidi returned to the table. "You and Amadeus are normal and you promised you wouldn't tell anybody about me, so you can't."

"Yes, I did promise this, but we did not know Booker then. And when we start to make our plans to go to San Francisco ... "

"But that's not yet," Marcela broke in, her lower lip quivering, "and when we go we say it's for vacation. We just lie about me, we always lie."

"Promised what?" Amadeus stood in the kitchen doorway, Gering at his feet. "Lie about what?"

"Do you want to weigh in with us about talking to Booker about how we are different?" Heidi asked.

"No, don't tell him," Amadeus said immediately. He slid down the wall to sit cross-legged on the floor and pulled Gering onto his lap. "He doesn't have to know—we just have to wait until Marcela gets her body."

"That is a long time away," said Heidi. "There will be many trips to San Francisco before that and Booker will have questions. This will be very many lies."

Amadeus looked at his sister. "I'm real good at lying, right, Marcela?"

"Right. And if Booker knows," Marcela's voice increased in pitch, "he'll think I'm *wrong*. Like Grandpa and those Riverton people. If Booker knows, he won't like me, he'll be like Grandpa ... Grandpa always said *teeyeihinoo*. He would point at me and say *cee'eseiht.*"

Heidi looked to Amadeus for translation. "*Teeyeihinoo* means that Grandpa was saying he was ashamed for him, for Marcel," explained the boy, his voice tinged with a weary resignation. "Mostly he said *cee'eseiht.* That's what he said about Marcela. It means 'he's different.' He got mad when we called her Marcela. He wanted it to be always Marcel."

"He had names for us," Marcela said. "Amadeus was *Hecesiwox*. It means 'Little Bear,' and he called me *Betei,* which means 'Flea.' He said the flea bothers the bear. And Mama, he called *nonsih'ebiihii.*" She looked at her brother.

"That was because Mama was drunk sometimes. It means someone who drinks a lot," said Amadeus. "She did, sometimes," he added softly.

Heidi saw the mixture of stubbornness and defeat on their faces. They were not yet eight. Amadeus had been thrown into the role of protector before he was five, they both lived with the fear of Marcela being found out. She had to reassure them Booker was safe and pray she was right.

"Booker is not like your Grandfather, he is not like the school people in Riverton. I feel we can trust him in here," Heidi pointed to her heart, "and I know it in here," she tapped her finger on her temple.

When Marcela started to protest, Heidi cut her off, "And if I am wrong, if Booker does not accept who we are, he will never eat another meal at The Crow's Nest, and he will not come to our apartment for Sunday lunch ever again! Not a crumb of food for Booker McNabb." Heidi held her thumb and forefinger together to indicate a tiny crumb.

She watched the children looking at each other in that way they had, together since conception, the two of them closing ranks.

"And Booker can not drink our water," Heidi continued doggedly. "No water for him."

Amadeus tried to hide his alarm, this was going too far. Nothing must come between him and Booker. And he could lose Cochise. He shook his head at Heidi, trying to tell her how dangerous all this talk was. If Booker had a problem with Marcela, he'd have to choose his sister over his best friend. Heidi caught his eye and mouthed, "Do not worry."

After a pause, Marcela said tentatively, "And if Booker doesn't like me, he can't come walk on our block."

Heidi nodded emphatically. "No, he cannot."

Amadeus searched for his own contribution. Aunt Heidi said not to worry and he had to believe her. "And if Booker doesn't like Marcela anymore, he can't even breathe our air," he offered.

Marcela grinned and for emphasis, the three of them inhaled deeply.

"He cannot even look at us, and if Booker *tries* to look at us," Heidi opened her eyes wide and looked intently at each child, "we will put a paper bag over his head and he will have to wear it even to take the shower!"

The twins erupted in laughter, delighted at the image of Booker taking a shower with a paper bag on his head.

* * * * * *

When the phone rang that evening, Booker answered, expecting it to be Heidi asking if he'd rather have this thing or that for lunch.

Her brisk, "Hello, Booker. I do not know if you will be staying for lunch tomorrow, I hope so," caught him off-guard.

"Okay," said he carefully. "Everybody all right?"

"Yes, but we have business to share with you."

"Business?"

"We have family business to tell you."

"Like ..." Booker cast around, "you guys aren't moving, going to Germany or something, are you? Do the kids know?"

"Why would we move?" Heidi sounded exasperated. "And of course Marcela and Amadeus know. This is *family* business. We will tell you about this tomorrow."

"But I shouldn't count on lunch."

"That will be up to you," said Heidi cryptically.

She said good night and hung up. Booker looked at the phone. Good God, she was an exasperating woman, but she had him hooked, she really had him hooked.

Family business meant something involving the kids. He got it, the kids came first, as they should, but spending time with Heidi had become such sweet agony. He lay in bed at night thinking of her, woke up in the morning aroused to the thoughts of her. He relieved his sexual tension by himself in the shower like a teenager, wondering how often she thought of him. He imagined she did, a lot. He could feel her desire when she warmed his hands on Sunday mornings, and when they gave each other a chaste good-bye kiss when he left in the afternoon.

CHAPTER TWENTY-NINE

JUST A PAPER BAG

Sunday morning broke bright, windy, and cold. Booker pulled over before reaching town and took off his gloves. He could see Heidi waiting for him on the steps when he arrived, his hands aching from cold. He turned off the motorbike, rocked it onto its stand, and dismounted, craving the brief moment of intimacy they'd have at the bottom of the stairs.

She opened the door without saying a word and he followed her inside. Before mounting the stairs to the upstairs apartment and Raul's office, she turned, reached for his hands, and placed them under her armpits. She clamped her arms to her side, head down, concentrating. The first time she'd done this, she said this was how her mother had warmed her hands in Germany in the winter. And now they would stand like this until Heidi was satisfied she had imparted enough heat. It was one of the most sensuous experiences he had ever had, standing with his hands trapped, feeling her warmth, the softness of the sides of her breasts, the firmness of her strong upper arms. Knowing he must not move, he clamped his lips together to restrain a smile. He inhaled slowly, deeply, trying to minimize his arousal, and exhaled softly—her mouth was so close.

Please, someday soon, let there be more, he silently begged.

Too soon, Heidi relaxed her arms and brought his hands to her checks to test their temperature. Satisfied, she let him go. He mounted the stairs behind her, wanting to reach for her, to pull her to him right there. He'd feel those soft breasts and lock onto the heat of her mouth.

Raul Diaz called, "Hey, Cousin," as they passed his open office door.

"Raul," Booker said with a nod.

"Working on a family trust," called Raul, as if thinking Booker was interested in why he was in his office on a Sunday.

"Sure," Booker called back.

Before Heidi opened the apartment door, she whispered, "Booker, you just listen first. Do not do the screw-up."

The children were waiting in the sitting room. Amadeus, wearing his usual t-shirt and jeans, lay stretched out on the floor, his face bronzed by the rosy sunlight filtering through the filmy red curtains. Marcela sat on the sofa. She had chosen to dress up for whatever occasion this was, in a light green dress, white socks, and shiny black shoes. Her braids were tied off with red ribbons interwoven with silver thread. Very fancy.

On the coffee table lay a paper grocery bag with the name 'BOOKER' written in large letters on the front. Heidi took a seat next to Marcela and nodded to the easy chair opposite, currently occupied by Gering.

"Sorry little guy," Booker said, picking up the comfortable, sleepy dog. He settled in the chair and placed Gering on his lap, grateful for the gentle warmth the little body radiated.

He smiled at the twins, then looked at the bag. "Is that for me?" he asked.

Marcela nodded. "Only if you don't like me anymore. Then you have to wear it, even in the shower."

Booker, mystified, examined the three of them in turn.

Heidi began, "Booker, we want to share ..." but she was interrupted by Marcela.

"No, I want to say it. I want to tell him!"

Heidi stopped, and her eyes met Booker's. Amadeus rose in one fluid movement and sat on Marcela's other side, slouching back to give her center stage. He placed his hand on her back.

With her brother settled, Marcela looked directly at Booker and said quickly, "I am a girl ... but under my clothes I look like Amadeus, but I am a girl and if you don't like me anymore, you have to go away. Aunt Heidi chooses me, so does Amadeus. They choose me, not you, if you think I'm bad."

Marcela pushed the paper bag toward him. She crossed her arms, pressed her lips together, and leaned back, glaring at him.

Booker fell his jaw drop. He closed his mouth and put his hand to his face. He glanced at Heidi. She had tears in her eyes. Jesus.

What the hell was Marcela saying? Heidi hadn't made a correction. Had he heard Marcela correctly? Was she saying she had male genitalia? Heidi should have said something to him over a cup of coffee or something. He stared at Heidi. How was he supposed to react? He couldn't ask questions with the kids there. Somebody should have said something. Ruth? Did Ruth know?

He felt the waves of doubt flowing from Heidi, he felt Amadeus's steady gaze. Heidi had him totally drawn in, he and Amadeus had that man-boy-horse deal, but Marcela? He hardly thought of her at all. She was busy with her little projects, was a pest to her brother sometimes. Esau got a kick out of her but to him, she'd just been a typical little girl. Maybe not typical, maybe more withdrawn and touchier than most, but he didn't really know. With the exception of Amadeus, it had been years since he'd had any dealings with kids.

He rubbed his hand over his chin and hazarded a glance at Marcela. She met his eyes and looked away. He was aware that what was happening here was between just the two of them, and Marcela held the upper hand. Heidi and Amadeus weren't going to help him at all. The silence lengthened—the only friend he had was the dog on his lap.

He'd heard of this, the essence of a person not matching the anatomy. There had been a rumor about another Army Ranger, but he had kept up and then some, so no one made an issue of it—not in the danger that had surrounded them in the Middle East and Northern Africa. Booker couldn't remember the name, something like trans-sexualism, maybe transvestitism, but that was just dressing like the opposite sex, trans-something.

Booker closed his eyes to block out the army of three opposite him. They were waiting for him to do or say something. He bit back a smile as he heard another slight push of the paper bag toward him. He placed his hands on Gering, feeling the gentle rise and fall of the dog's warm body. He was conscious of Amadeus now standing, impatient for his judgment, and yet he kept his eyes closed, searching for the words that would engender trust, that would allow him to join them, that would allow the paper bag to become just another paper bag.

He heard the exchange of air and the slight creak of the sofa springs. He opened his eyes and smiled at Marcela, but she looked away.

Growing up was confusing enough, he couldn't begin to guess how difficult this must be for her. Amadeus had shared some of their family's private stuff, Heidi's baby's ashes, Nara visiting him in the wind, but he had shared nothing, *nothing* about his sister being a boy. A boy? Booker looked at Heidi— he couldn't read her face but he felt her tension. He looked at Amadeus and saw the plea in his eyes.

Could he fake it? Booker wondered. Not fake it, but it was just so unexpected. He had known there was something hidden in this family and now they were offering it to him. Did Esau know? If Esau or Heidi had told him, he could have had time to get used to it, to act like everything was normal. How did that poor little girl cope? He heard a door slam, must be Raul taking off. They were looking at him, they wanted him to join them—he didn't want to lose them.

Booker cleared his throat. "Gering," he said to the little dog on his lap. Gering opened a round brown eye and furrowed his brow. "When is Marcela going to get to the part where I might not like her and that I am going to have to put that," he pointed to the paper bag, "on my head, even in the shower?"

He could hear Amadeus give a sigh of relief. Marcela slouched back on the sofa and gave him a hesitant smile, which he understood. She was thinking, who was he to share in this secret?

He looked at Heidi, motionless, as contained as a warrior ... until she smiled and invited him to lunch.

CHAPTER THIRTY

A DUTCH BABY AND A BURN

After lunch, they decided to walk down to the playground to play some basketball. A cold wind blew across the Green River Basin and Heidi convinced Marcela to change into sweat pants and a warm jacket. Gering rode in his wagon nestled in a blanket. They played Around the World on the basketball court, Gering barking his encouragement, the children putting the adults to shame. On the way home, Booker was invited to supper.

Before bed, the children stood in the sitting room doorway in their pajamas and suggested to the grownups that Booker spend the night.

Amadeus began their pitch by saying, "Aunt Heidi has a big bed, so you could spend the night if you want to."

Booker looked at Heidi—she seemed as surprised as he.

"If somebody has a nightmare they get to sleep in her bed," Marcela said. "Sometimes everybody has a nightmare, and then we all sleep in it. It's queen-sized."

Amadeus frowned at his sister, this wasn't part of the script.

"Sounds like even a queen-sized bed could get pretty crowded," Booker said thoughtfully.

"If you spend the night, nobody will have a nightmare, so there won't be four people in the bed," promised Amadeus. "That would be crazy."

Marcela remembered her part and chimed in. "And you could have breakfast with us before school and Aunt Heidi could make pancakes. Usually we just get them on Saturday."

The children looked hopefully at Heidi. She shrugged and said, "I suppose I could make pancakes, make even the Dutch Baby."

Marcela looked at her brother; Dutch Baby, this was going even better than they'd hoped.

"A Dutch Baby?" Booker asked.

"That's a fresh apple pancake," said Marcela, licking her lips. "It puffs up in a big pan then gets flatter and we have whipped cream and ..."

"Lemon syrup," finished her brother.

"It's been like a year since we got to have it," said Marcela.

"It was sooo long ago, I can't even remember." Amadeus flopped his arms over the easy chair dramatically.

"I made it two weeks ago," Heidi reminded them.

"What will you have for breakfast if I go home?" asked Booker.

"Scrambled eggs or cereal or porridge," sighed Marcela. "A Dutch Baby is so much better."

"We will let Booker decide where he sleeps tonight," said Heidi. She got up, turned the children around, and told them to brush their teeth as she turned down their beds.

Over her shoulder she said, "If you wish to go home, Booker, stay until I give you the articles I want you to read. I will be back after I tuck the children in."

Heidi returned to find Booker stretched out on the sofa with his shoes off. He had been thinking about her and opened heavy lidded eyes. "Well, that was a well-orchestrated performance."

Heidi laughed. "They really like the Dutch Baby."

He reached out a hand and pulled her down to sit beside him.

"I hate to disappoint children," he murmured, shifting his hips, conscious of his growing need. She leaned over and brushed her lips lightly on his.

"Good God, that all you got woman?" He pulled her head down with both hands and parted her lips with his tongue, kissing her deeply, probing, exploring, drowning in her liquid heat. When she put her hand under his shirt and dusted his nipples with her fingers, he thought he might explode. He grabbed her wrist to make her stop and whispered raggedly, "Take me to this king-sized bed, Wench."

"Wench, this is not rude? And it is the queen-size," she whispered back, eyes dancing.

He followed her down the hall, his erection almost painful. They entered her room and Heidi pushed the lock button on the door handle.

"This is so you will feel safe, but they will not come in," she said. "They learn early from their mother not to come in."

Her smile faded, she paused and cast Booker a troubled look. "Nara left me when they were fifteen months old," she said softly. "She and the twins went back to her father at the Wind River Reservation, until he died and they left. She started to drink again and there was a terrible cruel man who hurt Marcela and burned her with his cigarette."

He watched the shadows play across her features. He still felt the heat of the ardor that had threatened to consume him moments ago, but no longer the desire. This was about the children. He had avoided women with children for good reason.

"Oh yes, they want the Dutch Baby and they act in such a cute way," she said, almost mockingly. She looked to the black night outside the window and went to close the curtains.

"Heidi," he said, not knowing what she wanted. Should he go?

She turned and met his eyes. "I have not had a man since Amadeus and Marcela came to me, but they know what men

247

and women do. I think they saw it, I think they hid from it. I think it scared them. Their counselor in Riverton thought it might have even aroused them, titillated them, adult sexual things. Can you imagine how confusing for them? They are *five* when they came to me, the children of trauma, *five*. We have counseling for the death of their mother and all this while Marcela feels she cannot be who she is, even with the counselor. And Amadeus, with his guilt, his feeling of being responsible for Nara's death because of the clothes."

"Clothes?"

"Amadeus stole clothes for his sister, girl clothes, the boyfriend is so angry when he sees Marcela, and they run away. Nara is drunk but she drives anyway and this is the accident kills her."

There it was, the accent, the tense shifts—she was in pain. "Heidi," he said, reaching out for her, but she looked at his hand and shook her head.

"Amadeus feels responsible for this, and so guilty to be to be the normal one and to not have to hide like his sister," she said bitterly. "They tell you it is okay to spend the night because they want a treat breakfast, but I do not consider all this when we talk about you sharing my bed. I want them to feel safe."

Booker watched her. It was almost as if she'd forgotten he was there. This had been a bigger day than he had bargained for. Did he want to be with her enough to wade through all this? He had almost destroyed a family once before, but the circumstances here were so different—he wouldn't be moving into his own brother's territory.

This wasn't fair to anyone—he had to say *something*. So Heidi was never supposed to have a man again because of the children? She thought of the twins as being so damaged, but he saw a resilience there that maybe she couldn't see.

After a prolonged silence he asked, "Do you want me to go?"

COMFREY, WYOMING: MARCELA'S ARMY

Heidi stared at him blankly.

"Your call, Heidi. Obviously. But let me say, I'm not cruel...you know, *they* know I'm not cruel. They asked me to stay because they want this pancake, but maybe they also see I'm not a bad guy. Maybe a tiny part of them, beyond all the selfish kid stuff, wants you to have something too. They may be handling their past better than you think. They know that with you, they're at the top of the heap. The paper bag thing? That was impressive. I got an education today. When Marcela let me in, I realized I wanted in. I was *honored* by her trust. I want to be hanging on the outskirts of your little trio. I'm safe Heidi, I'm not here to hurt anyone."

That was a lot of emoting for him, and he was exhausted. He didn't have any more words. He had brought tears to her eyes, but they hadn't spilled over.

She gave him a weak smile. "Are you wooing me, Herr McNabb?"

"Now that you mention it, that might have been what I was doing, Frau Crow."

"Fraulein, I am not married, or Ms. Crow, if you would prefer."

"Heidi."

"Yes, Heidi, that is best," she said, looking at him, her arms folded.

"May I sit on your bed?" he asked. "Or, I could go but I'd suggest that if I go, you make this apple pancake for them anyway."

By her smile, he could tell she liked the pancake suggestion. After a moment she said, "You may sit."

She said something in German under her breath, appeared to listen, her head to the side. She nodded, walked to the dresser and withdrew small bag from the top drawer.

"Condoms," she said, holding the bag in her palm the way a person would offer an apple to a horse. "I bought them in Pinedale after the first time you come to eat dinner at my restaurant. You were so handsome, the way you watched me. I buy these just in case."

"You wooing *me* now?" He smiled.

"Yes, that is what I am doing."

"I see. And since we're sharing, I had a vasectomy a long time back. For the occasional interlude, I have worn a condom against disease, something the military drummed into us, but with you, I think we're good."

They exchanged a smile. She took a slow breath and threw the bag of condoms over her shoulder.

"And now we get down to business," she said.

He would always remember that, he knew he would—the way she said it, how she tossed the bag, how she advanced on him.

The moment their mouths made contact, they were consumed by a need so immediate there was no time to take off their clothes. He entered her with her corduroy pants and underpants pushed to her knees, his jeans barely to his thighs. They came together, faster than he could have imagined possible. Hearts pounding, he lay spent on top of her, both of them shuddering and gasping for breath. She wrapped her arms around him and held him tight.

It may have been ten minutes, it may have been half an hour before they began to slowly undress each other. Her hands stopped when they felt the scars on his shoulder and back.

"Booker?" she asked, but he shook his head and she didn't ask more.

He ran his hands over her body. He sucked gently at her nipples and her soft moan instantly hardened him again.

"Breakfast for dinner," he managed to say.

"Dessert before entrée?"

"That too."

"What are we talking about?" she asked with a soft laugh.

"Hell if I know."

He pulled her on top of him and ran his hands down her back. She parted her legs and straddled him, arched her back as his fingers messaged her, gasping as they entered her. Her head bent in concentration, she ground her hips and as she started to contract, she grabbed him and shoved him inside. The catch in her breath was the most erotic sound he'd ever heard.

He woke to find her looking at him. "What did you say in German, before you tossed the bag of condoms over your shoulder?" he asked.

"I pray to the Christian god and also to Athena and a little bit to Freyja, for their blessings."

"Mixed bag," said Booker.

"Yes, I cover the bases. The Christian god is safe, the pagan gods are more interesting. Freyja can be very good and very bad. The Greek gods are simpler. I know most people would say this is the overkill, but it does no harm."

"No harm at all."

Heidi looked at the clock. "*Mein Gott*, the time. You may rest while I shower. Would you like me to bring you tea or coffee before I make the Dutch Baby?"

"Can I shower with you and help make The Baby?"

"*Dutch* Baby, no one just says 'The Baby.'" Heidi gave him a mocking grin that he answered by rolling out her bed and following her. They made love in the shower, fast, slippery with soap, her back against the tiled wall, his arms braced on either side of her.

Cinnamon and apples wafting on the air brought the twins to the table. Marcela patted Booker's head as she sat down next to him.

"Are you staying tonight too?" asked Amadeus, his eyes lighting up when he saw two Dutch Babies on the table. Dutch Babies tomorrow would be almost too much to hope for.

"I am not. I've got a gate to finish, I'll be working until midnight."

"Did you guys have fun last night?" asked Marcela, giving him a knowing look.

Shocked, Booker caught Heidi's eye, not knowing how to respond.

"I do not care for your tone, Marcela," said Heidi sharply. "You are a little girl and we are adults, you need to respect this. If Booker stays again, you will not intrude on private matters, talking in that way. And do not blink your eyes at me, I know you understand what I am saying."

"Yes, Aunt Heidi." Marcela drew out the words. She pushed out her lips and slouched down in her chair. When the long-suffering look she cast around the table was ignored, she sighed and helped herself to another piece of pancake.

Before he left, Heidi handed Booker a folder and warned, "You will learn more anatomy and big, new words."

"I like anatomy and big, new words," he replied, and she laughed.

Once home, Booker went into the barn to feed Rosie, Cochise, and the cantankerous goat. He let the animals out to wander around their paddock. They had been shut in since yesterday morning and were not pleased. If he spent more nights at Heidi's, he'd have to work this out.

In his shop, he put the radio on. He had managed to orient an FM antenna to pick up a public radio station from Rock Springs, but today he searched for a country station. Love, angst, and plenty of passion suited his mood. He fired up the gas forge and lined up the final bars for the ornate gate Tyree or Armand Dubois were going to help him load up tomorrow and take to Jackson.

The paper bag, Marcela's situation, Jesus, Marcela's *situation*, Heidi, the sex, the sex ... if she were here, he'd take her right now, right on the shop bench. Distracted, he burned his right hand badly and swore so loudly, Rosie whinnied in alarm and he could hear her stomping her feet in agitation.

He examined his hand and realized the burn was more than he could possibly deal with on his own—right across the palm, three of his fingers past the second joint. His right hand, *damn it to hell!* He turned off the gas forge using his left hand and the tip of his index finger and thumb of his right. He got an ice pack and rested it in his burned hand as made his way down to Tom Magroot's—his first doctor visit since his military days.

"Ditch the ice. Shouldn't someone who works in a blacksmithy know better than that?" The doctor grabbed the ice pack and tossed it into the sink for emphasis. He whistled when he saw Booker's hand. "What did you do? Grab a red hot poker from the wrong end and forget to let go?"

"Something like that," said Booker sourly.

"You don't know better than ice?"

"Never been burned to this degree before. Any burn I've had, ice takes the pain away."

"Cold water for a minor burn, not ice, and this is beyond minor. Any more damage and I'd be driving you Rock Springs." Doctor Tom frowned at the hand. "Good thing I didn't close up early and go fishing as planned. We have our work cut out for us. Sit down, think pleasant thoughts, I'll be back in a jiff."

The doctor returned with a large syringe filled with fluid.

"What's that for? Don't I just need a dressing or something?" asked Booker, who was not a fan of needles.

"Local anesthetic. Lidocaine. Safe, even if you're pregnant, so I didn't ask."

"Good to know," Booker said, eyeing the length of the needle. "Don't think I need it, I have a high pain tolerance."

"Look, I have to pull this tissue off, here, here, and here," said Doctor Tom, pointing to the worst of the burn. "It'll hurt like hell if I don't give you something. When the lidocaine wears off you can test your pain tolerance and I won't have to be there to mop up your tears."

"Funny guy, Doc."

"Aren't I just? Now stop the chatter and let me work."

After gently peeling off the damaged tissue with tweezers, the doctor applied something from a tube and loosely wrapped the hand in gauze. He cautioned Booker to keep the gauze clean and dry.

"I have a gate to finish. I'll wear a glove over it."

"I don't think so," said the doctor. "Can't put any pressure on the fragile new skin when it starts to form, you're weeks away from using that hand. Now I need your left butt cheek."

The doctor selected what looked like a horse syringe and withdrew fluid from a vial.

"No thanks, I'll take the pain," said Booker.

The doctor laughed, "Oh don't worry, you'll have plenty of pain. This isn't an anesthetic, it's an antibiotic. Infection's a real concern with a burn of this size, you'll be on antibiotic pills for two weeks. Do not miss even one, and no alcohol."

"Beer?"

"Is beer alcohol, Frat Boy? How old are you anyway?" The doctor feigned disgust. "When was your last tetanus shot?" At Booker's shrug, the doctor grinned. "Oh good, another shot."

At the door, the doctor clamped a hand on Booker's shoulder. "Let's not shake hands," he said cheerfully. "I hear you're quite a metallurgist. You've got a show in Jackson, MacKenzie Gallery?"

"Yup." Booker gave a tight smile, his palm was beginning to hurt so much he'd broken into a cold sweat.

"Gotta go see it. I'll take Ruth Creeley, we're steppin' out."

"Ruth Creeley?" asked Booker, grinning, forgetting his hand for a moment. "Lucky man."

"That I am. And you know ..." the doctor said thoughtfully, "her grandson's living with her. Minkie Birdsong. Nice kid, anxious to please, he's twelve, not old enough to drive, but he'll be a cheap little serf. I think he'd get a kick out of helping you. Ask Ruth about him."

"I've met him. Ruth and I are close. She tell you that?"

"She's out of your league, son," said Doctor Tom with a chuckle.

Booker stopped by Ruth's on his way home. He'd have to get help of some kind. Ruth clucked over his hand and called Minkie.

"Hey, Booker," the boy said.

"Minkie." Booker nodded his head in acknowledgement. "Want an after-school job?"

"Sure, cool," said Minkie, He shifted his feet and looked at Booker's bandaged hand with interest. "Does that hurt?"

"It does. A burn, I don't recommend it."

Minkie nodded. "Okay."

"Tell you what, Booker," said Ruth. "I'll drive up in the morning, help you change that dressing, clean up. Tom wants the hand to stay dry. Then I'll go and attend to my own business and bring Minkie up after school. You bring him home. We'll do this as needed. If Minkie works out, who knows, marriage made in heaven."

Booker thanked them. How long since he'd left the doctor's? Ten minutes? Small towns, everybody talking to everybody *about* everybody, that's why he lived outside of town.

Once back in his cabin, Booker toyed with the idea of phoning Heidi. It seemed the thing to do after last night, but he hated phone calls. Maybe he'd read one of the articles she'd given him, they could have a brief conversation about that. He didn't want to see anyone, not even Heidi, for a few days. This hand thing—he'd been Special Ops, for Christ's sake, why was *this* getting to him? He hated relying on other people for anything. It wouldn't have happened if he hadn't been

255

distracted. His carefully crafted life was getting way too complicated.

Booker awkwardly opened a new bag of feed and scooped cups of it into a bucket because he couldn't heft the bag and just pour it in. Holding his hand high seemed to minimize the throbbing. He realized how ridiculous he must look as he carried a pitchfork of hay with his left hand, right hand up in the air. He shooed the horses and the goat in the barn for the night and closed the door—a mountain lion had been roaming the area.

He couldn't figure out how to open a can of stew with one hand, so he settled for bread, cheese, and an apple. He had his antibiotic, chased it down with a beer, and muttered, "Here's to you Tom Magroot."

He needed a dog. Dogs were loyal—a dog wouldn't think him an idiot for getting distracted and burning his hand.

He turned on a reading light, settled in his easy chair, and began to read the first of three articles from The Center for Transgender Research and Support, a clinic located in the Parnassus Medical Center in San Francisco. When he was done, he sat staring into space. Little Marcela Crow, the whole damn family for that matter...what a journey they were on.

In the morning, after taking a shower with his hand in a plastic bag, washing, drying himself with one hand, Booker phoned Tom Magroot. He left a message to please phone him on the answering machine and got a call back within half an hour.

"You running a fever?" was the first thing the doctor asked.

"No, I'm fine, I just have a question. When do little girls go through puberty?"

"Girls? Mind if I ask why you want to know?"

"Curious. It's nothing weird."

"All weirdos say that. Look it up. You have internet?"

"Not up here, not yet."

"Damn Wyoming," Tom Magroot grumbled. After a pause he said, "Well, since Ruth says you're okay, I'll tell you, but if you're bent I'll find out and come after you. So, let's see, lots of variables with puberty. Genetics, environment, it's getting earlier, surprisingly enough. Average these days I'd say ten to thirteen give or take a year. Race may be a factor; did I mention that? Although race is so loosely defined, some people are advocating just doing away with the whole construct, just talk about inbreeding populations ..."

Booker suddenly realized he'd asked the wrong question and cut the doctor off. "Boys, how about for boys, like what, a little later?"

"Yeah, usually. Wide range of normal there too, but you're thirty-seven so I'd say you're done, son."

When he heard Ruth's truck grinding up the drive, Booker realized he hadn't phoned the Dubois brothers to cancel, or his client in Jackson to tell her the gate would be delayed by a couple of weeks, or Heidi. His damn hand, he needed to get back to work. He *hated* phone calls.

Ruth came in with a bag of supplies and a gallon of sterile water from Doctor Tom.

"A couple more jugs in the truck, I'll bring them in before I leave," she said.

"I'll get them," Booker said impatiently. "I'm not completely helpless."

"Oh, don't get your panties in a bunch. Go bring them in if you're bound and determined. I'll set up camp on the kitchen table," said Ruth.

She shook her head, cranky, cranky, cranky. Out the kitchen window she watched him walk to her truck. Such an attractive man—when he'd arrived in Comfrey, there had been plenty of murmurings in the female community. Two hands, only one trip; one hand, two trips. That would frustrate him.

She smiled. Booker McNabb had become one of her favorite people. She had been his realtor and had managed to get the owner of this pretty piece of property to sell to Booker, instead of to the man from Taiwan who had offered far too much money and had given her the willies. Booker had qualified for a low-interest veteran loan, which had made financing easy. He hadn't settled back home in Pennsylvania after Uncle Sam was done with him. She often wondered about what had made him hightail it away from family and home.

Booker put the second gallon of water on the counter and sat down at the kitchen table, glaring at Ruth.

"You don't scare me, Booker McNabb," she said, and he begrudgingly muttered, "Sorry."

She looked critically at the wrapping around his hand. "How did a hand that's not being used get itself so dirty?" she asked mildly.

"I've just been reading," said Booker. After she raised her eyebrows at him, he added, "After, you know, taking care of the horses and goat and putting a few things away in the shop."

"Now that will be Minkie's job. He'll enjoy the horses, the goat, the shop. You'll think of all sorts of things for him to do," Ruth said with satisfaction. "I appreciate you putting the boy to work."

She held his hand gently as she dabbed the bandage with sterile water to loosen it where it had stuck to the wound. When she peeled the gauze back, she looked from the wound up to Booker.

"Nasty-looking but not infected. If you had a nice little sweetie, she'd be doing this for you."

"Workin' on it," Booker grunted as he placed his hand in the basin of warm soapy water Ruth put on the table.

Ruth smiled to herself. People were saying how Booker looked at Heidi when he came into The Crow's Nest, and she looked right back.

"Bring your hand to the sink, we'll rinse it with the sterile water," she said. "Have you had your antibiotic this morning?"

"Yeah, just twenty-two more to go."

"Oh, poor little me. If only Alexander Fleming hadn't discovered penicillin in 1922. Damn that *Penicillium* mold, damn its defense against bacteria."

At Booker's look she laughed. "Can't help it, I had a great teacher, Betty Ann Wolfe opened my eyes to the living world."

She patted the hand dry, smeared an antibiotic cream over the wound, and covered it in another sterile wrapping.

"You know, more people died in World War I from infection than weapons," she said. "Thanks to Sir Fleming, in World War II more people died of from weapons than infection. See what progress the human race is making?"

Booker groaned. "I can see why you and the Doc are perfect for each other."

"We do enjoy each other's company. We dated in high school. I should have married Tom from the get go, but we got distracted. I'm making us some coffee, you have any cookies?"

Booker shook his head.

"I'll bring some when I come back later," she said. "You could do with a cookie or two."

She tidied up, put a load of laundry in, and said, "I'll be back with Minkie after he's done at school. I'll hang the wash out to dry then. It won't hurt it to sit for a few hours, just open the top of the washer when it's done."

At Booker's frown, Ruth said, "Oh, lighten up, I know you've been doing your own laundry since you were a toddler. Take a break, read a book, go down and get lunch at Heidi's place. Life is damn good at times."

"Ruth, thank you, I mean it," he said, holding the door.

"I know you do. It's my pleasure," she said, grinning up at him. "You need a dog, Booker—nonverbal communication is right up your alley. I've seen a nice little Pitbull-mix puppy in the shelter in Pinedale."

"I don't do puppies," he said.

CHAPTER THIRTY-ONE

MICHELLE PRUITT MAKES HER ESCAPE

After finding Vera's pottery studio empty, Ruth knocked on the side door of Betty Ann's house—Vera's house now, she reminded herself. Vera called for her to come in and Ruth walked through a small mudroom into the kitchen where she found the young woman putting the finishing touches on a double-layer chocolate cake.

"My father would have been forty-five today," Vera said. "Chocolate cake was his favorite. Obviously."

"My antennae were waggling and it looks like I came along just in time to have a healthy piece," said Ruth, who had, in fact, written the date on her calendar. After Betty Ann died, Ruth had transferred pertinent dates from Betty Ann's calendar to her own. Forty-five years old...Rick McNabb would have still been a young man. That baby would now be a teenager.

"I hope you're thinking of tucking into it right away." Ruth put her finger in the frosting bowl and took a taste. "I have a lot on my plate today."

And that was the thing about receiving a big smile from someone who smiled so seldom, thought Ruth, putting on the tea water. A smile like that lit up the room and made the recipient feel blessed.

As Vera reached for two plates, Ruth observed her middle. The girl was putting on some weight. It must be all that sitting at the potter's wheel—Vera had been working feverishly as of late.

"Looks like Michelle Pruitt's done a runner," said Ruth, watching with surprise as Vera selected an *herbal* tea bag for herself. That was a first. "Flew to her sister in Florida."

"Michelle's gone for good?"

"According to Raul Diaz," Ruth said, adding honey liberally to her Darjeeling tea, "she left right from the hospital before Riley's temperature dropped more than a couple of degrees. She phoned Raul about handling her affairs and of course, he then phoned me about selling the house. Michelle didn't even go home to get her clothes, she drove straight to the airport. Raul said she told him to pick up the car and either keep it or sell it."

"The Ford Fairlane?"

"The very one. Over thirty years old, but only 70,000 miles on her. Raul says if I go and get her, I can have her. He's a little put out Michelle didn't discuss any of this with him ahead of time but I told him no one thought Riley would die from a broken ankle. Only sixty, smoker, so there was that, but he developed a blood clot and was gone in a day. Raul had to arrange for the body to be picked up and dealt with, add that to the reasons he's perturbed with Michelle. Their daughter, Lia, you remember her, she's somewhere in Africa now, working in an orphanage. Well, Raul still hasn't been able to get in touch with her. Maybe Michelle's tracked her down but I don't think Lia cared for her father any more than her mother did. That's what you get for being a man like Riley Pruitt."

The phone rang and Vera excused herself, saying she was expecting a call from a gallery owner in Landers who wanted more of her ceramic koi fish. As Vera talked, Ruth got up to say hello to Jada and congratulate him for being the model for Vera's highly successful pond art series. The fish must be over twenty years old now. Goldfish were a different genus and species from koi, but they were in the same family. With the addition of colors and two sets of barbels flanking the mouth, a goldfish could become a fine artist's model for a koi.

Vera returned and sat down with a sigh. "It's hard to keep up with demand for the koi but they have big profit margin. Is there such a thing as being too successful?"

"Well of course there is, if you insist on flying solo. You need to hire someone to help you," said Ruth, knowing that Vera would balk, too independent and solitary by half.

"Good for Michelle," said Vera. She took a sip of her peppermint tea.

"I couldn't agree more. Riley was a rat-ass bastard, if you'll pardon my French." Ruth looked up from her cake in time to catch Vera's grin.

The phone rang again—another request for koi, from Pinedale this time.

"You're not delivering to Landers and Pinedale in the same day," said Ruth. The girl already looked beat. "You'll be running all over the map, Vera. Raul's son is back for a week or two, rope him in to deliver, he's a decent young man. He lives in Hawaii. Raul's very proud of him."

When Vera hesitated, Ruth offered to make the call and Vera accepted.

"Thank you, strangers ..." began Vera.

"I know, Vera, I do know how you abhor them, but everybody's a stranger at some point. Now you owe me some cake to take home for my dinner."

Vera nodded. "Tyree is coming by to change the water in Jada's tank. I can get rid of more of it then."

"Get rid of? That's no way to talk about a chocolate cake," said Ruth, scraping her plate with the side of her fork to get last remnants of frosting. She looked at Vera thoughtfully. The girl had always been a challenge to read, but something was off.

"You alright, Vera?" Ruth asked, cutting herself another

263

thin sliver of cake. "You usually take care of Jada yourself."

"I strained my back. Too much work. I'm tired."

"Hire some help in the studio, then you can spend some time outside," Ruth wouldn't mention the weight gain, "get some exercise, do some planting and weeding, when the back's better of course."

"Armand will do the garden tomorrow. I have to build up inventory. I might take a little time off to visit..." Vera grimaced, trying to think of something, "... to help out a college roommate that, ah, is recovering from surgery."

"Huh," said Ruth. "That's kind of you. When might this mission of mercy be taking place?"

"Middle of October maybe."

"Oh, I had the impression your friend had the surgery already. I must have misheard."

The conversation lapsed. They both looked at the kitchen clock. Vera cut a generous slice of cake for Ruth and put it on a paper plate to go. She didn't wrap it, knowing Ruth's aversion to the overuse of plastic.

"Heidi Crow might be interested in the Pruitt place," Ruth said as Vera walked her to the truck. "She, those two kids, and the dog are still crammed into that apartment upstairs from The Crow's Nest, next to Raul Diaz's new digs. I promised little Marcela a cat when they came to Comfrey, but she's been good enough to wait for them to get a house. Think of the space they all have and an easy walking distance to the school."

Vera gave Ruth a bleak look. She was fine without having to deal with neighbors. Ruth, the Dubois brothers, and her clients were enough.

* * * * * *

"Everything is as Michelle left it, a lot of junk," Ruth warned Heidi as she unlocked the front door to the Pruitt house and ushered Heidi, the children, and the dog inside.

"Riley was a smoker. I should have gotten the key yesterday and opened some windows. He was supposed to smoke outside only, but smokers are a sneaky lot. So imagine new paint, roof and appliances, fresh curtains, and a redo of the master bedroom and bath. That's where I understand Riley spent most of his time."

The twins and Gering ran straight down the hall, through the kitchen, and out the backdoor.

"Look, Gering runs like he is a puppy," Heidi said with a delighted laugh.

Ruth chuckled. "Plenty of good dog smells out there. They'll all be safe enough in the yard. I walked the fence line yesterday."

Heidi looked around. The house was beyond dismal, although the electricity had been turned off, so the interior might have looked grimmer than it really was. Halfway down a long hall to the kitchen at the back, a short hall led to two bedrooms and a nice surprise—a newly renovated bathroom, spotless, new fixtures, tub and toilet.

Ruth proclaimed the bathroom to be Michelle Pruitt's pride and joy. Michelle had inherited five thousand dollars from her brother, and Riley, a controlling man if ever there was one, wouldn't let her touch the kitchen or the master bedroom or bathroom, so Michelle had poured all her money into redoing the guest bathroom and one of the smaller bedrooms.

"Then I think she left Riley to stew in his own juices on the other side of the house and moved in here," Ruth said.

"*Traurige Familie.*" Heidi shivered.

"If you're saying, 'sad family,' I'd agree," said Ruth, whose German was rudimentary at best. "But this is a nice sized place, and you and the twins and Gering, let's not forget the cat, all of you could make this a happy home."

Heidi looked around doubtfully. Living above the restaurant was so easy and she wasn't sure she was ready to move, especially to a house that required so much work. She asked where the master bedroom was.

"Down a bitty hall off the dining room, other side of the house. Strange set up but in the end, it put some welcome distance between Riley and Michelle, I'd guess. We'll check out the kitchen, then go through the dining room to the master suite." Master suite, even to Ruth that sounded much too grand. "The sitting room is to the right of the front door, if you recall. You could go from your bedroom, through the sitting room, and into the kid's rooms pretty efficiently. Consider knocking down that wall between the living room and the hall to open things up. We can get a crew in here and with enough people, we could have you in here in a month. And the master bedroom has a window on the street so you can watch the twins come home from their dates in a few years."

"*Gott schütze mich*," said Heidi with a shudder. She gave Ruth a wry smile. "I ask God to protect me."

"Oh, He will," Ruth promised. "I see good things for you in this house."

The kitchen was spacious, but smelled terrible. Ruth opened two windows over the sink. Dirty dishes on the counter fought for space with moldy bread in a plastic bag and a carton of milk left out and souring.

"Michelle leaves in a hurry," Heidi observed. An escape from an oppressive house.

"Never came home from the hospital, flew right to her sister in Florida. Raul talked to her yesterday and said she was already stepping out with a retired Jewish gentleman, who likes to dance and has plenty of money," said Ruth with a grin. "She married Riley because he knocked her up, got a nice daughter out of the deal and now she's got a fella to match."

So Michelle Pruitt was not so sad now. Heidi felt the atmosphere in the room lifting. She looked through the window to see the twins chasing each other in the yard, Gering at their heels. They looked like pictures in the reading primer she'd bought the twins, *Dick and Jane, Go, Go, Go.*

There was an empty lot behind the back fence and she asked if it was up for sale. Ruth said it was.

As far as Ruth was concerned, Heidi was Comfrey Citizen Number One. She had renovated the old Taylor's Refresher eyesore on Main Street, had brought more jobs to Comfrey than any other enterprise, and now she was looking at the Pruitt place *and* the lot behind it. And she had caught Booker McNabb's eye.

Heidi watched the twins disappear around the side of the house. Almost immediately, Amadeus reappeared alone and faced the wind, hair blowing back, mouth moving. She knew he was talking to Nara. Suddenly Marcela reappeared with Gering and they were off, chasing each other, leaving the dog to dig in a determined manner under an apple tree laden with small red fruit.

"Gering digs like a real dog, I thought he was past that," said Heidi when Ruth came up behind her.

"He'll have a new lease on life, with his own yard."

Heidi nodded. "What kind is the apple?"

"That is a Frostbite apple. Two Winter Nell pears, two North Star sour cherries, and a great frolicking bramble of huckleberries are planted along the more sheltered strip on the south side of the house."

"A Frostbite apple," Heidi repeated. The name promised it would do very well in Wyoming.

"Hardy, pretty little red things, sweet, intense taste, they'll be ripe in a month or so. They're from Minnesota and cold hardy to minus thirty-five Fahrenheit. I wouldn't object to it becoming Wyoming's official State Fruit Tree."

"A state has an official *fruit* tree?" asked Heidi. She found the American obsession with official birds, flowers, reptiles, gems, songs impossible to keep up with. To have a state tree *and* a state fruit tree was just too much.

"Not that I know of, but it's not a bad idea. Now, let's take a look at the rest of your house."

Heidi smiled to herself. *Your* house—under Ruth's not-so-subtle ways, the house was beginning to feel like theirs. She had never owned fruit trees before.

"*Ach je,*" muttered Heidi as they peered into a dark bedroom smelling of mildew and cigarettes. She went to the windows and, with Ruth's help, managed to open them wide. In the bathroom, both women started back when Ruth pulled open the shower curtain. The amount of stain on the tub was quite stunning.

"Gut it," said Ruth shortly. "You've enough room for a separate tub and shower. Remember the fruit trees, the proximity to school, the size of the yard and the kitchen. Think how happy Gering and the cat will be," Ruth urged. "An added bonus is having Vera McNabb right across the street. You saw her at the funeral, sitting between Elizabeth and me, she's Betty Ann's girl. I know you sent her a note thanking her for the plums but I'm not sure you've actually met. She's a potter, a reserved sort of person but pleasant, industrious. She'll make a very good neighbor."

"Vera, it means truth does it not?" Heidi asked. "Veracity?"

"It does," said Ruth.

The children burst through the back door, announcing there was lots of stuff in the shed. Heidi and Ruth exchanged a glance.

The apples were sour, they complained. Could they eat the blackberries behind the back fence?

"Michelle is what we call 'a motivated seller,'" said Ruth as they followed the children outside. "We will get the price down low enough to pay for the Dubois brothers to clear the place out and paint. We will contract out the bathroom and kitchen and have the place renovated in a wink, a blink, and a nod."

Two days later, Ruth went to check on Vera, using banana

bread as an excuse. She also wanted to tell her the Crows were buying the Pruitt's house. She walked behind the house to the pottery studio, stopping to admire the calendula beds in full bloom. From reading her three-times-great grandmother, Greta Magroot's diaries, she had learned Greta used calendula as an anti-hemorrhagic and antiseptic. Greta had planted it liberally and descendants of the original plants still festooned gardens in Comfrey. Betty Ann had used it to flavor stews and decorate salads.

The door to the studio stood open, the room was silent, and there was Vera, sitting at the potter's wheel motionless, head down, her mane of auburn curls almost in the clay.

"Vera," said Ruth sharply, and Vera looked up with a start.

It might have been the oversized men's flannel shirt, but Vera looked even weightier than the previous week. She also looked pale and exhausted.

"Oh Vera, honey, what's not right with you?" Ruth put the banana bread down on a bench and put her arms around the young woman. Vera stiffened, but to Ruth's surprise, she did not pull away.

"I can't ..." Vera began, her voice catching.

"Of course you can," Ruth soothed. "Betty Ann used to say, 'Bear a friend's burdens and you'll be the better for it,' Corinthian's I think."

"Bear one another's burdens, and thus fulfill the law of Christ," corrected Vera, quoting Galatians 6:2 in a weary voice.

"That's the one," said Ruth. "Now let's have a part of this burden."

"If I tell you part, don't ask any questions about how it ... about how it ..."

"No questions," Ruth broke in. "You've known me two-thirds of your life. You know I can keep a confidence when asked."

"I am asking," said Vera. Betty Ann had always said that

although Ruth was in everybody's business, she didn't gossip and she could keep a secret.

One sentence, that's all Vera delivered, and when she'd said it, Ruth kissed the top of her beautiful thick waves of hair. Vera was a good-looking girl but her solemnity had put the boys off in high school, that or her total lack of interest in men and now some scoundrel had left her with a baby. Had it been her first foray into dating? How could she have been so careless? Ruth would have bet good money the girl didn't drink. Had this been an act of rebellion on Vera's part? Somehow, Ruth could not imagine such atypical behavior on Vera's part.

Afraid she wasn't going to be able to refrain from asking questions when she'd promised not to, Ruth went into the house to get a knife for the banana bread and said she'd also bring out suitable beverages. Was the father going to offer help in any way? Was he a married man? A one-night stand? Did the man even know he had fathered a child?

Pouring milk into two tall glasses, Ruth considered the situation. Traumatic to find yourself pregnant and, Ruth assumed, alone, but nothing like the horror Vera had faced as a child. Look how Vera had hunkered into her own silent little world after the fire and it had taken Betty Ann months, and the assistance of that African gentleman, to help Vera find her voice again. If Vera shut down again, there was no way Ruth was going to be able to help. But perhaps Vera would allow her to break the 'no question promise' to ask for one piece of information. They had to concentrate on the health of the baby now.

Ruth managed to slip in, "Have you had prenatal care?" as she cut into the banana bread. Vera cast her a cautious look but nodded.

"Sensible girl and you know I'll help however I can," said Ruth, watching with satisfaction as Vera followed a bite of the banana bread with a gulp of cold milk. "And I told you Heidi

Crow and the children are moving in across the street. They'll make good neighbors. She'll be busy at the restaurant and school's starting up again in a month, so I doubt you'll see a lot of them but, it's nice to know they'll be there."

Vera felt like asking why? For years she had only nodded to Michelle Pruitt or her miserable husband. What had any kind of neighbors got to do with her?

CHAPTER THIRTY-TWO

MARCELA GETS A JOB

"I'm taking you over to meet them, Vera," said Ruth. "They've been moved in five days and you still haven't knocked on their door. I'm not saying you have to be close friends, but not even going over?"

Vera sat at her kitchen table hoping to quiet her morning nausea with saltine crackers and peppermint tea. Betty Ann had never bullied her into meeting people.

"Do you still have some of those oatmeal cookies I brought over yesterday?" Ruth asked, opening the door to the most likely cupboard. "We're in luck that they're home today and we'll have to bring something as a house warming gift. The Crow's Nest is going gangbusters but with Esau Aoah, another person you have yet to meet, she has excellent help. Booker McNabb, who I know buys clay from you on occasion, helps with the boy—bought him a *horse* for heaven's sake—so you might consider helping out with the girl. Marcela is bright and capable, from what I can see. She could do a few chores for you."

"I ate the cookies. I have nothing to bring them," said Vera, "and I'm not interested in babysitting."

"Not every interaction with a child is babysitting, Vera. I said, perhaps you could use the girl's assistance. She's a funny little thing, reminds me of you as a child, private around people she doesn't know. They've been in Comfrey for almost two years and the girl has yet to make a friend. According to Heidi, Amadeus is popular at school. He's very good at sports, so that helps. She claims Marcela is equally athletic but has no interest in team sports—a pity as I'm sure you'll agree. That might have been you, if Betty Ann hadn't insisted you participate in softball."

Vera looked at the table and wished Ruth would just stop. It was true, softball had allowed her to interact with her peers, and she loved being out on the field, winding up for a pitch, diving for a ball. But the team dinners, the award nights, and the accolades had been a chore, even in college. She knew she should come to the girl's defense and tell Ruth if the child wanted to be left alone, she should just be left alone, but she didn't feel like she could marshal the energy to the defend anyone at the moment.

She watched Ruth angle her head to look out the kitchen window at the Italian Plum, laden with so much fruit, its boughs bending. Vera knew what was going to come next.

"There's no better housewarming gift than a bag of plums," said Ruth. "Heidi has swooned each time I've given her some from this tree. She makes a German plum cake with them. Wash your face, get your shoes and I'll go pick 'em."

Ruth grabbed a shopping bag and marched into the yard.

They found Heidi and the children behind their house, trying to get the little dog to chase a red plastic frisbee. Marcela threw it the furthest, Amadeus's throw was the most level, and Heidi's was hopeless. The dog was thoroughly confused.

Shaking her head, Ruth marched over, angled Heidi's hand, and showed her how to grip the disc with all four fingers wrapped under the rim, thumb pointed along the rim. Ruth positioned the disc so the rim touched the inside of Heidi's forearm, told her to take a few steps, twist her waist, and let it fly. After a couple of attempts, Heidi gave a credible throw and the twins clapped enthusiastically.

"Good job, just like I taught Vera to throw for Porky's Dog," Ruth said, pleased as punch.

Vera stood holding the bag of plums, wondering when they'd get to the introductions and exchange a few pleasantries so she could go home.

"Now, Vera," Ruth waved her over, "come here girl, show us what you've got."

Reluctantly, Vera put down the plums and said hello. She accepted the disc Heidi held out to her and gripped it as she had done so often for Porky's Dog. She took three steps, awkwardly twisted her expanded torso, and let the disc sail. It flew level and true over the back fence and into the empty lot behind. The kids howled with delight and ran to get it.

Porky's Dog had been a champ at catching frisbees and Vera could almost see him now, leaping with his powerful legs, prancing back to her with a drool-festooned disc. To lose both her dog and Betty Ann within a year of each other had been so very hard, but Vera turned to receive Heidi and Ruth's congratulations with an attempt at a smile. Amadeus and Marcela wanted her to throw the frisbee some more and show them how to get it over the fence so she obliged, while Ruth followed Heidi inside to take a quick peek at the new appliances.

"Vera is pregnant and she is alone?" asked Heidi as they examined the new stove.

"I'll not deny she's pregnant and except for me, I'd say alone, yes," said Ruth. "She's in a difficult situation and it's best not to ask questions about the circumstances surrounding the conception, if you would be so kind."

"No, of course we will not," said Heidi. "I will talk to Marcela and tell her not with the questions. She will notice, but I doubt Amadeus will. We will offer help when she knows us better, but we will not do the prying."

Ruth liked that. She liked how Heidi usually said *we*. They

COMFREY, WYOMING: MARCELA'S ARMY

were a little family unit that placed adult and children on equal footing in many things, leaving no doubt who was the boss, however.

* * * * * *

The young men in Rock Springs loaded Vera's truck with forty twenty-five-pound plastic-wrapped blocks of clay and she drove home with no clear idea on how she was going to unload it. Betty Ann had turned the short driveway along the side of the house into a vegetable garden because it was the sunniest part of the yard, so there was no easy access to Vera's studio now that parking had been relegated to the street. Someday she might put a driveway on the other side of the house, but that would involve removing the Peachleaf Willow she and Betty Ann had planted.

Vera thought she had arranged with the Dubois brothers to be on hand to help get the clay from the curb to the studio, but when she phoned from Rock Springs to confirm the time, there had been a message on their answering machine notifying callers they had gone fishing on the Snake River. They gave no indication when they would return.

The brothers were usually very reliable so she thought perhaps she had given them the wrong date. Ruth would have come to help, probably bringing a hefty young man, but she was pitching in once again at the Rock Springs community college, substituting a Mandarin class for a few weeks. Raul Diaz's son had already left town. Booker McNabb was a possibility, but Vera had only met him a couple of times. She liked his brusque manner, but it would be terribly difficult to ask him to help. The clay could stay in the truck overnight, she supposed. She'd work up the nerve to phone Booker tomorrow unless a better idea came to her.

The 'better ideas' sat eating popsicles on front the steps of their house with the little dog at their feet. To her surprise, Vera found herself walking across the street. She asked the twins if their aunt was home. The boy nodded and said she was inside doing stuff. They had been helping but they were taking a break, Vera could just go in. They scooted aside to give her room and Vera knocked on the door.

Amadeus couldn't see the point in knocking when he had already given Vera permission to enter so he got up, opened the door, and yelled, "Aunt Heidi, that frisbee lady is here."

Heidi came to the door smiling and ushered Vera into the kitchen, where it was obvious a lot of organizing was going on. She accepted Heidi's offer of a glass of water and wondered how to begin her request.

"You are well?" asked Heidi.

Vera nodded. "I know you're busy ..." she started, looking at the gaping cupboards waiting to receive the contents of the open boxes on the floor.

"Not so busy that you cannot ask a question, Vera," said Heidi, examining the young woman's flushed face. "You need some help. What can we do?"

Vera drank some water and blinked back tears. She had felt so emotional lately. The baby book she'd bought in Rock Springs had a chapter on pregnancy hormones and increased emotions but she hadn't thought it would apply to her.

"I have a truckload of clay, forty bags weighing twenty-five pounds each," she said.

"Do they need to be taken out of your truck and brought to your studio?" asked Heidi. "Ruth said it was behind your house."

"Yes. Do you think the twins could help me? Is twenty-five pounds too much for them to carry?" asked Vera, relieved to just get the words out. "I will pay, of course."

"Oh yes, I think together they can carry that much," said Heidi. "They pick up each other, but just for the moment, for the joke, but if Amadeus and Marcela work together, that will be just over twelve pounds each. They have a new wagon, a red one, and they would like to use it, I am sure. I would say no to the money, but for people of their age, earning a little money will make them feel important."

The twins were delighted with the idea of a job and ran to get their wagon. With a little bickering on how best to shift the clay out of the truck and onto the wagon, they settled into a rhythm. Three bags at a time made the wagon difficult to pull over the uneven terrain, but two bags not only fit better in the wagon's bed, one twin could pull it with little resistance, giving the other twin a little rest. Gering, who had been guarding the twins since the day Heidi had given him the job three years ago, trotted back and forth, following the wagon, his tail beating to the tempo of a slow metronome.

They had the truck unloaded and the clay stashed in Vera's studio within two hours, pausing for lemonade partway through. When they finished, Amadeus reminded Marcela they had to go home because he had to go to his basketball practice.

"It's not *my* basketball practice," said Marcela, thinking that a better option may have presented itself. "Tell Aunt Heidi I want to stay here and help."

Amadeus hesitated and Marcela suddenly realized she should have asked Vera first, and then the grownups would have to talk and decide if she could stay, as if she was a little kid. She picked up Gering, who knew what a good helper she was, and they both looked at Vera. The woman gave a smile that was a little bit sad and a lot tired, before saying to Amadeus that it would be fine to go and ask if his sister could stay.

After Amadeus left, Marcela said, "I can do a lot of stuff, like sweep and dust and ..." She looked around, spied the bubble wrap, and pointed. "... and I can use that to wrap things."

A dozen ceramic koi did need to be wrapped in bubble wrap by tomorrow for shipping, but could a child do that? The floor badly needed sweeping, ceramics tools needed to be taken out of the sink and dried so they didn't rust. A helper—Ruth was going to love this.

"If your mother says it's okay, you can stay and make a little more money," Vera said, before remembering she should have said *aunt*.

"Our mother's dead," Marcela corrected. "Heidi's our aunt and she's our guardian. She won't care if I stay, but she'll have to say, 'If you're sure Marcela won't be in the way,' then she'll have to say, 'thank you, thank you, thank you.' She's German, so she's very polite."

Trying to think of more ways to ingratiate herself, Marcela decided a little flattery might be in order. "And then she'll probably tell you how 'glorious' your hair is. She says that each time she sees you out our window. '*Meine Güte, was für einen Kopf voller herrlicher Haare diese Frau hat.*' That's what she always says, it means 'Oh my goodness, what a glorious head of hair that woman has.'"

Vera smiled. Like most of Cora and Faolan's direct descendants, she was used to compliments on her hair. She had inherited what the locals called 'McNabb' hair. When Cora and Faolan McNabb had perished crossing the North Platt River in 1852, and their four children had been absorbed into the Magroot family, who had gone on to found Comfrey. Cora's kinky African hair and Faolan's wild, red Highland tresses had combined in their descendants, even four or five generations down the line, to produce a magnificent mass of loose, copper-colored, corkscrew curls. Defying the laws of genetic probability, outsiders who had sown their seeds or provided eggs to succeeding generations had been unable to dilute the trait. The lucky inheritors, both male and female, wore their hair long, rarely tying it back, allowing the Wyoming winds to toss and tousle their ringlets with abandon.

Vera looked at Marcela's earnest face, amused. "You speak German?" she asked, tucking a spiral curl behind her ear. Amadeus had done most of the talking earlier, and she hadn't been sure at first if the girl spoke much of anything.

"Yes, and I'm pretty good. Heidi and Karl say so. Karl is our uncle who lives in Germany, even though Beppe—that's man he's going to marry—lives in Italy. Beppe has a vineyard so he has to live there. They phone every week and we went to stay there, in Germany, for a month. Amadeus won't learn German. He says he has to save his brain for Arapaho so he can talk to Nara in secret and if he had to stuff in German, it would fill up his head too much. Aunt Heidi says his brain has plenty of room, but Amadeus says no. He learned Arapaho from Nara and our Grandpa and some more from Esau. Esau works for Aunt Heidi and he and Amadeus talk in Arapaho a lot. Grandpa didn't like me. He didn't talk to me, but I don't care. German is better anyway. Not that many people speak Arapaho, not many at all." Marcela's voice trailed off. She was ashamed of having a grandfather who hadn't liked her and now she was guilty of sharing Amadeus's private business and she was talking way way too much to get this job.

"Who is Nara?" asked Vera, but the girl's eyes had shuttered and she refused to answer.

When Heidi walked over to thank Vera for having Marcela for the rest of the afternoon, she asked for the assurance that this was as much Vera's idea as Marcela's.

"I am grateful for her help," said Vera. "There is plenty for her to do."

"Tomorrow, we will drop off a fresh peach pie," promised Heidi.

"That is not necessary," Vera protested.

"We have it on the dessert menu for my restaurant this week. I will make one extra," said Heidi. "When you have a piece, you will see it is very necessary."

When it appeared the push broom in the studio was too much for a child to handle, Vera sent Marcela into the house for the kitchen broom. The girl was thorough and efficient. Vera wasn't sure how much a seven-year-old could read, but she made a list and Marcela read through it, asking what a few of the words were, sounding them out competently.

"Dry ceramic tools, what's ceramic?" asked Marcela, frowning at the word.

"It refers to clay, pottery, things made with clay."

"Why don't they just say clay?"

"I misspoke, I meant ceramic refers to *fired* clay."

"You put the clay in a fire?"

"Usually you use a kiln, at least I do." Vera pointed to one of her three kilns. "They are ovens that get very, very hot. Native Americans used to dig pits, or build mounds and fire their pottery in them."

"But now they use kilns," said Marcela.

"I imagine so, although many potters continue to use pits sometimes. I still do on occasion. The effects are different."

"What do you mean different?"

Vera sighed. Since Betty Ann's death, she had sunk into the comfort of her own company and having this child launch question after question was getting too much, especially since recently this had been the time in the afternoon when she went inside to lie down for half an hour. She couldn't do that with the girl here.

"Marcela, do you think we could have some quiet time now?" Vera forced a smile. "Every time you come, I could teach you maybe one or two new words."

Marcela looked at Vera a long moment. "I know lots of words, plus German words," she said, her voice mixture of defiance and embarrassment.

Gering, who had been curled up on Marcela's sweatshirt,

slunk over, tail held low, and the girl picked him up.

"I know, I know you do," said Vera. "I'm just not used to..."

Marcela looked down at the dog nestled in her arms. She had been asking too many questions—why this and why that all over the place—and if you were being paid for work, you should act like a grownup and pretend you knew everything already.

"Let's take a break," said Vera, because even if she couldn't put her feet up, she needed to eat. "I'll get the boxes we're going to need if you get us some apple juice and the loaf of bread, the peanut butter, strawberry jam, and a knife. The tray is in that slot next to the fridge. The food is in the fridge or on the counter. After we eat something, I'll show you how to wrap the ceramic fish that Tyree is going to deliver for me tomorrow."

Marcela nodded silently. She'd get the apple juice and stuff and wrap the fish perfectly and keep working hard with *no questions* and maybe she could still keep this job. Vera had said a dollar an hour and that was so much money.

When Heidi returned to bring Marcela back to The Crow's Nest for supper, she consented to Marcela coming back the following day. Booker McNabb had offered to take Amadeus to the lake, and if Vera had work, and if Marcela was really being useful....

Marcela rolled her eyes and showed Heidi how she'd used the bubble wrap to make the koi fish safe in their boxes.

"Koi fish like we feed at the restaurant in Cheyenne?" asked Heidi.

"Yes, but better," said Marcela, "because these are ceramic. Ceramic is what potters call *fired* clay."

"I see," said Heidi. "Can you open the wrapping a little more so I can see the whole fish?"

Marcela looked at Vera, who nodded.

"Okay, but be careful," said Marcela.

Heidi shared a smile with Vera and promised Marcela she'd just look and not touch.

On her second day on the job, Marcela showed up with the peach pie and Gering and the red wagon, in case they needed to take things to or from the truck. "Good idea," said Vera.

Marcela swept, fetched, wrapped, and labeled and Vera was relieved to find the girl's brief flood of chatter on the previous day had dried to a trickle. And, although not overly fond of little dogs, Vera found herself liking this one. He stayed out of the way, and either slept in a patch of sun in the garden or trotted behind Marcela as she went about her business.

After Marcela finished her other chores, Vera showed her how to load the smaller kiln with another dozen koi fish. They stopped for a lunch of meatloaf sandwiches—the meatloaf courtesy of Ruth. Vera poured herself a glass of milk. Marcela, who said she was lactose intolerant and could only drink special milk, had a glass of apple juice. A little later, Ruth stopped by and said she heard there was a fresh peach pie. Vera looked at Marcela, who went into the kitchen and brought the pie back on a tray with plates, a knife, and three forks.

"So in two days, she knows her way around your kitchen," said Ruth, smiling in satisfaction. Booker and Amadeus had each other, and now Vera and Marcela were taken care of.

After Ruth left, Vera offered to show Marcela how to wedge and knead clay.

She cut off what she considered a large enough chunk of clay for the girl's hands and said, "First, we need to wedge the clay to make it easier to work, and more importantly, to remove the air bubbles."

"What happens if we don't remove the bubbles?" asked Marcela, breaking her no-questions rule.

"The pot may explode in the kiln, destroying not only

itself, but lots of others."

Standing on a stool, Marcela followed Vera's example of slamming the clay on the bench, wedging it, cutting it with a wire, restacking and slamming.

"Now we can make something," said Vera.

Marcela wanted to use the pottery wheel immediately but Vera said she needed to become more familiar with the clay first. The wheel could come later.

"Native Americans didn't use a wheel," Vera said.

"Well, I'm mostly German."

Vera regarded the stubborn little face. "I was just saying that as a point of historical fact. We'll start with a pinch pot. That's how my father started me off. He said the reason some Native tribes made such beautiful pottery is that they held the clay the whole time."

"I bet Germans never pinched pots," muttered Marcela, glowering at the tennis-ball-sized piece of clay Vera held out to her.

"Roll your piece into a ball and make a depression in the middle with your thumb," Vera said, demonstrating with her own piece of clay. This prickly, German-obsessed child was easier to talk to today. "I've always wished I was mostly Navajo," she continued. "Their pottery is incredibly beautiful. Maybe in my next life. Now pinch like this." Using both hands, thumbs in the depression, Vera pinched the pot's walls, rotating the clay around and around as she pinched. "Make the walls as thin as you like. If you pinch through, roll it back into a ball and start again."

Marcela had to start over four times, but in the end she had a nicely formed pot, only a little thicker on the bottom than Vera's.

"Some people say a pinched pot has more soul," said Vera.

"That's because you're holding it the whole time so your soul can get in there," said Marcela. She cast a look at Vera and saw the woman was smiling.

Before Marcela left for the day, Vera offered her employment through the rest of the summer and maybe even in the afternoon after school started, unless she had team sports or playdates with friends.

"I'm almost eight. I don't *play* and I don't like *teams*," said Marcela, her voice dripping with disdain.

Chastised, Vera realized she should have respected the girl just as she presented herself. Playdate—even as she'd said it, Vera had cringed at the term.

Several weeks later, Marcela asked Heidi if Vera was going to have a baby because her tummy was looking bigger and bigger. Heidi told her yes, in a few months according to Ruth, but not to talk about it, unless Vera brought it up.

"Is it a secret?" asked Marcela. "Doesn't she want to have a baby?"

"I do not know what she wants, but Ruth has asked us to respect Vera's privacy, so we do."

Marcela gave Heidi such a grownup look that Heidi realized the secret they held themselves would ensure the girl's discretion about many things. But how sad, how very sad not to welcome and plan for the arrival of a new life.

CHAPTER THIRTY-THREE

WHAT IF?

On a cold night in the last week of September, the light from Vera's headlamps illuminated the wall opposite Heidi's bed. Grabbing her bathrobe, Heidi made it outside in time to see the taillights of Vera's truck disappearing into the dark, one light a brighter red than the other.

So Vera had decided to drive herself—Heidi wasn't surprised. She had felt Vera pulling back, shying away, and Rock Springs wasn't so far.

She turned when she heard the front door open. Marcela, barefoot and wearing a pink flannel nighty, came to stand next to her and said, through chattering teeth, "Where's Vera going? We were supposed to take her."

"She has decided to keep us at the arm length," said Heidi, drawing Marcela's shivering body close. "She will be okay. We will not worry."

"But what if she crashes?" asked Marcela. "We should follow her. What if she has to talk someone? You know how she gets all red and nervous."

"She will not crash," Heidi said.

Once back inside, Heidi put soymilk in a pan on the stove and Marcela retrieved cocoa and sugar from the cupboard. The girl dragged a kitchen chair close to the stove and perched with knees bent to her chin and her nighty drawn over her legs for warmth.

"What if her truck breaks down or the baby starts being born on the way and she's all by herself?" asked Marcela, watching Heidi measure cocoa into the milk.

"How hot would you like the milk?" asked Heidi.

"Hot," said Marcela, momentarily distracted by her toes; the purple nail polish Heidi had bought after refusing to allow her to wear make-up was beginning to peel off.

"Why aren't you answering me?" said Marcela, poking at Heidi's bottom with a pointy finger. "I said ... what if Vera goes off the road and goes unconscious and the baby dies?"

Heidi batted Marcela's finger away. "Vera is a sensible person. The baby is not due until next week. If Vera's labor already started, she would let us drive her, but she tells us last week she may leave early and stay next to the hospital to wait. We will respect her wish to be alone."

"But what if the truck goes off the road? What if she crashes and she's in a ditch and nobody comes and then she has the baby when she's in the ditch?" asked Marcela stubbornly. "And then they die. Both of them die, a baby can't do anything."

Marcela appeared to study her toes, but in her mind saw herself and Amadeus getting out of the car, leaving Mama behind the wheel, unmoving. But they hadn't been babies, they had been five and they had done something. They had crawled up the bank and stood in the dark on the gravelly side of the road, waiting for someone to stop and help. That Shit Sean didn't have a car, so they hadn't been afraid it would be him. They had waited for hours and hours before the first car appeared over the hill. The whole time they stood there, they looked down the bank to see Mama's face through the windshield, her head back, her eyes open a little bit.

Heidi had said the Highway Patrol thought a car came along in less than twenty minutes. Marcela scowled at her toes. *They* didn't know, no one knew, *they* hadn't been there, watching Mama not move for such a long, long time.

A baby would die if its mother crashed the car and it had to wait like they did, for hours and hours.

"Mein Schatz," said Heidi, gently tilting Marcela's head so the child would look up at her. "Listen to me. Vera will not crash. She will drive slowly and carefully and she will come home with a baby and then she will let us make the fuss. We do not get too big for our britches and follow her when she wants to be alone."

"What's going on?" Amadeus appeared in the kitchen doorway, his voice husky with sleep. His eyes narrowed to the light and he shook his hair out of his face. Gering sat trembling at his feet and looked up at Heidi and Marcela, his brown eyes moist and half-open.

"Why are you guys up?" Amadeus sniffed the air. "I want hot chocolate." At Heidi's look, he added, "Please."

"We wake up when Vera leaves to drive to Rock Springs where she is going to wait until her labor begins," answered Heidi. "She will be safe."

"Maybe safe," muttered Marcela, twisting a lock of her hair tightly around her finger.

Amadeus got the milk carton from the refrigerator and handed it to Heidi with a huge yawn. "A big cup *please*, and why's she going in the middle of the night? She's weird." Vera *was* weird. She had that thing about talking to strangers, especially men. If a man was around, she sometimes pretended she had a sore throat or something and wrote notes on that pad she kept in her pocket. She talked to Marcela mostly, then came Heidi, and he was last. She talked to Booker and Armand and Tyree little bit, so maybe she wasn't totally weird.

Amadeus looked at his sister's toes. "The purple's coming off. You should use red next time."

"Pink," said Marcela. "No ... green."

Gering stood up, opened his mouth, and a tiny sound came out. Heidi shooed the twins to their beds, saying Gering was cold and needed to be under someone's covers, she would bring the hot chocolate when it was done.

Heidi placed the drinks on a tray, stopping first at Amadeus's room. She sighed when she found his bed empty. No point in checking Marcela's room, it was going to be another of those nights when she wished she had followed social worker Lily Brown's advice and bought a king-sized bed.

Amadeus lay asleep on his stomach, legs splayed, head on her pillow. Gering was presumably the small lump under the covers nestled at his hip. Marcela sat upright next to her brother, shoulders hunched, long black hair obscuring most of her face. She had one foot out of the blankets and was about to add a flake of purple polish to the little pile on the nightstand.

She looked up guiltily. "I'm done, I didn't get any in the bed." She scooted over to make room for Heidi. "Amadeus farted. Boys are so stupid, and I don't know why you made him a cup of chocolate, he's asleep. He asked for a big cup and he always falls asleep."

"It is a blessing to fall asleep so easily," said Heidi, handing Marcela her cocoa and admonishing her not to spill. Before claiming her third of the bed, Heidi swept purple flakes into her hand and deposited them into the small wastebasket by the dresser.

"How long does it take for a baby to be born?" Marcela asked, examining the skin forming on the top of her drink.

"With Peter, we went to the hospital too early and they told us to go home," said Heidi.

Marcela flicked a glance—there it was, that smile that looked like it hurt whenever Aunt Heidi mentioned Peter. "Why did you go when it was too early?"

"We go when the contractions start, but when we get to the hospital they stop and the opening to the womb is still very small. We lived close to the hospital and they say when the contractions get stronger and closer together to come back.

Peter took twelve hours when we go back. Twelve hours is not so long for a first baby."

Heidi wrapped both hands around her cup and closed her eyes. She no longer remembered the pain of labor, just the warmth of her baby placed on her chest. She tried to forget that he had been taken from her almost immediately, an oxygen mask clamped to his tiny face.

"That's too long." Marcela scowled into her cocoa. "That's like longer than a whole day at school. It's longer than breakfast to dinner. All he had to do was go from your tummy to the outside."

"It is the womb or uterus, not the tummy," Heidi corrected, causing Marcela to roll her eyes.

"Your voice gets funny when you talk about Peter," said Marcela.

"I know."

"But you have us now," Marcela said, bumping her head against Heidi's shoulder for emphasis and causing both of them to slosh their drinks.

CHAPTER THIRTY-FOUR

LEO

Vera had told Heidi she was going to deliver in Rock Springs but she left Comfrey just after ten P.M. and drove the three hours to Riverton instead. Arriving in town, she pulled into a Walmart Supercenter and headed directly for the restroom. As she sat on the toilet, she felt herself grinning at the sheer pleasure of voiding her bladder. She pulled her XXL t-shirt down tight over the purple stretch marks that snaked their way across the enormous belly that rested itself on her thighs.

She sat a couple of extra minutes to practice the technique Betty Ann had taught her. 'Project yourself beyond your difficultly, Vera, and see how strong and well you are,' the old lady used to counsel in her firm and gentle way.

Eyes closed, Vera imagined herself a month from now. She stood in the meadow where the stream from Wild Horse Valley descended toward Comfrey. Slender once more and strong, her face to the sun, she heard the babble of the water, the whisper of wind, she smelled the rose geraniums someone had long ago planted by the stream. Perhaps the slipper orchids would still be in bloom.

She got up from the toilet slowly to avoid dizziness. What she hadn't been able to imagine was a baby in her arms.

Vera braced herself with her hands on the restroom sink and waited to catch her breath before washing her hands. The bathroom mirror was covered by plywood, which was a relief. She dried her hands on a rough paper towel and tossed it on top of a pile of towels in an overly full trashcan. Her towel teetered a moment before falling to join a number of its brethren littering the floor. Vera regarded its crumpled form with a moue. She'd never left her trash for someone else to pick up in her life, but this time had to be different. If she tried to retrieve it, she'd pitch forward, right onto her front, an enormously pregnant woman wallowing on the floor of an almost deserted Walmart at 1:20 in the morning.

Leaning heavily on her cart, Vera headed toward a large yellow sign suspended from the ceiling over the infant's section, miles away. She bought a diaper bag, a package of six tiny white onesies, and three receiving blankets. She managed to wrestle a car seat into her cart. She paused in front of the socks before deciding a newborn didn't really need socks, and headed for the stacks of disposable diapers.

Cherubs smiled at her from white plastic packages of twenty-four, thirty-six, forty-eight, one hundred and twenty-eight diapers. White babies, always blond, Asian babies, black babies. The black baby had the brightest twinkle to its eye, so Vera selected his package of thirty-six, although she might not even need a dozen.

Exhausted, she halted, wondering if she should head all the way back to the restrooms when she was now so close to the checkout registers. The motel was close, her truck was close—through the store's front doors, she could just make it out illegally parked in a handicapped spot, another first.

The lone cashier waved from a register, calling her over in a friendly fashion, so Vera pushed her cart forward.

"When ya due? Yesterday?" The girl grinned at Vera, light flashing off her purple-rimmed glasses. She looked to be about fourteen.

"Next week," said Vera.

"Oooo, nearly there. You're small, like I was, small for all my babies. This your first?"

Vera nodded, faintly amused that this child, who'd apparently whelped a brood, had called her 'small.'

The girl adjusted her glasses and chuckled knowingly. "Just getting your essentials now, right?" she asked. "I was in denial 'bout my first too. Couldn't believe I was going to have to actually go through the whole pushing a pumpkin through your you-know-what. Like how's a baby gonna fit through that? And he was late, like by two weeks almost. Lotta first babies late, but he was *ridiculous*. Then after my labor started, he didn't make his grand entrance 'til the next day. My other two, like boom, boom boom, Indy 500."

"Are you saying they were born really fast, or that they were on time?" Vera asked the experienced mother of three, who now looked to be a little older than fourteen.

"Well, both I guess, but with my first? When he was just refusing to get goin'? I *kinda* thought, that maybe it was all just a big joke, like maybe he wouldn't come at all. Not really, but maybe he was just a big old tumor that they'd have to cut out, throw in the trash or grind up."

The cashier adjusted her glasses, caught Vera's grimace, and added quickly, "I'm sayin' if he was a *tumor*, not a baby. He's a good kid, not a tumor at all." She rang up the final item. "Credit or debit?"

"Cash," said Vera, handing over five twenties.

The cashier counted them carefully and tucked them under her drawer. Not bothering to count back the change, she handed Vera some coins and a fistful of ones. "I've asked people but...well, you look educated, so maybe you'll know." She looked at Vera hopefully. "What do they do with all that stuff they cut out of you? You know? You ever wonder about that?"

"I think it's either incinerated—burned—or sometimes it may be used for research," said Vera, beginning to push her cart forward.

"Hey, wait a sec', I mean I just wanna say, I *knew* it. Hubby's brother said they made it into dog food, like in Korea or something. Didn't believe him for one second, he blames everything on the Koreans, but he read that somewhere. Are you a nurse?"

"No, I'm a potter," said Vera, again starting to push her cart.

"Hang on, a potter? You make pots and like that?"

"Like that." Vera nodded.

"Well, that's cool I guess," said the cashier doubtfully, perhaps wondering if a potter would really know how human body parts were disposed of. "Hang on a seccy while I lock my drawer and I'll walk you out," she said. As a mother, she had more to say.

"Like I was tellin' you," she said, slowing down Vera's cart by holding onto the side, "I didn't have a thing ready for my first baby. His name's Johnny by the way, for 'Mr. Johnny-Come-Late-to-the Party.' You pick out a name yet?"

Vera shook her head.

"Yeah well, Baby's gonna *do* something or *look* like something and you'll figure it out. But like I was sayin', I didn't have a single, solitary nuttin' for Johnny. Hubby's family don't believe in baby showers, say they're bad luck, tempting the devil and like that. It's all 'don't count your chickens 'til they're all hatched out' with them, and I don't have family beyond his. Anybody throw you a shower?"

Vera smiled and shook her head.

The glass doors swung open with a hiss, and the cashier leapt forward to right the car seat as it threatened to topple. "I'd walk you to your car but they don't let us out," she said apologetically, keeping her feet just inside the threshold. "But I'm just sayin' from the bottom of my heart, that you're doin' real good. You got the basics now, and Baby's not even due 'til next week. And who needs a baby shower? People will give you plenty of stuff they didn't like or their babies grew out of."

"Thank you," said Vera. "You are very kind."

"And *you* are *very* welcome." The cashier gave a formal little bow from the doorway. "And congratulations in advance. Hope you bring that baby by. I work graveyard and it's dead quiet."

Her voice followed Vera to the curb, "With Johnny? I made Hubby stop on the way to the hospital, and it wasn't even a Walmart, so we couldn't get our discount."

When Vera had phoned to make a reservation at the Prong Horn Inn, the motel closest to the hospital, she had intended to book for two weeks at a discounted weekly rate, which she assumed would be much more than enough time. She had extended the booking to three weeks when the brisk young voice on the phone offered an even greater daily discount, assuring her prices could be adjusted should she need to shorten or lengthen her stay.

Her map had deceived her and it took longer to get to the Prong Horn than Vera had anticipated. The motel loomed, two stories on one side, three on the other. She hadn't thought to ask for a downstairs room. She stepped out of the truck into air heavily infused with chlorine from the kidney-shaped pool in the middle of the parking lot. Through the bars of a high, black metal fence, she could see turquoise water glowing with a surreal underwater light. The pool lit the surrounding white plastic lounge chairs from beneath, one lay on its side, another partially submerged on its back in the shallow end, its legs protruding into the air like a giant bug.

A neon pronghorn antelope stood on the roof of the office, its tail flicking up and down with an irritating electrical hum. Through the window Vera could see a young night clerk sitting behind a desk. Male. She forced a smile to her face and opened the door.

The young man checked his computer screen and looked up at Vera with a face so shiny, it might have been coated with

Vaseline. "Ms. McNabb?" he asked.

Vera nodded and pointed to her throat. She opened and closed her mouth, shaking her head with a grimace. "Lost your voice? Laryngitis? Bummer," he said sympathetically. "Had it last week, still have a little tickle. Driver's license?" He held out his hand, his eyes widening as they traveled to her belly. "Pregnant too? Man, double, triple bummer."

Vera shrugged in a 'what can you do?' manner and he grinned. "Yeah, really. I have *five* sisters, so I know. Two of them knocked up—excuse me, *impregnated,* in high school. All still living at home with the folks, but, whatever, family's family."

He paused and examined Vera closely. "You look like you're plenty old so I'm not saying you didn't know what's up," he said apologetically. "And ..." he drew out the word and rapidly typed into his computer, "I'm thinking we'll change you to a downstairs room," he said. "How's that?"

Vera gave him a grateful smile and he sat up a little straighter. This was his second night on the job, he informed her. Would she mind if he just read off his checklist? He took her nod as permission and picked up a laminated page. He asked her if she would need an extra key or if she had any valuables to store in the safe. He informed her that swimming or lounging by the pool was limited to the hours between nine A.M. and eleven P.M., there was no lifeguard on duty and no food or running was allowed in the pool area.

He winked at her belly and grinned up at her. "You get the part about *no running*?"

She managed a smile and shifted uncomfortably. She nodded at him to keep going, she needed a bathroom.

"Sure, sure," he said, running his finger down the list to find his place. "Coffee, tea, orange juice, and Danish are available in the office between seven A.M. and eleven." He paused and looked up. "We have real half-and-half, by the way, and the coffee is unlimited, but we request you limit yourself to two pastries."

Vera nodded vigorously and raised her eyebrows. She *really* had to use a bathroom.

"Gotcha, probably have to pee, excuse me, *urinate*. My sisters had to *urinate* it seemed like every ten minutes, when they got close. And let me just say, you can't take a pregnant girl on a long car ride." He grinned at her, one adult to another. "But what am I telling you for, right?"

He went back to his list. "Sooo ... let me see, tokens for the washing machines? Yeah, here we are, tokens are available right here at the office, and if you need extra blankets or towels, let us know. We have sample menus for your perusal and recommendations for your entertainment, including riding stables, jeep rides, and nightlife. Wind River Casino, one hundred percent Arapaho owned, two miles south on 729."

He looked away from his list and added enthusiastically, "It's the biggest casino in Wyoming, my cousin heard of a guy who won ten thousand quarters at the slots, last week. Insisted on keeping it as quarters, made them put 'em in sacks and just walked out with them. Must have weighed a ton. And, by the way, the All-You-Can-Eat is outstanding, I highly recommend it."

Vera exhaled loudly and he looked back at his list, "Okay. And finally ... if another guest books on your recommendation, you'll receive a twenty-five percent discount on your next stay. And we are *done*," he said, finishing with a flourish.

He took a key off a pegboard and jostled it in his hand. "Thanks for listening, I really mean it," he said earnestly. "The guy before you was pretty rude, stopped me right after the valuables in the safe, and guess what? Bet he's out there tomorrow morning before nine, eating, dropping food all over, watching his kids running around the pool. I'll be off by then so I'm glad I won't have to see it."

After using the bathroom, Vera went back to her truck. She

hung the few outfits she'd brought in the closet, the diaper bag with its baby things might as well stay in the truck. Tomorrow she'd unpack the car seat, figure out how to strap it in, and get rid of the box.

She filled the plastic ice bucket from a machine that sweated and shuddered under the stairs near the end of the building. An giggle wafted through the screen of a partially open window as she passed, but most of the rooms were dark and heavy with slumber, not surprising at 3:15 a.m.

Returning to her room, she brushed her hair into a soft auburn cloud, washed her face, brushed her teeth, filled a glass with water, and looked around for something to use as a coaster. She picked up a garish pamphlet from the desk next to the television, a handsome, laughing couple sat at a gaming table, a phalanx of newly-made best friends beaming behind them. Winners all.

As Vera folded the pamphlet in half, she noticed, written in a whisper of elegant script across the bottom, the number for a hotline for those experiencing 'the *psychological, physical, social and vocational disruptions of problem gambling.*'

Betty Ann would have certainly said to these suffering souls, *'The Lord giveth and the Lord taketh away.'* Betty Ann had liberally sprinkled words from The Book of Job over many of life's travails.

Vera placed her water glass on its coaster and turned the television on. She flipped through channels until she found a PBS special on marsupials. A baby kangaroo the size of a small fawn was attempting to squeeze itself back into its mother's pouch as the commentator said with a nasal Australian twang, "Mind you, just when Mum thinks she's free, this little joey has other ideas. Never too old to snuggle back inside."

"Idiot," said Vera to the screen. A female commentator wouldn't have made that comment. "No snuggling back inside for you, Baby," she muttered, her hand resting on her distended abdomen.

"A human inside a human, a cat inside a cat, a rabbit inside a rabbit," Vera said as she sat down heavily on the bed. The mantra had come to her soon after she realized she was pregnant. The words had helped her make peace with the being growing inside her. Did a cat or a rabbit give a first or second thought to the life within, or the circumstances of its conception?

"Thaaat's it. Good on you, mate," the commentator chuckled as the little joey finally managed to fit most of himself back into his mother's pouch, leaving only the lower portion of his hind legs sticking out to the side at a rakish angle, like enormous hat feathers.

With an exhausted sigh, Vera lay down and rested her hands on her belly, waiting for a kick or the thrust of an arm against her uterine wall. Strangers at the hospital would do their job and deliver the baby. Then the two of them, a baby and the woman who'd birthed it, would be sent on their way. She tried to say to herself, 'a mother and her son,' but she couldn't.

For a few weeks, Vera had considered Heidi's offer to drive her to the hospital. But what if the baby was repellent? She couldn't possibly keep him then. What if he looked like a complete stranger? The sonogram showed a boy—a girl might have been easier.

If Heidi had come, and the children probably, if they knew where she was and they stayed to bring her home, she wouldn't be able to leave the baby at a police station or a fire station in town in Utah or Colorado. She had given this baby life but she might not be able to do more than that. Someone else could love and raise him. She would return to Comfrey and say the baby had died. She would have to endure their sympathy, the small number of people who were aware of her pregnancy, but everyone would be anxious to help her forget there'd ever been a baby. They wouldn't keep bringing him up.

Vera hoisted herself off the bed and made her way to the bathroom again, the light from the television illuminating her elephantine body in the mirror along the wall. She returned to bed and curled onto her side. She clamped her hand over her ear, trying to keep at bay the dark and hairy voice that had visited every night for the past thirty-nine weeks as she dropped off to sleep.

And once sleep has descended, he enters her dreams and stakes his claim.

The dream's main event, which took just a few minutes, plays over and over, and often she doesn't wake for the better part of an hour.

The event's preamble varies in length. Sometimes it begins earlier in the day as she's delivering boxes of bubble-wrapped, pit-fired pots to three downtown galleries in Casper. Friendly, helpful people welcome her, grateful she's come to restock her popular wares. Sometimes the preamble starts later, as she drives down a broad and dusty street in the industrial district. She is seeking a small business that has advertised a used kiln for sale.

Broken buildings, crumbling concrete with twisted re-bar protruding like tentacles, offer little shade. She parks. Always, the dream includes the wind playfully tossing wrappers, always she hears the hollow sound of the empty aluminum can that bounces and rolls ahead of her. Then a darkness falls; this is the part of the dream that expands and contracts, this is the main reason the dream takes so much longer than the deed itself.

The darkness pauses, waits, then the dream may reboot and she is again driving down the broad and dusty street, parking and locking the car, the wind, the wrappers, the bouncing, rolling can, the darkness, the pause, the waiting. Another reboot? But the moment she steps into the alley, the dream launches itself forward.

How had she been so unaware?

Suddenly, so suddenly, with no warning, without a vibration to the air, without a smell or a shadow, his strong hand grips the back of her head as if it were a melon. He presses her cheek against the mustard-colored, stuccoed wall. His other hand does the rest, unsnaps her jeans, pulls them down. He positions her hips to an angle where he can enter her from behind. His meaty fingers probe her first, tentative, exploring. She smells his sweat, his salty, oily sweat.

He rests a firm, rotund belly against her, his fingers leave her, a grunt followed by the sound of the teeth of his zipper parting. A penis, held in a hand that is the companion to the one that immobilizes her head, pushes into her. She feels no pain, she feels nothing, but later she will find blood.

"I'm sorry, I'm sorry," he rasps as he thrusts into her, a 'sorry' for each thrust. His breath is warm and moist upon her neck. He finishes and she stands absolutely still, her eyes squeezed shut, her face remains against the wall, her cheek scraped raw, a sticky fluid leaking down between her legs.

She almost laughs when he says, "Stay quiet, no screaming, I'll watch you. I'll kill you if you scream." As if she could, as if she *could* make a sound.

If it's a good night, the dream stops here, on a bad night, the dream continues. She walks from the alley, an automaton. She stands with her head pressed to her truck window, craving the safety inside, unable to find her keys. She must return to the alley. She can't remember—were the keys in her pocket, her hand? A low grey creature scuttles before her as she walks, looking for a sign this is where it happened. Under a dark mark, blood on the wall from the abrasions to her face, the keys lie crumpled on the ground.

After the dream releases her, she wakes drenched in sweat and gasping for breath. She places her hand on her throat. It is familiar, this contracture that hardens her vocal cords. It visited her after the immolation of her family sixteen years before, now it steals her voice when she attempts to speak to men.

She lies in the dark wondering how she could have been ... how she could have been so *completely* unaware. Later in the night will come the dream of her return to Betty Ann's house, a sanctuary now devoid of Betty Ann. She roams the house, leaving the lights off, pulling the curtains, showering, washing, scrubbing, changing the towels each time she dries herself, unable to get clean.

Vera knew if Betty Ann had still been alive when she returned from Casper, ravaged, defiled, unable to speak, they would have negotiated doctors and the police, together. Betty Ann would have comforted her, turning to the Book of Job, the King James version of course. She would have urged Vera to have faith and not to question why the Lord had heaped another suffering upon her.

Betty Ann would have closed her faded eyes in concentration—she liked to get things right. She would have skipped right to the end of Job, and quoted in her reedy voice, "*So the LORD blessed the latter end of Job more than his beginning... fourteen thousand sheep, and six thousand camels, and a thousand yoke of oxen, and a thousand she asses.*" Then with eyes open, her gnarled hand on Vera's head, Betty Ann would have promised, "And, Vera honey, we can forget about all this livestock business, but the Lord is promising our faith will be repaid. He has his plan."

Vera prayed the Lord's plan included taking away these dreams after the baby arrived. She hadn't thought she would die in that alley in Casper. She hadn't died in the fire that had consumed her parents and baby brother. But would it really matter if she had died, either time?

Betty Ann would have said God and Satan weren't done with their game of testing her yet.

To Vera's relief, the human inside the human decided not

to take the option of being a late first baby and her water broke with a gush of pale yellow liquid in the shower during her third day at the Prong Horn. "Oh God," she gasped when she thought she'd shed it all. What better place than in the shower?

She'd bought *The Essential Pregnancy Guide: from Conception to Birth* at a second-hand bookshop in Rock Springs, the only time she'd gone to a clinic to be checked by a doctor. The book had predicted that some labor pains would precede this rush of amniotic fluid, but they hadn't.

"Water breaks, they keep you," she said aloud as she dried herself and dressed. At least now, if she arrived at the hospital, they wouldn't tell her to come back later. She found stationary in the desk drawer and wrote in block letters, 'I AM MUTE. MY WATER BROKE.' She might be able to speak, even if the doctor was a man, but it would be easier not to. There was such comfort in her silent world.

Vera returned to the bathroom to collect an extra towel to place on the seat of the truck in case she leaked. She put a pair of drawstring pants, underwear, and a sweatshirt in a tote bag, and opened the motel room door to chlorine and the happy cries of children chasing each other around the pool in the center of the parking lot.

When the nurses at the hospital tapped her on the shoulder to get her attention every time they were about to speak to her in their loud, precise voices, she realized they assumed she was deaf as well as mute. She shook her head when offered an epidural. The book said an epidural often delayed labor and she wanted her body back.

In one chapter, women had described their experiences with labor, the intense stabbing pain, the dull cramping, the disbelief that an immense child could make its way down a passage so narrow, but no one had mentioned the crushing pressure in her abdomen and back. She made no sound beyond panting, no grunting, not a squeal. She strained, bore down, relaxed, pushed, pushed, vomited twice. The nurses were kind, placing cold cloths on her head, tapping her on the shoulder, and mouthing encouraging words. She was doing well; it had only been three hours but it wouldn't be long now. They told her of the joy she would feel when they placed her baby on her chest. She wouldn't remember the pain once her baby lay there, skin to skin.

With a final massive push, Vera felt the baby pull away. A nurse laughed with delight, the baby's cries filled the room, and Vera closed her eyes tight, afraid to look when the loaf-sized, naked form was placed on her. The nurse shook Vera's shoulder until she opened her eyes.

"Take a look at your son, look how beautiful, I've never seen such a head of hair," said the nurse, exaggerating the movement of her lips. She took Vera's hand, placed it on the baby's head.

Vera looked down tentatively, opening her eyes wide in shock. She felt her tears break then ... not a stranger. She *knew* him, this baby who waved his fists in the air and roared, this baby with his mane of tawny hair. McNabb hair, she'd seen it over the generations in the family photographs that had burned in the fire. She looked down into the face of her baby brother.

"No doubt who this baby belongs to," said the nurse, smiling at Vera. "Does his daddy have hair like the two of you?"

"Have you seen the head of hair on the deaf woman's baby?" Vera heard one nurse say to another in the hall several hours later.

"Hush, not so loud, she hears. What made you think she doesn't hear?" said the other, almost as loudly. "She just can't talk, not all people who can't talk are deaf. The doctor says her throat's real tight, that maybe it's an emotional thing."

"Emotional? How's someone so emotional that she can't talk going to parent a baby?" the first nurse asked.

"Keep your voice down, she's okay. She doesn't *seem* emotional," said her companion. "The doctor alerted Social Services, you know, like he has to when something's off, but they say she's good. Very calm and competent. And you see *her* hair. My God, what I wouldn't give, and she put his name down as 'Leo.' A perfect little lion with a mane like that."

CHAPTER THIRTY-FIVE

THREE WHITE COTTON HANDKERCHIEFS

Vera found Bakari Silberstein's address while poking through a drawer looking for stamps. It was on the envelope of a sympathy card that he had sent when Betty Ann died. Vera waited another week before writing her letter. Leo had just turned three months old.

She started the letter the way most letters begin. She inquired about Bakari's health, she stated she was well, her business was good. She congratulated Bakari on his new book, she had read it and found it very interesting.

The baby cried from his room and she ended her letter quickly. *"For a while I lost my voice again, but mostly to men this time. I'm better now, but I need to tell someone how I came to have a son. His name is Leo. I want to love him but I need help. Will you be visiting your aunt anytime soon?"*

His aunt always emailed, so it had been several years since he'd received a letter from Wyoming. Bakari didn't recognize the writing on the envelope but the return address was Betty Ann's. It would be from Vera.

Bakari read the letter several times before picking up the phone. Vera had left Betty Ann's greeting on the answering machine and it was a shock to hear his old friend's voice again. His aunt was due a visit, he said in his message, and he would like to meet Leo. His agent had promised to release him from his book tour obligations soon—he would phone again with a date.

When Betty Ann was alive, Bakari habitually took a day to visit Comfrey when he visited his aunt in Pinedale. His friendship with Betty Ann had deepened through the letters they shared. Her thank you for the book he had sent on African folk tales, his thank you for the book on Irish wolfhounds. She had become a Grandmother—the only one of his Grandmothers who wrote and sent cards. They corresponded monthly, Betty Ann ruing the corruption of their political leaders, railing against educational inequality, Bakari questioning if America had an impenetrable upper class, if college was for everyone. They shared stories of their childhoods, they pondered an afterlife, reincarnation, the physical reality of heaven.

Betty Ann's death came without warning. Pneumonia, devoted visitor of the aged, had stolen her in a heartbeat. His aunt had notified him after seeing Betty Ann's obituary in the newspaper. There would be no more letters with the colorful commemorative stamps Betty Ann favored, just emails with colleagues, no more acerbic commentaries on the state of the world, just lectures to give, treatments to debate, papers to pen.

He had felt the loss of his old friend acutely but he had taken some comfort in the thought of Betty Ann joining her Ralph at the hand of a loving God; a forgiving God she had almost gotten him to believe in.

When Vera answered the door, Bakari was surprised to see she'd gathered her masses of hair at the nape of her neck with a scarf. As a child she had hidden behind that hair. Although she couldn't be more than twenty-five, the years had stamped their wear upon her features, but her face seemed the stronger for it, her mouth resolute. Her eyes were guarded—she would be doubting her decision to contact him—but with her hair back, she was exposing herself to him. The sleeves of her green turtleneck, a hint of clay on the cuffs, were shoved to her elbows, revealing the muscular forearms of a potter. Her jeans were spotless.

Three years after Betty Ann's death, he hadn't expected to be back, sitting in her garden, surrounded by her calendulas, bright yellow, hardy, and dependable. The baby slept on a blanket in dappled sunlight. When Vera excused herself to make the tea, Bakari crouched by the child. He wasn't someone who found all babies pleasing to look at, but this one was. His face was unusual, a broad nose, pale lips, tawny springy hair like his mother's. His lashes were thick, blond, and lay on his cheeks like caterpillars. Bakari restrained the impulse to touch them. The baby rolled his head, punched the air with his pudgy dimpled fists, grimaced, burped, and quieted.

He took his seat when he saw Vera returning with tea on a tray.

"In my village, we would have said your son has the blood of a lion," he said, accepting the cup she offered. "You named him Leo. You have seen it too?"

"It is the coloring," said Vera.

Bakari laughed. "Oh, let us hope it will be more than that."

She looked at him uncertainly. "More than what?"

He shrugged off her question and blew on his tea. Steam rose like smoke from its surface and he cautiously took a sip.

"Very nice," he said. It was Prince of Wales, mild, lyrical with a slightly woody flavor. Both he and Betty Ann had agreed it was the best of the Twining teas, and apparently Vera remembered it was their favorite.

They sat quietly—he tired from his journey, she most certainly wishing he hadn't come. He glanced at her face and the set of her mouth and said gently, "I have come to hear the story of your son."

He doubted she would be prepared for the tears that were sure to come if she shared her story honestly. In his office he had Kleenex of course, but a person couldn't carry a box of Kleenex to someone's door. He hoped the three white cotton handkerchiefs he carried in his pocket would be enough.

She started mechanically. She had been raped, she said, pausing as if waiting for his exclamation. Leo had been rape's legacy.

"I am listening," Bakari said quietly.

It had happened almost a year and a half ago; she took a shuddering breath and continued. She had gotten over the worst of it. She slept fairly well now, ate well, she worked and tended the baby. She had, for the most part, regained her ability to talk to men. She stopped, raised her eyebrows, and gave him a tight smile.

After a prolonged pause, he said, "I see, but then you wrote to me."

Yes, like she had said in her letter, she had read his most recent book about women raising children conceived during the violence of war. How did they do it? How did a mother learn to love a child conceived through rape?

A slight darkening of the sky. A large black bird passed over them as it swept down from a pine. It alit on a Thornberry bush and examined the baby on his blanket. Vera stood and took a step, the bird tilted its head and watched her with its bright, intelligent eyes. It dipped its head, opened its black beak, and emitted a series of clapping, clicking sounds as it fluttered his throat. Vera turned and she and Bakari shared a smile. They both had expected the harsh sound of a caw, but this sound was more pleasing.

Vera returned to her seat at the bird's departure, and the momentary pleasure faded from her eyes.

"Vera," Bakari said, and she shook her head. "You need to speak of the rape." She shook her head again. "Vera?" he pressed.

"It is over, I don't think about it anymore," she said, untying her scarf and releasing her hair.

"You wrote to me," he said.

She inhaled deeply, put a hand to her throat, willing her muscles to relax. She started with a description of the alley in Casper. Where else to begin? The alley, dark, narrow, littered with paper, brought back the sweaty stench of his body and his fumbling, clumsy, meaty hands, the thrust of him in her, the coarse heat of his breath.

Unbelievably, because the actual act was surely so much more horrific, it was memories of the waves of loneliness and despair that had drenched her as she gave birth among strangers in a hospital that released her tears. She hadn't expected to cry. When the rapist stole her voice and planted a seed that grew in her belly for forty weeks, she had endured most of it without shedding tears. She had hardly cried since Porky's Dog died, the year before pneumonia stole Betty Ann with such astonishing rapidity.

Bakari pressed a handkerchief into her hand. She had feared she'd recoil from the sight of her child, she said—he would be stranger she would be forced to abandon to social services. They would have surely found him a good home. But he had looked like her baby brother and she thought maybe she would grow to love him—but it hadn't happened. She accepted a second handkerchief.

By the time Marcela found them in the backyard, Vera's tears had dried and the third cotton handkerchief lay damp in her hand.

Marcela introduced herself to Bakari as Leo's babysitter. She glanced at the sleeping baby. "*Ich kann es nicht glauben.* You shouldn't let him sleep so long, he won't sleep tonight." She gathered the baby up and looked at Vera critically. "Don't give Leo your cold," she said. "I'll tell Heidi to send over *Hühnersuppe.*"

With a cursory wave to Bakari, she took Leo into the house for a change and a bottle.

"A purposeful young lady," remarked Bakari. "How old is she?"

"Nine. She lives across the street."

"Do you know what she said, the foreign words?"

"German. The first was one of her favorites, something along the lines of 'I can't believe it!' A lot of things exasperate Marcela. The second was 'chicken soup.'"

"Beloved worldwide, the cure for all that ails," said Bakari.

It was time to decompress, to focus on something beyond the rape. Her answers would give him a sense of how far she would be able to heal.

"Tell me about this Native American child who speaks German," he said.

"She's Arapaho, when she's not being German," said Vera. When talking to and about Marcela, her words came easily. "She and her twin brother are being raised by a very German aunt," she said, relieved Bakari's focus had turned from her to her neighbors. "I hired Marcela to help in the studio when they moved in. I was pregnant and needed help. She's young, I know, but she asked for the job. Her aunt thought it was a good idea."

"What's the brother like?" Bakari asked.

"Amadeus is almost as tough as his sister." Vera smiled. "He won't speak German. He's fluent in Arapaho; he never lost it from early days with his grandfather. He was the favored child, according to Marcela. She says Amadeus speaks Arapaho to their mother, who visits in the wind. The mother died when they were five."

"The mother doesn't talk to Marcela?"

Vera shook her head.

Bakari shut his eyes to envision the image of a boy talking to his mother on the wind—a mother the daughter refused to hear. Interesting.

"And the aunt?" he said when he opened his eyes.

"She had a baby who died young, cystic fibrosis I think.

She divorced, moved to Riverton. She became the twins' guardian after their mother died. She changed her last name to match theirs. When they arrived in Comfrey, the school had a hair length limit for boys. Amadeus has always had hair as long as his sister's. Heidi threatened a lawsuit. The school relented, now all three native boys at the school wear their hair long."

"Progress can be slow, sometimes it takes an immigrant to give it a kick in the butt," said Bakari.

Vera smiled—she'd find a way of mentioning to Heidi she was a butt-kicking immigrant.

"You said were considering moving. How do you feel about leaving these neighbors?" asked Bakari.

"Not good. But a fresh start, away from questions about Leo, might be a relief. The lot where my family's house caught fire still hasn't been built on, the foundation just sits there."

"The fire was nearly twenty ago, Betty Ann has been dead for three, yet you stayed because *her* house is *your* house. This family ..."

"The Crows," Vera supplied.

"The Crows, do you think the Crows intend to stay in Comfrey?"

Vera nodded. "Heidi owns a restaurant in town, she has a boyfriend, man-friend I mean. The children like him. They're doing well in school."

"About the prying questions people ask about Leo, you know, Vera, you are not obligated to explain him to anyone. Your history is yours alone to share as you wish. Do the Crows press you with questions?"

Vera shook her head. "They have their own secrets, we respect each other's privacy."

"Then think of what you'll lose if you move," Bakari cautioned. "Neighbors who respect your privacy, yet make you chicken soup, are not so common. You and Leo need the Crows and young Marcela will be devastated if you leave. Living for other people is not a bad way to live."

At the door they shook hands; they were not people who derived pleasure from a casual hug. Both were tired but they had lanced an abscess so healing could begin. Tomorrow would be better, the next day more so.

As Bakari drove back to Pinedale in his aunt's car, he allowed images to float gently on the surface of his mind. It was a technique his adopted father had taught him when he needed help keeping the horror of his childhood at bay.

He needed to step back from Vera's story now, and he allowed one image to replace another—Betty Ann with her twinkling eyes, Vera sitting by the fountain with Porky's Dog, a Mexican sage tiara dancing over his brow, a baby with a lion's coloring being picked up by a determined little Arapaho girl, her twin brother speaking to his mother in the wind. The wind, the elders of his village would have approved. Betty Ann, Vera, Porky's Dog, Leo, the twins ....

Fodder for a new book. A work of fiction? Only partially— he'd use a pseudonym; any similarity to actual people and events would be coincidental.

CHAPTER THIRTY-SIX

FALLING IN LOVE WITH LEO

Her response to her son didn't change in the days after Bakari Silberstein's visit, but the relief of being told that leaving Comfrey was perhaps not the best move brought comfort. She would be a competent parent. Marcela had enough affectionate parenting for both of them. When Vera had asked Marcela how she knew so much about baby care, Marcela had rolled her eyes and said, "Your magazines. The ones Aunt Heidi gave you a subscription to and I'm telling her you don't read them."

Parenthood arrived every single month, a gift from Heidi that Vera hadn't yet found the time to read. "I do look through them," Vera had replied.

"Then why don't you know more?" Marcela had demanded. "Like you're supposed to hold him more."

"He likes his baby seat and his animals." Vera's protest had sounded half-hearted even to her own ears.

"And you're supposed to talk to him more. It'll make his brain bigger. You don't want him to grow up and be ..." Marcela had closed her eyes as if seeking a phrase from *Parenthood*. "We don't want him to be *emotionally disabled*," she had finished triumphantly.

When Vera told Heidi that Marcela appeared to get a great deal of satisfaction out of telling her how to be Leo's mother, Heidi said Marcela was born with a strong maternal instinct, other women had to learn the hard way.

As the edges of night faded to gunmetal grey, Leo emitted his first cry of the day. Vera rolled over and groaned. She checked the clock—6:02, today promised to be like all the others.

A typical morning consisted of feeding Leo, bathing Leo, doing laundry for Leo, an hour of housework, and an hour of gardening with Leo nearby on a blanket. At one o'clock, Leo went down for a nap and Vera escaped into her studio. She left the baby safe in his crib as long as she could, but made sure to have him up, changed, and propped in his baby seat in the kitchen before Marcela arrived after school to liberate them both. Vera knew better than to have Marcela find the baby lying upstairs, alone and fretful.

She pulled a sweatshirt on over her pajamas and walked down the hall to the baby's room in her woolen socks. She turned on the overhead light and Leo stopped mid-howl. They blinked at each other as she leaned over the crib.

"It's Tuesday," she said, picking him up. Talk to him more, Marcela said.

Vera sighed as she felt the damp sheet beneath him.

"You have soaked through your diaper again. Marcela says we should be buying special overnight diapers," she said. She changed him and stripped his bed.

In the kitchen, Vera strapped Leo into his baby seat and pushed it to the middle of the table. She gave the colorful plastic animals arranged along the horizontal bar in front of the chair a spin. The baby grabbed for them but they were just out of his reach.

"But if we hope for what we do not yet have, we wait for it patiently," Vera said, quoting one of Betty Ann's bible verses, Romans 8:25. That didn't sound very encouraging, so she added, "Someday your arms will be long enough to reach for the stars."

There, Marcela would like that, positive parenting. Vera sighed, talk, talk, talk, all this talking felt so foreign to her. She frowned at Leo and he frowned back. She gave the animals another spin.

"Just trying to appease little Miss Crow," she said as she went to turn on the radio. The sensible voices of the people at KUWZ, the public radio station out of Rock Springs, were a comfort, and the radio would stay on until evening, whether she was in the kitchen or not.

"Going to get the newspaper," she said to the baby as she headed down the hall.

The newspaper had landed once again in the hedge that separated her yard from her neighbor's. Vera took off her socks so they wouldn't get wet and picked her way across the damp grass, trying to avoid the litter of prickly leaves from a variegated English Holly. Despite her ministrations for tar spot, the tree continued to drop its leaves at an alarming rate. Looking over the hedge, she saw her neighbor's newspaper had landed neatly outside his front door.

Vera heard Leo working himself up in the kitchen as she reentered the house. She grabbed her socks and wiped her feet hurriedly on the hall rug.

Dangling the socks in front of Leo, she said, "Socks. The newspaper landed in the bushes again, and now I'm going to put my socks ..." she gave them a little shake, "back on my cold, cold feet."

Vera periodically gave the plastic animals a spin as she started the coffee maker and measured out Leo's powdered formula, stirring it carefully as she added water so it didn't clump. When their beverages were ready, she sat at the table and held Leo's bottle with her right hand, checking the angle periodically so he didn't ingest air, while she awkwardly used her left to pick up her coffee cup and flip through the pages of the newspaper.

After breakfast and bathing Leo in the kitchen sink, they

went upstairs so she could take her shower. Leo was still unable roll over or sit up unaided, so she put him in the middle of her bed where he would be perfectly safe.

She watched the baby from the bathroom doorway as she toweled her hair dry. He lay on his back with his arms out to the side like a gingerbread boy. Suddenly he lifted both legs, slammed them down, and started to whimper. Vera looked at the ceiling. He was bored—who wouldn't be? Not tired, not hungry, looking at an ivory-colored plaster ceiling for ten minutes as she took a shower. She looked at the clock, twelve minutes she amended.

Without thinking, she dropped to her hands and knees and crawled to the end of the bed. Raising her head, she called, "*Peekaboo*," as she'd seen Marcela do. Leo startled and looked at her bug-eyed. She thought he might cry and she ducked her head in shame, but he remained silent. She could feel him waiting.

She raised her head. "*Peekaboo,*" she called, and he let out a peal of laughter.

Leo seemed to have an unlimited capacity for the game, but Vera considered seven times enough. She stood up, put a knee on the bed, and leaned over, peering into his eyes. He sucked on a fist and looked up at his mother expectantly, eyes wide. His irises had lost their last vestiges of blue and had become light brown. The blood of a lion, Bakari Silberstein had said.

Vera sat on the bed and rested her hand on Leo's little drum of a belly. She didn't know how long she talked, she might have described the series of botanical tiles she had designed for a culinary store in Landers, garden herbs drawn in fine detail on a stark white background with underglaze pencils. She would add hints of color to the leaves, berries, and flowers with a paintbrush. She might have mentioned the pruning she still needed to do on the quince and apple trees and the new treatment Tyree had recommended for the holly.

Leo watched her mouth, looked in her eyes, and appeared content to listen. She touched the tip of his nose and made a grab for his little pink tongue when he stuck it out.

"*Ew*," she said and he giggled.

She wormed her finger into his little clenched fist and felt him squeeze it. "Leo, Leo, Leo," she said.

He rolled his head, kicked his legs, and waited. She stood up—they would go to Pinedale today. She would leave a note for Marcela that they'd probably be home late.

Leo hadn't been to Pinedale before. No one would ask questions about the other half of his parentage there. They would go to the ceramics supply store, buy more firing cones and another drying rack, then to Ridley's for Marcela's list of baby items, including a teething ring and Orajel. Marcela said Leo was drooling so much because he would be teething soon.

The young man stocking the shelves at Ridley's found the Orajel for Vera but said he'd never heard of a teething ring. His mother just put a rag in the freezer for his baby sister and let her chew on that. Marcela would be scandalized when Vera told her.

At the register, the cashier and another woman were discussing a moose cow and calf that had taken up residence in the county park. Although not an uncommon animal in Wyoming, Vera had never seen a moose in the wild.

"Is it safe to go see them? Are they dangerous?" Vera asked.

"Oh, they're not territorial, pretty much solitary. You ever see a moose herd?" asked the cashier with a chuckle.

"Plenty of people have gone over to visit. Just don't get between her or her calf," warned the other woman. "Keep a respectful distance, the mama will ignore you."

"There's something wrong with her foot," said the cashier. "The vet went over with binoculars and studied it, didn't want to get too close, he's mainly for cats and dogs. He thinks maybe she got it caught in a trap, says it doesn't look infected but she's real lame."

"Guess she'll just be our moose for now, she'll be safe with us as long as she stays in the park," said the other woman. She studied Leo a moment. "Beautiful head of hair you and your baby have."

"Real pretty," agreed the cashier. "Boy or girl?"

"Thank you, a boy," said Vera.

"Well, you take that little boy of yours over and see if you can catch sight of our moose," said the cashier. "Then you can tell your baby about the time the two of you spent with a mamma moose and *her* baby. The vet says our moose baby is a boy too."

Pine Creek flowed quickly in this part of the park, eddying around boulders and fallen branches. In the shallows, long brown strands of vegetation tugged by the currents floated like hair above rocks turned golden by the sun. A chilly wind kicked up and Vera decided it was time to head back to the car rather than cross the creek at the wooden bridge.

As soon as she turned around, Vera caught sight of the moose. She stood camouflaged in a thicket of aspen and cottonwood on the opposite side of the creek. Her calf, redder than his mother, watched them warily as his mother ignored them, methodically stripping tender shoots from an aspen with her rubbery prehensile upper lip.

"A moose and her baby, look Leo," Vera breathed, but Leo was more interested in a twig with an oak leaf attached, which his mother had given him to hold.

The calf's compact, short-necked body perched on impossibly long knobby-kneed legs. The cow paused in her feeding to look across the creek at them and bob her head up and down. A long black scar slashed jaggedly down her faded brown face and disappeared into a nostril. Favoring her right foreleg, she took a few stumbling steps toward another tree and placidly returned to her shoot stripping and rhythmic chewing.

Such a scar, and now a foot damaged in a trap. "An exception or the rule?" Vera silently asked Betty Ann. On their way to Farson years ago to celebrate Vera's eighth-grade report card with ice cream, she and Betty Ann had seen a coyote limping along the road with his head down.

"All God's creatures suffer," Betty Ann had said. "But suffering is not a reason to stop loving life. Bad times are followed by good."

"What if all your skin burns off?" Vera remembered asking. "Then you can't love life. There's no good after that."

"Oh, Honey," Betty Ann had said, "I'm talking about the rule, you're talking about the exception."

How did a moose get a scar like that? What if her foot became infected? What if she left the protection of the park? How much suffering before the rule became the exception? Vera watched, absorbed, as the calf turned his bony haunches toward them and began to suckle. He twitched his short tail rapidly back and forth in his concentration, nudging his mother so insistently she staggered to the side for a few steps before righting herself.

Vera suddenly jerked her head back as Leo's twig came perilously close to her eye. She removed the twig from his fist and squeezed her son's solid little body.

"Sorry I didn't breastfeed you, I just didn't have it in me," she whispered, burying her face in his hair. "But I would die for you, Leo McNabb," she added, shuddering at the wave of relief that washed over her.

Heidi was taking Marcela to San Francisco in a week, but now she knew she and Leo would be able to cope until the girl returned. Co-parenting with a nine-year-old, Vera laughed aloud—a sound she hadn't heard escape her body for years.

CHAPTER THIRTY-SEVEN

OCEAN BEACH

Two days before their flight to San Francisco, Amadeus balked at going. He said his basketball team was playing a Reservation team, and they couldn't win without him.

"And Gering can stay at Booker's with me so he doesn't have to go to Vera's. You know he'd rather be with me." Amadeus tried for a winsome smile. "You and Marcela can go by yourselves. They're just talking to her, right? They're not going to do anything to her yet."

Heidi didn't say this focus on basketball at all costs could wait until high school and that Gering would be perfectly fine with Vera. Instead, she leaned back against the kitchen counter and said, "I already told you the clinic just needs to talk to you this first time. They say it is so unusual for identical twins to be different in this way. They have heard of few other cases. If you were the other kind of twins, it would be two different eggs and two different sperms and your genes would be different from each other, but one egg and one sperm makes your genes the same."

"I *know* that, you say it bazillions of times. I get it."

"A bazillion is more than several?"

She waited for Amadeus to finish releasing a very annoyed sigh before adding that two of the researchers were not convinced Marcela was a girl but three others thought there was more than genes at play.

Amadeus scowled. "What do you mean 'genes at play'?"

"I just parrot their words. When I told them it will take us three flights and many hours to get to them, they talked to me on the phone for quite a long time in what they call a conference call."

"Why three flights? You said there were two."

"Rock Springs to Denver and now they tell me they add a stop in Seattle before San Francisco," she explained. "Who understands why airlines do what they do? But when we come home, there are only two."

"So a bazillion hours to get there?"

"I think perhaps two bazillion to get there, but less than one bazillion to come home."

The long flight wasn't the issue—flying actually sounded pretty cool—but not worth missing playing a Rez team for. Amadeus tried another tactic.

"I know why Marcela is in the wrong body," he said, hoisting himself up on the counter. "When I tell you, you can just tell them and I can stay here."

"You tell me and I will listen, but you come to San Francisco for Marcela just this one time," Heidi countered. "We will stay in a hotel and eat food at restaurants and have room service and buy a big present for each of us."

When she started with the bribes, Amadeus knew she wasn't going to back down, so with a sigh, he said he wanted a Michael Jordan jersey—an *official* NBA jersey. It would cost a lot.

"Okay, I agree," Heidi said immediately. "Now tell me why Marcela is born in the wrong body."

"Well ... once upon a time," Amadeus rolled his eyes for effect, "there were two spirits in the spirit world. They were very, *very* best friends. One was a girl and one was a boy and when it was time for them to come down and enter their baby bodies, they made a mistake." He shrugged, raised his hands palms-up—everybody makes mistakes. "Marcela's spirit wanted to be with me so she had to enter the other twin body inside Mama, otherwise some other spirit would go into it and then that spirit would be closer to me than Marcela. Our spirits didn't know how hard was going to be for Marcela to be in the wrong body." He looked away. "Maybe my spirit made her spirit do it."

"Or maybe your spirit tells her not to do it but she does it anyway," said Heidi. "Your sister is very stubborn."

"More stubborn than me?"

"Oh yes." Heidi took his face in her hands and pressed her forehead to his. "You are the best brother, Amadeus. You tell the doctors what you know, but let them also do their tests. We need their help to get Marcela her body."

* * * * * *

Booker offered to drive them to Rock Springs-Sweetwater County Regional airport and pick them four days later, but Heidi turned him down. She claimed she found flying relaxing and they were returning in the early morning hours of the day a major client was coming to pick up one of his gates. She knew how much work he still had to do. She wrapped her arms around his waist and squeezed so hard he gave a loud, "Oof."

She buried her face in his chest and said, voice muffled, "You will see, we will soon be home with spunk and the bushy tails."

Booker laughed and said he was looking forward to seeing that. He told her to phone before their return flight left San Francisco.

"Why?" she asked.

"Just do it, Heidi," he said, "then let me know when you get to Rock Springs, you know, so ... ah ... so maybe I can be at your house to ... ah ...."

"*Ach*, you want to see our spunk and bushy tails," said

Heidi, grinning up at him.

* * * * * *

Their two days at The Parnassus Clinic began with morning interviews and lab tests, done under the cold light of fluorescent tubes. More interesting were the afternoons, when they were separated into groups, Heidi with parents, Amadeus with siblings, and Marcela with other transgender children at varying stages of transition.

Both days, they ate lunch at a Chinese restaurant near the hospital. Authentic Chinese food was a first for the twins. In the evenings, they ordered room service, Amadeus and Marcela carefully examining the menu before selecting their usual hamburger and fries.

Over dinner the first night, Amadeus puzzled at terms Marcela was already familiar with and Heidi realized how often he hadn't been present when she and Marcela had talked about the path ahead.

"Gender identity disorder, gender *dysphoria*, they make Marcela sound like she's sick," said Amadeus, as he tore open a package of ketchup with his teeth. He frowned at his sister. "You're not sick, your spirit just went into the wrong body. Why can't they just say that?"

"They use the terms they are taught," said Heidi as she unwrapped her chicken sandwich. "I looked it up. They put ancient Greek words together to come up with dysphoria." She wrinkled her nose. The kitchen had used too much dill, such a common mistake.

"What does it mean?" demanded Amadeus.

"Dys means ..." Heidi paused before deciding not to lie, "it means imperfect or wrong or ill."

"Told ya," said Amadeus, triumphantly. "It's not a good word, and what about the 'phoria' part?"

Before Heidi could answer, Marcela broke in, glaring at

them. "Don't make such a big deal about their dumb words because if they get mad and won't help me, I'll have to kill myself."

Heidi put her sandwich down carefully and took a sip of water. She never should have gotten into this back and forth with Amadeus within Marcela's hearing. At her afternoon parent session, a psychologist had shared the suicide statistics for transgender youth.

"Over forty-five percent of your children have or are thinking about it," the doctor had said. "If your child talks of suicide, even casually, pay attention."

The following day they walked back to their hotel from the clinic for the last time and Amadeus was full of high spirits. He leap-frogged over a fire hydrant and spun himself around parking meters.

"A guy in my group said his sister turns eighteen next month," he said, panting, when Heidi and Marcela caught up to him, "then she's getting her penis cut off."

"Not everyone decides to do this," said Heidi. "Not everyone wants to go this far."

"I do," said Marcela.

* * * * * *

Their flight back to Denver didn't leave until early that evening, so at the hotel concierge's suggestion, they left their bags at the front desk and took a trolley to Ocean Beach, a three-mile expanse of sand that bordered San Francisco's western side. They got off at the end of the line and walked north toward a promenade. The wind was cold and seemed to come from all directions. They passed a parking area, empty save several vans with surfboards propped against them. The surfers, at various stages of peeling off their black rubber wet suits, stopped to return Heidi's smile, their skin pimply and tinged with blue.

"Ew, White People skin," Marcela whispered with a giggle before being shushed.

Signs along the promenade warned of dangerous currents, rip tides that could sweep a person out to sea so that even wading was discouraged. The twins begged to dip their toes—*just* their toes—in the Pacific Ocean, so the three of them descended steep cement steps to cross a broad expanse of almost deserted beach, littered with broken shells, seaweed, bits of paper, and plastic.

Amadeus ran ahead, his long hair streaming behind him as he danced around the incoming waves and chased them back out to sea. Heidi and Marcela stood with arms wrapped around each other for warmth and faced the incoming tide, backing up a few feet each time a wave swept over their toes.

"Your mother would tell us this is a neap tide," said Heidi. "The sun and moon are at odds with each other, their pull on the water is not so strong."

"I don't get why she was so crazy about the ocean," said Marcela. "She never even got close to an ocean."

"She had her big book," said Heidi. "It was her comfort from when she was a child."

"Most of the pictures in it aren't even in color. In the book, the ocean just looks grey but look at all the green out there." Marcela waved her hand toward the sea. "How did she even get that book?"

"I think she took it from someone who she thought did not deserve it."

"She *stole* it?"

"No, she ... it was something we did not talk about, but she took it for justice I think."

"She stole it," said Marcela. "She should have stolen one with colored pictures."

"Your mother did not steal things. This book was a special circumstance," Heidi said, ignoring Marcela's smirk.

The wind stilled, the sun shone warm. Heidi closed her eyes and inhaled the briny air. The book had become a permanent feature on the coffee table of her house in Riverton the day after Nara had moved in. She now kept it safe in her closet.

She smiled at the memory of Nara, hugely pregnant with the twins, lying on the sofa. She had the book open to a photo of the rear end of a sea turtle in the process of delivering another egg to a growing pile in a sandy hole.

"Climate change will increase sand temperature which will affect the sex ratios of sea turtle hatchlings," Nara had said, speaking in the superior tone adopted by the scientifically minded when talking to one more interested in food preparation. "Oh, I know cousin Karl introduced you to birding, but I bet neither of you truly grasp how many more females will hatch in a turtle clutch, or crocodilian clutch for that matter, if it's warmed during its thermo-sensitive period."

"What are you smiling about?" asked Marcela suspiciously.

"I think of a time your mother lectures me from her book."

"Yeah, well Amadeus and I just ran away when she started."

"You remember nothing of what she tried to teach you?"

"When the mom seahorse puts her eggs into the dad using that tube thing, I guess that's pretty interesting," admitted Marcela begrudgingly.

The tide continued to advance, they continued to retreat. When Heidi looked back to see if their shoes were still safe, she realized with a surge of fear Amadeus was nowhere to be found. His footprints on the compact sand at the water's edge had been swallowed by soft grey fog that was advancing with astonishing rapidity.

Hand-in-hand, she and Marcela chased his footsteps, their cries for him muffled by the rush of the waves, the density of the fog, the calls of the gulls. They became disoriented in their panic—one moment they entered the water, the next they were on dry sand and stumbling through a cloud of tiny insects rising from the broken body of a pelican, its bill grotesquely large. The water again, the dead bird, they were spinning in circles. They stopped and stared at each other, their faces shiny with sweat and fear.

Marcela suddenly tugged at Heidi's hand. "Wait, wait, listen," she whispered hoarsely. "I hear him singing. It's the song Mama used to sing before the wine made her sleep."

Heidi heard the song too, but not Amadeus. It was Nara singing. Nara was here.

They found Amadeus on his knees, crouched over, his arms stretched out in the sand toward the ocean, as if he were an Arab supplicant in prayer. They saw the retreat of an outgoing wave that must have just swept over his arms and pulled at his hair.

* * * * * *

Booker took a break and came in from the studio around the time he expected Heidi's call. When the phone rang, he caught himself grinning. She was a punctual woman.

He quickly sobered when he heard her voice. She sounded exhausted.

"I almost lost Amadeus at the beach," she whispered into the receiver. "I thought he might leave forever."

"But you're all okay? You're about to get on the plane?"

After a pause she said yes, they would soon be boarding, and yes, she would phone when they got to Rock Springs, if that's what he wanted.

Booker made himself a sandwich. Heidi had sounded completely...he didn't know quite how to describe it ... drained? Defeated? He thought back to his mother's panic

327

when they lost his brother at the county fair. He had been six, Simon four. They finally found Simon under a tree, sharing in another family's picnic. His mother, who rarely raised her voice, had yelled at the other mom for not taking a lost child to one of the authorities right away. Then both women had started to cry, his mother apologizing for yelling, the other woman apologizing for not thinking. Soon Simon's disappearance had just become part of the family lore. Except maybe not for his mother, who for a while hadn't even let the two of them play in the yard unless she had been out there with her mending.

He took a cup of strong, black coffee back to his studio. He placed a thin sheet of hammered copper on the workbench and laid the template of a maple leaf over it. When the leaves developed their patina over the life of the gate, they would look better and better. He paused before making his first cut and looked at the clock. Another dozen leaves to cut out, they'd still need to be attached, add a couple of hours to see Heidi—he'd be pushing it.

At midnight, when his reconstructed shoulder ached more than he could endure, he went back to the cabin for an ice pack and to try for a few hours' sleep. Just before dawn, Heidi phoned from Rock Springs. She sounded better, business-like. She said he sounded very tired. He should finish his gate, rest, and come down in the evening.

He didn't let the animals out because he wouldn't be gone long. His shoulder still hurt too much for the motorbike so he walked to his truck. He swore when he saw a partially deflated right front tire. Someone somewhere would think the powers-that-be were agreeing with Heidi and he should finish the gate first and go down to see her after it had been picked up.

"Just like a dog, you sorry ass bastard," he muttered under his breath, conscious of his need to see her now. He examined the tire. A nail—he couldn't just add air, he'd have to change it. Maybe the bike was a better idea, just ignore the shoulder.

He rolled the bike out of the barn. Its engine refused to catch. He let out a howl of frustration so loud, the horses stamped and whinnied. He watched a large dark shape leave its perch high in a tree and envied the freedom of a wild creature.

Despite his delay, he still should have beaten Heidi to her house, and he shook his head when he saw the Mercedes already parked out front. Heidi's penchant for driving fast was so at odds with her methodical approach to life, it never ceased to amaze him. The kids must have fallen asleep in the car or they would have reined her in.

The front door was unlocked and he let himself in. The twins habitually slept with their doors wide open and he glanced in their rooms to find Amadeus flat on his back snoring and Marcela asleep curled around Gering. The dog opened an eye and lifted the tip of his tail. Someone must have rapped on Vera's door pretty damn early to get him.

He heard the shower in Heidi's bathroom and was almost tempted to join her, but he was just so damn tired. Her bed would be easier. He locked the bedroom door, took off his boots, and stretched out to wait. A hot shower, the twins safe asleep, she'd be feeling better by now.

She came out of the bathroom looking warm and enticing. He reached out a hand and murmured, "Hey," but instead of lying down next to him, she remained standing and covered her face with her hands. He sat up when he realized by the slight movements of her shoulders she was crying.

Had he ever seen her cry? An angry, frustrated tear on occasion, but no, this wasn't her way. What the hell had happened in San Francisco? He went into the bathroom and brought back a damp washcloth. She pressed it to her face and when she was done, she folded it into a neat square and handed it back, a gesture of trust that touched him. He took the cloth into the bathroom and hung it on the shower door.

"I thought Nara had taken Amadeus at the beach," Heidi said hollowly when he returned. "Then we found him and I thought she was pulling him into the sea."

He sat next to her on the edge of the bed and rested his forearms on his thighs, hands clasped between his knees. He looked at the floor and said she'd better start at the beginning.

In a voice devoid of intonation, Heidi described the beach, the fog that had appeared from nowhere, and Amadeus's footprints running away from them, how they had frantically called for him.

"When Marcela tugs at my hand she says she hears her brother singing, but I hear Nara," said Heidi.

"But Marcela heard Amadeus," Booker repeated quietly.

"It is true Marcela did not hear her mother, but then she never does." Her eyes searched his face as if imploring him to understand. Then she turned her face away and said, "It is so difficult to walk on sand carrying a wet, fifty-pound child who is limp, like the dead weight, but I had to get him far from the water and Nara."

Booker wanted to say San Francisco is known for its fog. He wanted to say they'd gotten disoriented—the warnings along the promenade were there for a reason, they were home safe, it was over. But he knew that wasn't what she wanted to hear, so instead he lay down and pulled her on top of him. He held her until he could feel her resistance fading and their heat beginning to build. They made love slowly, tentatively at first, and then with increasing urgency. He managed to hold off his release until she'd had hers.

They both knew he had to get back to work on the gate so they rested only a short while before he went to take a shower. He aimed the showerhead at his shoulder and turned the water to as hot as he could bear for a solid ten minutes until some of the ache eased.

Leaving his flannel shirt hanging off the back of the chair, he put his leather jacket on over his t-shirt. He leaned over, kissed her goodbye, and told her to get some rest.

She nodded. "You get rest too," she said, turning her face away.

Esau got out of the van with a thermos of coffee and a white paper bag just as Booker was walking to his truck.

"She phoned me about half an hour ago while you were apparently in the shower," said Esau, holding the bag out to Booker. "She said she's coming in later this morning, but she sounded like hell, so I'm here to head her off."

Booker opened the bag, extracted a scone, and nodded his thanks.

"She thinks Nara tried to take Amadeus into the ocean," he said, his eyes searching Esau's face.

Esau shrugged. "She mentioned something about Nara, but I told her to try and get some rest and we'd talk about it later."

"She's obsessed."

"Who, Heidi or Nara?"

"Don't you start," said Booker, voice hard. "Don't you encourage her."

Esau knocked on Heidi's bedroom door and entered to find her standing at the window. Over her nightgown she wore a large plaid flannel shirt, which he recognized as Booker's. She had been watching them.

"Brought coffee and scones," he said, holding up the bag and thermos.

She gave him a wan smile and said, "Except for Karl and Beppe, you are my very best friend."

He chuckled and went into the kitchen. He poured their coffee into mugs, cream for Heidi, black with a teaspoon of sugar for him. There had rarely been a day in the last three years when one of them hadn't prepared coffee for the other. He took two scones out of the bag and left the rest on the counter.

He returned to the bedroom, took off his shoes and the two of them sat, backs against the headboard, legs stretched out before them. They drank their coffee and nibbled their scones in silence for a bit. Heidi dusted her crumbs onto the bed and told him to do the same. Gering would take care of them.

"It is the job of a dog to clean up after his people," she said.

"It's certainly liberating," he said. After another moment's silence, he continued, "Sooo, what's this business with Nara at the beach?"

When Heidi had finished, Esau brought his hand to his cheek and rubbed at his scars as he habitually did when deep in thought.

"What do you think?" she asked.

"Give me a moment," he said.

Amadeus knocked on the door and, at Heidi's call, came in. He didn't seem surprised to see both adults sitting on the bed like that. No doubt he knew they had been talking about the beach and didn't want him or Marcela to hear.

"Two-part question," the boy said, wiggling his second and third fingers. "One, can we have the rest of the scones, and two, even if we're not going back to school 'til tomorrow, can I still go to basketball practice later?"

"Yes, to both," said Heidi.

Amadeus backed out and closed the door with exaggerated care. With a hoot, they heard him thundering down the hall. Esau rolled his head to the side and looked at Heidi.

"Yes, I know he seems okay," she said, "but what do you think about what I tell you? I *know* Nara was there."

"What I think," he said slowly, "is that you have assembled an army to stand behind Marcela. There's me, Booker, your cousins. Even people who don't know her story are enlisted, like Vera, Ruth, little Lucas Darcy, who is still fixated like a bird dog on her, by the way."

Heidi gave a soft chuckle. She had a drawer full of Lucas's pictures, delivered by Esau and refused by Marcela. She saved them because she thought someday Marcela might like evidence of a boy loving her since he was four.

"So Marcela is set," Esau continued. "She knows what she needs, you know what she needs and together the two of you are going to get it done. She's not open to having Nara in her life anymore. But Amadeus?" Esau paused and rubbed at his scars. "There's no doubt he's open to the idea of his mom hanging around. You said Nara had that book on the ocean that she escaped into. Both you and Amadeus are conscious of how important the ocean was or is to her. So here he is at the beach, feeling the power of the waves, feeling the power of his mother and you're feeling it too."

"This is not about my feelings or Amadeus's feelings," protested Heidi. "Nara *was* there. She tried to pull him in. How do I protect him from his own mother?"

"The thing to fear isn't Nara, it's your response to Nara," said Esau. "To you guys, a small dust devil that flings pebbles and leaves isn't sun-heated air and wind currents, it's Nara reminding Amadeus that she's there." He looked around the room, out the window, and smiled at her. "Maybe she just wants to remain a part of your lives. Marcela's not open, but you and Amadeus are. But here's the other thing —the ocean is just too much, maybe for all three of you guys. There's too much energy there, it's too big and too powerful for vulnerable people."

Heidi bit her lips to prevent herself from saying she wasn't a vulnerable person. After a moment's silence, she said, "Marcela and I have to go back in three months. On the airplane home Amadeus says he wants go back with us, but he knows the trolley goes right to the beach now. He must stay here in Comfrey with you to be safe."

"I agree he should stay here, but not with me if Booker's available. He'll keep Amadeus even if he doesn't believe Nara still has influence."

"He said this to you?" Heidi was surprised. Booker wasn't

one to share his thoughts with anyone.

"He didn't say it in so many words," admitted Esau. "It's Booker, he's too shut down for his own good. But to take care of Amadeus, he doesn't have to believe. He's invested in you and the kids."

"Invested? You do not want to say he is in crazy love with us?"

"Nope, he's in crazy love with me and Ruth, and maybe that horse of his," said Esau. "He's just fallen under your bewitchment."

"Bewitchment is not a real word," said Heidi, taking Esau's hand and giving it a squeeze. "But about Nara, you believe she was there?"

"Luisa would believe it's possible," he said, with that slight wince he made at his wife's name. "For me, the jury's still out." He rubbed at his scars. "So you go back in three months, then what?"

"I think they will play this by the ear as Marcela develops, but we will return many times and Amadeus cannot come. Except I think when the twins are eighteen and she has her operation. They will want to be together then and I will not stop him. He says their spirits bonded in the spirit world. He also tells this to the researchers."

Esau chuckled. "Did they have a better explanation?"

"No, they did not."

"Well, there you go," said Esau, swinging his legs off the bed. He bent over to place Gering on the bed so the dog could take care of the crumbs. "In nine years Amadeus will be strong enough to keep himself safe. Now, I need to get back. Elizabeth has a full house so she can't come in for prep or the lunch crowd. Tyree will have to take care of the front by himself."

"I will come in," said Heidi immediately.

"No you won't," said Esau, stretching and rolling his shoulders. "Stay here and I'll scratch one of the favors you owe me off my list."

After Esau left, Heidi got up, because of course she must go to The Crow's Nest if Elizabeth couldn't be there. Vera would be happy for Marcela to go over and help with Leo, and Amadeus could choose to come to the restaurant with her or go to school for the rest of the day. She took Booker's shirt off and buried her face in it, inhaling his scent of smoke, metal, hay, and horses. The man she was in love with wouldn't let himself believe Nara had been there in the ocean, but her dearest friend, except for Karl and Beppe, thought it possible and said his wife might think so too.

A sharp yap, and she turned to see Gering at the edge of her bed, looking at her expectantly. His muzzle was mostly white now, his joints stiff, his back unstable. The bed had become too high for him to jump down safely and she thanked him for waiting.

"Do you know what my mother would say to us right now, Gering?" she asked, placing him on the floor and supporting him a moment until he got his bearings. "She would say, '*Zähl die guten Sachen in deinem Leben, nicht deine Probleme.*' Count the good things in your life, not your problems."

She walked out the backdoor with the dachshund and sat on the stoop to listen to the bees in the lavender. She'd have the twins pick some blackberries from the bush outside the backyard fence on the weekend. Blackberry sour cream muffins, she licked her lips, not enough berries to supply the restaurant, but enough to make muffins for Vera, Ruth, Booker, Esau, and the twins.

In nine years Marcela could be offered the surgeries that would transform her body into one that fully matched her spirit and the burden of their family secret would lift, but until then, there would be many things to celebrate. Vera said Marcela was gifted with clay. Marcela called herself Leo's second mama and took great pride in his developing vocabulary. Booker had taken Amadeus under his wing and would keep him safe. Rumor had it homosexual marriage would be legal in the Netherlands soon and Karl and Beppe were already planning their wedding. They wanted Marcela to be their flower girl and Amadeus their ring bearer.

When she had told Nara that Karl and Beppe would marry one day, Nara had said she would bring the boys to the wedding and they could be the ring bearers.

"The time is coming, Nara," she said to the rustling leaves of the apple tree, "but so much has changed."

A sudden gust of wind caused an apple to drop, and then another. Nara had been amused by Gering's penchant for apples, and not wanting more apples to fall, Heidi called the dog to her. He trotted over with a small red apple in his mouth. She knew he wouldn't give up Nara's gift, so he could take it with him to The Crow's Nest. Now they had leave, so she could work side-by-side with Esau in preparing the most innovative meals possible, within the confines of a small town on the Green Basin side of the Wind River Range.

ACKNOWLEDGMENTS

I am deeply grateful for the support of my family and friends as I endeavor to give voice to the people in my head.

In particular, I would like to thank:

Jocasta Mettling: for her eagle eyes, late night critiques and lifelong friendship.

Marsha and Rich Niemann: for letting me read every last word of my books to them and cheering me on.

Fred Larson: a quirky, charming and peripatetic soul, who has distributed my books far and wide.

Anke Hamsen, who once again kindly checked my German. Any errors are mine.

ABOUT ATMOSPHERE PRESS

Atmosphere Press is an independent, full-service publisher for excellent books in all genres and for all audiences. Learn more about what we do at atmospherepress.com.

We encourage you to check out some of Atmosphere's latest releases, which are available at Amazon.com and via order from your local bookstore:

The Embers of Tradition, a novel by Chukwudum Okeke

Saints and Martyrs: A Novel, by Aaron Roe

When I Am Ashes, a novel by Amber Rose

Melancholy Vision: A Revolution Series Novel, by L.C. Hamilton

The Recoleta Stories, by Bryon Esmond Butler

Voodoo Hideaway, a novel by Vance Cariaga

Hart Street and Main, a novel by Tabitha Sprunger

The Weed Lady, a novel by Shea R. Embry

A Book of Life, a novel by David Ellis

It Was Called a Home, a novel by Brian Nisun

Grace, a novel by Nancy Allen

Shifted, a novel by KristaLyn A. Vetovich

Because the Sky is a Thousand Soft Hurts, stories by Elizabeth Kirschner

ABOUT THE AUTHOR

Daphne Birkmyer's background as a teacher and biologist continues to exert its influence on her written work. She observes Americans through an immigrant's eyes and is currently working on book three of the COMFREY, WYOMING series.

Visit her at www.daphnebirkmyer.com